German Yearbook on Business History 1987

German Yearbook on Business History 1987

Edited by
the German Society for Business History, Cologne

In Cooperation with
the Institute for Bank-Historical Research, Frankfurt/Main

Editors:
Hans Pohl (Editor in Charge) and Bernd Rudolph

Editorial Staff:
Beate Brüninghaus, Monika Pohle and Manfred Pohl

Springer-Verlag
Berlin Heidelberg New York
London Paris Tokyo

Advertisements' Management by Springer-Verlag Berlin Heidelberg New York

ISBN-13:978-3-642-73932-3 e-ISBN-13:978-3-642-73930-9
DOI: 10.1007/978-3-642-73930-9

2142/7130-543210

Table of Contents

List of Contributors and Translators

Contributors

Beate Brüninghaus M.A.
Geschäftsführerin der Gesellschaft
für Unternehmensgeschichte e. V.
Bonner Str. 211, D-5000 Köln 51

Dr. Otmar Emminger †

Stephanie Habeth-Allhorn
Am Domplatz 27, D-5305 Alfter

Manfred Mai
Verein Deutscher Ingenieure
Graf-Recke-Str. 84, D-4000 Düsseldorf 1

Dr. Jürgen Mura
Deutscher Sparkassen- und Giroverband
Sparkassenhistorisches Dokumentationszentrum
Simrockstr. 4, D-5300 Bonn 1

Professor Dr. Hans-Werner Niemann
Blumenstr. 33, D-2900 Oldenburg

Professor Dr. Hans Pohl
Historisches Seminar
Abt. Verfassungs-, Sozial- und Wirtschaftsgeschichte
Rheinische Friedrich-Wilhelms-Universität
Konviktstr. 11, D-5300 Bonn

Monika Pohle M.A.
Geschäftsführung, Institut für bankhistorische Forschung e. V.
Goetheplatz 9, D-6000 Frankfurt am Main

Professor Dr. Dr. h. c. Wilhelm Treue
Otto-Wallach-Weg 13, D-3400 Göttingen

Dr. Immo Zapp
Hochschule Aachen
Templergraben 55, D-5100 Aachen

Translators

Stuart Christie
Deutsche Bank AG, Zentrale Internationale Abt.
Taunusanlage 12, D-6000 Frankfurt am Main
(article by Otmar Emminger †)

A. Llewellyn
Bayerische Hypotheken- und Wechsel-Bank AG
Theatinerstr. 11, D-8000 München 2
(report by Monika Pohle)

Eileen Martin
19 Evelyn Gardens, GB-Richmond Surrey TW9 2PL
(articles by Hans-Werner Niemann, Hans Pohl, Wilhelm Treue, reviews by Beate Brüninghaus and Monika Pohle)

Ingrid Scheben
Akazienstr. 9, D-5357 Swisttal
(report by Jürgen Mura)

Carol Trevor
72 Talbot Road, Highgate, GB-London N6 4RA
(reports by Beate Brüninghaus, Stephanie Habeth-Allhorn and Immo Zapp)

Anne Wegner
Fischenicher Str. 28, D-5000 Köln 51
(report by Manfred Mai)

The Evolution of the Exchange Rate from "Sacrosanct" Parity to Flexible Monetary Policy Instrument[1]

Otmar Emminger

1. The Three Evolutionary Phases of the Exchange Rate System After the War

Deutsche Bundesbank's refusal to continue supporting the dollar at a fixed rate after the dollar nose-dived on March 1, 1973 triggered off an avalanche in the international monetary landscape. It resulted in the collapse of the Bretton-Woods-system of fixed parities and in the introduction of the mixed system of free floating and the European "snake".

Even if the dollar crisis of spring 1973 had been resolved in some other way, sooner or later the system of fixed parities would have had to capitulate in the face of other world economic shocks, e.g. the oil shock at the end of 1973 and its repercussions on the international balance of payments structure and inflation. No less a figure than the Managing Director of the International Monetary Fund, Mr. J. Witteveen, attested to this when in a programmatic address held in London in January 1974 he declared: "Given the new circumstances, a considerable measure of floating is not only unavoidable but even desirable".

The evolution of the exchange rate system over the last 40 years can be broken down into *three phases.* In the first phase after the Second World War, currency parities were still regarded as almost taboo or "sacrosanct", more so than would have been necessary or advisable under the Bretton-Woods-system. This was followed, particularly under the pressure of the currency tensions and crises of the sixties and the initial years of the seventies, by a period of ad hoc parity adjustments which were always overdue and often inadequate. This phase was, in turn, replaced in 1973 by the new system of group floating against the dollar which, on the one hand, meant flexibility versus a number of major currencies and, on the other, a system of fixed but adjustable parities within a regional group in Europe. This mixed system has, in turn, undergone several evolutionary phases since 1973.

All this was of such decisive importance for both the world economy and German stability policy that it justifies a brief review of the entire postwar period. One motivating factor for me here is the fact that I lived through all these developments and changes since 1949, often playing an active role. Besides, it is my

[1] The present article corresponds in large parts to chapter 9 of Otmar Emminger: D-Mark, Dollar, Währungskrisen. Erinnerungen eines ehemaligen Bundesbankpräsidenten, Deutsche Verlags-Anstalt GmbH, Stuttgart 1986.

German Yearbook on Business History 1987

impression that the essence of, and the reasons behind, the present mixed system of free floating and a regional monetary system can only be understood properly if its emergence is shown in greater detail.

2. Exchange Rate Parity as "Taboo" – a Look to the Distant Past

In looking back to the evolution of the exchange rate system, I should like to go back to the pre-war period because of my personal experiences. I was probably one of the first people in Germany to show an active interest in the phenomenon of floating. My doctoral thesis, the bulk of which was conceived during my stay in England in 1932/33, was entitled "Discount policy or currency-floating as a means of squaring payments balances". In it, I treated both the abortive sterling revaluation of 1925 and England's abandonment of the gold standard as well as its transition to floating in September 1931. My assessment of this transition to floating was on the whole positive. In the main, I saw in it an effective defensive measure against the deflationist tendencies emanating at the time predominantly from the U.S.A.[2]

The section of my doctoral thesis published in the "Weltwirtschaftliches Archiv" caused a fair bit of commotion at the time. It was discussed in seminars at various universities. Immediately after its publication, I received an invitation from Ministerialdirektor Lautenbach, the acknowledged currency expert, to a lengthy discussion with him and his staff at the Reich Economics Ministry. Lautenbach was very much taken by my pladoyer for exchange rate adjustment and greater exchange rate flexibility, but he could not prevail over Schacht. The publication of my thesis also resulted in an invitation to join the international section of the Berlin Institute for Business Research, which I did in spring of 1935. In 1936, the President of the Institute, Professor Wagemann, instructed me to write an opinion opposing the then prevailing 'Schacht' system. This consisted of a vastly overvalued official Reichsmark rate, but de facto of a number of different exchange rates (types of blocked Marks etc.) which varied depending on the type of transaction and often on the country involved, the whole thing coupled with numerous payments and trading restrictions. The Reichsmark had been the sole currency to maintain gold parity, even when the dollar was devalued by roughly 40% at the beginning of 1934. By 1937, the Reichsmark was overvalued by no less than 51% compared with the average of other major currencies. At the time, I proposed a strong devaluation of the official Reichsmark parity (I also estimated how much it would have to be devalued) and the abolition of the many exchange rates. I do not believe that my opinion ever reached the addressee Wagemann had in mind, the then President of the Reichsbank Hjalmar Schacht; but, in view of the well-known attitude not only of Schacht but of practically the entire Reichsbank, it probably would not have achieved much even if it had. I should like to add here

[2] For reasons too complex to discuss here, the theoretical part of my doctoral thesis was never published, and the manuscript was lost in the confusion of war. The practical section, my analysis of English monetary policy from 1919 to 1933, was published in two essays in the "Weltwirtschaftliches Archiv" in September and November 1934.

that I met with Schacht on several occasions in the fifties and on one occasion crossed swords with him in front of a larger circle when he criticized the central bank's monetary policy with a highly impertinent line of argument (something he also did in a number of articles in obscure publications). The main reason for Schacht's fury at the Bank deutscher Länder and later the Bundesbank was our decision from the outset never to publish comments made by him (as one of the men behind Hitler) in our press extracts.[3] Nor could he ever understand how it was that we had such high foreign exchange surpluses while he, as head of the Reichsbank, was always facing the trauma of a lack of foreign exchange.

Some of today's economic historians share the view – rightly or wrongly – that Brüning and Luther had no other course of action open to them in 1931 and 1932, above all because of the conditions imposed on Germany in the Young Plan, other than to stick to the excessively high Reichsmark parity and to pursue a corresponding deflation policy. In my view, these conditions did not justify the disastrous policy adopted at the time. Besides, it certainly did not apply to Schacht, who took over the helm of the Reichsbank in 1933.[4]

I should like to show just how deeply rooted the ideological dogma of exchange rate immutability was with the help of another example. From 1930 to 1932 there was a triumvirate of experts in Berlin known to be the main ideological supports for Brüning and Luther's deflation course, namely Gustav Stolper, Moritz Julius Bonn and Melchior Palyi. Bonn emigrated to England in 1933, Stolper and Palyi to America (where Palyi later became professor in Chicago). Both Bonn and Palyi visited us on several occasions in the fifties at the Bundesbank or Bank deutscher Länder, as it was then called. Both still shared the view that Brüning and Luther's politically disastrous deflation policy was the only correct one. A quotation from an opinion Professor Palyi wrote for the Institut für Bankwirtschaft und Bankrecht in Cologne in 1961 will perhaps provide an impression of the way both regarded the fixed parity as sacrosanct. At one point he writes: "Before the era of the World Wars ... economists, irrespective of their school of thought, were unanimous that the fixed parity vis-à-vis gold was valid for all time ... even the 'Staatliche Theorie des Geldes' by G. F. Knapp (1905), the standard work of the anti-metallists (opponents of the gold standard) culminated in the sentence that 'a fixed exchange rate was the ultimate goal of monetary policy'. ... To throw overboard a principle accepted by all noteworthy economists of the last centuries denotes a lack of scientific tradition". Professor Bonn had a similar attitude towards currency parity. So it is little wonder that in a speech we organized for him in Frankfurt he condemned England's abandonment of the gold standard in 1931 most categorically as a great mistake. That contrasts most sharply with the assessment in my doctoral thesis published in 1934 where – among other things – I wrote: "The point

---

[3] One of the ways Schacht had his revenge was to accuse the President of the Bundesbank at the time, Blessing – whom Schacht himself had recalled from the BIS in Basle to the Reichsbank in 1933 and who was considered his "right hand" for quite some time – at the end of the fifties in a most unfair way of being a Nazi sympathizer, something which – being totally unfounded – wounded Blessing deeply.

[4] The other argument that official devaluation would result in a corresponding increase in the Reichsmark value of German external debt most of which was denominated in dollars was untenable, at least after the dollar devaluation in 1934.

of the English experiment in 1931 was to avoid the compulsion to deflate. ... The whole difference between England and America during the crisis was in a nutshell that America was an active deflation site, while England was compelled to deflate from without. ... Certainly, the success would have been more secure and greater, had England distanced itself from the deflation of the gold countries earlier, say at the end of 1930. ... At any event, the payments balance crisis was solved by this step, the independence of English credit policy restored" etc.

Although I considered England's transition to floating in 1931 as the right decision under the given circumstances, and although I was in the thirties one of the small circle of younger economists who criticized the enormous overvaluation of the Reichsmark, I was not one of the dogmatists who regarded floating at any price and in every situation as the sole valid panacea. On the contrary, I was always a pragmatist in external monetary policy. In the postwar period I, of course, followed the academic discussion on flexible exchange rates very closely from the outset, from Professor Milton Friedman to the well-known German proponent of floating, Professor Egon Sohmen. In the sixties we invited Professor Sohmen, who was then teaching in Heidelberg, to discussions at the Bundesbank on various occasions.

3. Exchange Rate Adjustments on an Ad Hoc Basis (1961–1973)

In the fifties and sixties I did not speak out in favour of floating the D-Mark, except that at the end of 1956 in an internal paper on a possible D-Mark revaluation one option I did propose was to greatly increase the fluctuation band and to allow the D-Mark to float up to a possible upper limit. But at the time it still looked as though the inflation differential which kept opening up between the Federal Republic and other major European countries could be compensated by ad hoc parity adjustments, thus safeguarding the external stability of the D-Mark. From 1956 I pleaded passionately on several occasions for timely adjustment of the D-Mark exchange rate. I can probably say that I was one of the first monetary pragmatists to defend the view that our stability policy would only have a chance in the long run if it was protected on the external flank. At the end of 1956 my ideas on a possible D-Mark revaluation were thrown out by the central bank directorate by seven votes to one (mine).

I simply accepted it as inevitable that my 1956/57 proposals were doomed to failure with the central bank president at the time, Vocke. Vocke used to hold marvellous speeches against inflation, but he was incapable of comprehending this new external threat to the stability of the D-Mark. He was too greatly influenced by his pre-war experience characterized by the trauma of a constant shortage of foreign exchange while we, since the mid-fifties, had been suffering from an undesired influx of foreign exchange. To the end he denied the very existence of a currency dilemma as the result of our stability policy in the midst of an inflation-stricken Europe. Towards the end of his term, he frequently repeated – the last time in a speech in May 1957 – the contradictory statement: "We do not want to revalue the D-Mark, nor do we want to adopt the inflationary line taken by some other countries". He simply could not accept that the creeping inflation of the early sixties was the very result of the long delay in revaluing. He revealed just how entrenched he was in his pre-war ideology in a 1972 essay in which he made a passionate plea – as a cure for the currency dilemma – for a general return to gold convertibility, proposing a large international "gold bond" issue to the U.S.A. (a bond issued in real gold!).[5] Vocke resented my early lobbying for a D-Mark revaluation and other clashes to the end of his life (which bothered me little).

A source of true regret, however, was that between 1959 and 1961 I also had differences of opinion on the exchange rate question with the revered and very likable president Blessing. He, together with a majority of votes on the central bank council, over which he had great influence, was responsible for the D-Mark revaluation which would have been due at the beginning of 1960 at the latest to avert imported inflation being postponed to March 1961. The Bonn Government was divided, and the view adopted by the Bundesbank often tipped the scales. Two convictions determined Blessing's negative stance: on the one hand, he had firmly believed – not least under the influence of Per Jacobsson, at the time Managing Director of the IMF – that the inflationary danger had been overcome in the world economy and that a new era of stability had dawned, with the result that an inflationary danger from without no longer existed. On the other hand, he had, like Vocke, taken over from his pre-war activity at the Reichsbank the ideological belief of the inviolability of the exchange rate parity into the postwar period. At the press conference held on March 5, 1961 to mark the announcement of the delayed and insufficient 5% revaluation of the D-Mark, Blessing said: "The Bundesbank has long resisted an exchange rate adjustment. For any central bank, currency parity is simply sacrosanct and may only be changed when all other means have failed".

The postponement of the revaluation was one reason for the inflationary wage-cost spiral the Federal Republic found itself in from 1960 to 1962 and which was difficult to get under control again. Some critics of the 1961 D-Mark revaluation pointed out ironically afterwards that the inflation rate *after* the revaluation was for a time higher than *before* the revaluation, and from that they deduced the inefficacity of using the exchange rate to protect the external flank. These critics included Vocke, Abs, Klasen, Strauss and others. Apart from the fact that the 5% revaluation in March 1961 was naturally totally inadequate, these critics overlooked above all the fact that, once under way, wage inflation was a phenomenon that could continue for years, particularly if monetary policy was fettered by the exchange rate.

Blessing and I were very close friends, so I know how difficult it was for him in February 1961 to come around to the D-Mark revaluation; at the time, he had even openly toyed with the idea of resigning. All the more credit to him then that he learned the right lesson from the experience in 1960/61, and that in autumn 1968, when domestic stability was again being threatened from without, he immediately and with all his energy joined the camp of those in favour of a quick D-Mark revaluation and that he advocated this viewpoint in the face of criticism from the

---

[5] Wilhelm Vocke, "Bemerkungen zur Währungskrise" (Comments on the Currency Crisis), Neue Zürcher Zeitung dated September 22, 1972.

Federal Government. In 1960/61, Blessing had long hesitated before agreeing to a 5% change in the D-Mark parity, but in October 1969 in a speech on the occasion of the 300th meeting of the central bank council he said: "I hope that in future exchange rates will no longer be treated like sacred cows. ... After 12 years I have come to the conclusion that if we wish to maintain some degree of stability in our own house, we must adjust exchange rates from time to time, or we shall have to join the rest of the world on the inflationary roller coaster".

Moreover, in the period prior to the transition to floating, I myself often had to face the problem that I had to deny any intention of a change in the D-Mark rate – often very much against my own convictions and intentions – to avoid greater damage that would have been caused by the inflow of undesirable speculative money.

But there were also occasions when I spoke out publicly against exchange rate adjustments and more flexible exchange rates, not out of consideration for any tense monetary situation but because the situation did not demand any parity measure. This was, for example, the case when in its first annual report at the end of 1964 and in the ensuing period the "Board of Experts for the Assessment of Overall Economic Trends" spoke out in favour of somewhat more flexible exchange rates, underpinning this view with an attached opinion by Professors F. A. Lutz and E. Sohmen. I rejected these and similar proposals at the time in interviews and lectures. I cited the usual counterarguments, not least of which being that we should not unduly hamper the cooperation that was just getting under way on the currency front within the European Community. But for me a much more important reason was that in those years there was exceptionally no necessity to protect the foreign trade and payments side via parity measures. From mid-1964 to mid-1966 we had, for the time, a high current account deficit (over DM 9 bn.) which was also not fully offset by capital inflows, with the result that the overall balance was in deficit and that there had to be a net outflow of foreign exchange. Our import prices fell by 3% between mid-1965 and mid-1968. All this meant that this was one of the few longer periods prior to the transition to floating in 1973 when Bundesbank monetary policy was free of the nightmare of imported inflation. At the beginning of 1965 we then also stated in our annual report for 1964 (page 23) that imported inflation was over, at least for the time being. So the proposals of the Board of Experts and the other professors were wide of the mark and outdated.

My stance on the D-Mark parity at the time did not, however, mean that I now regarded fixed parities as taboo. I was always clear on the fact that there would always be situations where the exchange rate would have to be adjusted in as flexible a way as possible.

Even at the time when we remained pretty well untroubled by the dilemma between the fixed exchange rate and domestic monetary stability, my support of the system of fixed exchange rates, above all against the dollar, was only conditional. I stated as much in the mid-sixties in several speeches and essays. I did so in very basic terms in a paper I delivered at the annual meeting of the Verein für

Socialpolitik in September 1964.[6] In it, I outlined that a system of fixed but adjustable exchange rates could only work if

- "through its domestic stability, i.e. monetary and economic stability, the key currency country makes it easier for the other member countries to maintain fixed parities without causing too great tensions with respect to their own domestic stability;
- any possible tensions between fixed exchange rates and domestic economic objectives are lessened successfully through close cooperation and common rules for balance of payments policy;
- adequate (but again not excessive) elasticity in the financial bridging of temporary imbalances is ensured, whereby of course abuses of such elasticity must also be prevented".

These key statements, dating from 1964, do not yet, of course, contain the reservation indispensable on the basis of later experience that vis-à-vis the dollar erratic capital movements can be a particularly disruptive element in a class of their own, making fixed rates impossible.

4. Change in the Nature of Currency Crises

Up to and including 1968, the currency crises we had to face were caused mainly by European tensions. This is particularly true of the sterling and franc crises in the sixties. The last step in this European theatre of crises was the D-Mark crisis in September/October 1969. It was in the main a crisis of omission. What had been left undone in November 1968, despite the strong urging of the Bundesbank, now had to be done by means of a more general and stronger D-Mark revaluation. But the D-Mark crisis of October 1969, unlike that of November 1968, was no longer an entirely European crisis. Dollar tensions now also played a role, primarily as a result of disruptive short-term capital movements between the D-Mark and the dollar in both directions. From the end of 1969 there was then a fundamental change in the nature of currency crises in two aspects:

- Firstly, the dollar replaced inner-European currency tensions as the main crisis factor.
- Secondly, destabilizing capital movements now came to the fore as the cause of the crisis, relegating price and demand differentials to the second rank.

The Bretton-Woods Agreement had not been very kind towards capital movements. When payments business was liberalized, it was to come after goods and services business. Now the tables almost seemed to be turned. Today, there is at times the danger that the capital flows triggered off by distorted interest rate

[6] Otmar Emminger, "Grundprobleme der internationalen Währungsordnung" (Basic Problems of the International Monetary System), address delivered at the 1964 annual meeting of the "Verein für Socialpolitik" in Travemünde.

relations or other disruptions will distort payments balances and exchange rates to such an extent that goods and services business must suffer. Capital movements have not only become a driving force for the world economy since the seventies, but also a potential disruptive factor of the first order. *At any rate, the superiority of international capital movements over goods and services has radically changed the nature of our currency system.*

It was not by chance that from the beginning of the seventies the interest rate differential and speculative financial flows increasingly dominated the monetary policy stage. It was at the beginning of the seventies that international financial flows and the mutual interdependence of the financial markets increased enormously, with the dollar at the centre of attention. The continuing liberalization of international capital flows as well as the greater mobility of capital as a result of modern communications technology were instrumental in the increasing importance of capital movements.

Naturally, loss of confidence in the dollar, which had repeatedly resulted in destabilizing capital movements from the end of the sixties, was not uninfluenced by the deterioration in the U.S. trade and current account balances, particularly in 1971 and 1972; confidence in the dollar was also undermined by lax U.S. budgetary policy and burgeoning inflation – in part a consequence of the Vietnam War. But if we look at the orders of magnitude for the crisis period from 1970 to spring 1973, the U.S. current account deficits were more than overshadowed by the disequilibria in the U.S. balance on capital account. Over these $3^1/_4$ years in question, the U.S. foreign exchange balance (official reserve transactions) showed a deficit of roughly $ 62 bn. The current and capital accounts made up roughly $ 25 bn. of this total, the rest was short-term capital movements (including unclassifiable residual items). The situation elsewhere was even more one-sided. *From 1969 at the latest, the D-Mark had – most unwillingly – become the main counterpart to the dollar.* Of the huge foreign exchange surpluses from the beginning of 1970 to March 1973 (DM 74 bn.), only one-seventh (DM 10.7 bn.) came from surpluses on the German current account, the other six-sevenths from monetary and capital inflows due to interest rates and confidence; and that despite the fact that out of pure desperation the German side had in those years repeatedly tried to stem capital inflows through administrative or price restrictions (including cash deposits). The extent to which the world was inundated with dollars at the time can be seen at least approximately from the inflation of global foreign exchange reserves. Between the beginning of 1970 and March 1973 they trebled from $ 33 bn. to $ 103 bn. This meant that aggregate currency reserves almost doubled. In the same period, *the foreign exchange reserves of Deutsche Bundesbank climbed more than sixfold* (from DM 11.7 bn. to DM 73.4 bn.), which resulted in overall reserves more than trebling.

The change in the nature of currency risks from the sixties to the seventies was recognized early on. I myself said in an interview[7] in November 1969, i.e. shortly after the overdue D-Mark revaluation of October 1969 that, with the sterling, franc and D-Mark parity adjustments behind us, we were now facing a dollar problem which would impose a strain on the world monetary system in future. In this

[7] Industriekurier dated November 15, 1969.

context, I of course cited in the main the deficit on the U.S. "basic balance", the deficit on current account, plus the balance of longer-term capital movements. It was only in 1970/71 that it became apparent what huge disruptive potential was also harboured in the to and fro of all types of short-term funds (vagrant dollars). I repeatedly drew attention to this in lectures and essays.

In one lecture delivered to an Italian banking conference in June 1971 entitled "Short-Term Capital Movements as the Cause of Crisis"[8] I said: "Whether we like it or not, we need greater exchange rate flexibility for our own protection. A broader exchange rate fluctuation band will not be of much help in such cases. ... For special emergencies, the International Monetary Fund should therefore under all circumstances be given the possibility of permitting a country whose monetary situation is seriously threatened to let its exchange rate float".

5. Greater Exchange Rate Flexibility Becomes International Topic

The currency crises of 1967 to 1969 had demonstrated how ad hoc adjustments of individual parities encountered political and psychological barriers, and how large the damage could be if adjustment were postponed. These new insights resulted in ever greater discussion worldwide of how to improve the monetary system through greater exchange rate flexibility. Nor was such discussion merely limited to academic circles anymore. From 1969 at the latest, the IMF, the EEC and the OECD also tackled the problems connected with greater flexibility of the exchange rate system. As a rule, consideration was given to extensively widening the fluctuation band around a fixed parity and to promoting timely parity adjustments by relaxing the rules or even by introducing a system of continuous minor adjustments ("sliding parities").

I myself was involved in such deliberations, but not only on various official and unofficial international bodies of which I was a member. Our own experience in Germany in November 1968 and May 1969 had made it clear to me just how much timely adjustment had been prevented by political and ideological prejudice as well as by lobby groups, so I made a number of sallies in favour of greater exchange rate flexibility in Germany too. Even though my proposals did not yet advocate freely floating exchange rates but merely that the IMF should grant a country greater flexibility in special cases, in Germany I was nevertheless regarded more and more often as a pioneer of exchange rate flexibility.[9]

I went one step further in an interview I gave the Handelsblatt in September 1970. I predicted, not at once but in a not-too-distant future: "We shall decouple from the dollar, and if possible *together with other* EC currencies". The first practical opportunity to do so would have been the dollar crisis in May 1971. The block float Minister Schiller and I wanted to introduce against the dollar did not,

[8] Otmar Emminger, "Kurzfristige Kapitalbewegungen als Krisenursache" (Short-Term Capital Movements as the Cause of Crisis), address delivered to an Italian banking symposium at the invitation of the Italian central bank, June 1971.

[9] Cf., for example, Industriekurier dated November 15, 1969, page 13: "Asked about his favourite topic, limited flexibility of exchange rates, Dr. Emminger said ...".

however, materialize because France and Italy could not be convinced to join in. This was half a defeat for me, too, as in May 1971 I had – in opposition to Klasen's view and the majority of the central bank council – been an energetic proponent of block floating. The May 1971 crisis also provided an object lesson that floating made it possible to bridge a fairly long period, namely in this case May to December 1971, and even to withstand the "Nixon shock" of August 1971 relatively unscathed. During this period of floating we were able to get rid of several billion dollars we had previously been compelled to take up through intervention, whereas those countries which in the summer of 1971 initially maintained their fixed parity against the dollar (e.g. Japan and France) had to take up substantial dollar amounts at excessively high rates.

The Washington exchange rate realignment of December 1971 did not, as Nixon had claimed at the time, turn out to be a lasting monument but merely an intermediate stage on the way to floating the dollar. Britain threw in the towel as early as June 1972 and let the pound float downwards – and since then it has been floating in isolation to this very day.

When in spring 1972 I saw that the December 1971 realignment kept running aground because of a lack of U.S. cooperation and that the only way we could maintain it was by instigating a monetary policy geared one-sidedly to the payments balance in conjunction with renewed capital import restrictions, it became pretty clear to me that sooner rather than later the switch to floating against the dollar would have to come.

I had an interesting and amusing experience around that time during a meeting with the later Nobel Prize winner Milton Friedman. We were both members of a panel discussion at an international banking conference in Montreal in May 1972. During the panel discussion there were no noteworthy points on which we disagreed. During the ensuing press conference Professor Friedman was asked by a reporter: "Professor Friedman, you have been in favour of a general floating of currencies for some time now. When do you think it will come about?". Friedman replied: "It will probably never come about for one simple reason. It would put the world's central banks out of business. Fixed exchange rates always result in renewed currency crises and crisis meetings where central bank chiefs can make themselves important and show off". Just under a year later, it was none other than some central banks – specifically the Swiss and German – which gave the impulse to floating (and block floating). By chance, or perhaps not by chance, it was in both cases the deputy chairmen then in office – Leutwiler in Switzerland and myself in the Federal Republic – who in February and March 1973 took the decisive step. The end of the fixed-rate system was heralded in by the Bundesbank ceasing to buy dollars, thus forcing the Council of Ministers of the EEC to resort to block floating against the dollar. To describe the details of this dramatic development would go beyond the scope of this paper. The result was that we decoupled ourselves from the international inflation convoy – a revolutionary step for our stability policy.

6. The Long Road to the Legalization of Floating

It took quite some time for the new system of floating to be finally accepted and legalized, namely until January 1976.[10] When we sounded the alarm on March 1, 1973 by no longer buying dollars at the fixed rate and when, ten days later, at German insistence the EC Council of Ministers passed its resolution to block float with the majority of members against the dollar, many thought that it was only a transitional phase, a temporary emergency solution. The reason was that, at the time discussion on the future exchange rate system was in full swing in the IMF's reform group, the so-called Committee of Twenty, and they were not yet considering a longer-term transition to floating.

On March 23, 1973, I had to report to the Group of Deputies[11] of the reform committee on the preceding monetary crisis and our transition to floating. I emphasized that destabilizing capital movements had been the villain of the piece, and that the massive influx of foreign exchange into the D-Mark (within four weeks over $ 7.6 bn., i.e. almost DM 24 bn.) had virtually nothing to do with a German current account surplus. I also stated that interest rate differentials had been of scant significance, since at the height of the crisis penal interest had even had to be paid on short-term D-Mark deposits. I came to the conclusion that as long as the combination of a weak dollar and huge liquid dollar holdings persisted, greater exchange rate flexibility would probably be unavoidable, not only temporarily but also over the longer term. This was not contested, but too little notice was taken of it in the committee's further deliberations. To begin with, even the Committee of Twenty treated the dollar/D-Mark crisis of spring 1973 as a gust of wind, which – although strong – would nevertheless die down. The preferred formula for the future reformed system which was accepted by the ministers and central bank governors at the end of March 1973 was as follows: "The exchange rate system should remain based on stable but adjustable par values. It was also recognized that floating rates could provide a useful technique in particular situations".

There were signs as early as late autumn 1973 that the work of the reform committee would come to a dead end on all major points. The centrepiece of the reform, "fixed but adjustable parities", had been slipping further and further away since March 1973. This became even clearer when towards the end of 1973 the first oil crisis erupted. Then – as already mentioned – even the Managing Director of the IMF stated that under the new circumstances extensive floating was not only unavoidable, but even desirable. But other parts of the planned general reform had also been too ambitious or far fetched from the outset. Even under more favourable conditions it would have been almost impossible to implement them. All these theoretical projects never left the drawing board; in the end, the reality of the inevitability of exchange rate flexibility caught up on and overtook them.

---

[10] If the day the revised IMF Articles of Agreement came into effect is taken as the date of legalization, then it took until April 1978.

[11] This Group of Deputies, under the chairmanship of the Englishman Jeremy Morse (at the time still Bank of England), did the real work; meetings of the Committee of Ministers were only seldom.

What remained was a small piecemeal programme including, for example, the appointment of the Interim Committee of the IMF as ministerial advisory and steering group. Or the guidelines promulgated in the summer of 1974 on how to deal with floating exchange rates. Some of these were taken over into the revised IMF Articles of Agreement.

The Reform Committee of the IMF was dissolved after presentation of its last report in June 1974. But that by no means saw an end to discussion of the future world monetary system, because the system of extensive floating had not yet been accepted by everyone as being final. Even the Germans and the Americans, who had almost always adopted the same position on the exchange rate question since March 1973, still disagreed on the nuances. One example of this is the discussion which took place at an international banking conference in Williamsburg in July 1974.[12] In my address[13], I had stated that floating, or at least much greater exchange rate flexibility, would probably remain the dominant element in any exchange rate system for the foreseeable future. This address was my farewell to the Reform Committee of the IMF (which was in the process of being dissolved). My friend Paul Volcker stated at a press conference at the same meeting that he was "more optimistic than Dr. Emminger about the possibility of making progress towards the stated aim of the reform, namely to fixed but adjustable parities", and perhaps even of achieving a certain degree of convertibility of major currencies into reserve assets, particularly special drawing rights. Certainly, that would not be possible without a reduction in global inflation and "sensible inner stability" in the major countries. Even Jeremy Morse, Chairman of the Group of Deputies of the Committee of Twenty, still fostered certain illusions about monetary reform. At the same conference he said: "If world inflation abates and the oil price problem is gradually resolved, we can then achieve a measure of cooperative control over floating from which we could then advance to stable but adjustable parities".

Nor did the completion of the work of the Committee of Twenty put an end to the differences of opinion on the future exchange rate system. Discussions continued in the various bodies, because the Articles of Agreement of the International Monetary Fund still had to be adapted to the new situation. In the process, the situation escalated to seemingly irreconcilable differences between the American and French viewpoints. The Americans wanted an exchange rate system which was as liberal as possible. The new U.S. Treasury Secretary, William Simon, was an out and out advocate of free exchange rates. The French, on the other hand, insisted on a gradual return to a system of fixed but adjustable parities, at least as the ultimate goal. Their view at the time was that the European "snake" should only be a transition to a general system of parities. But the future treatment of gold within the IMF was also a source of long-running disagreements with the French.

---

[12] Cf. New York Times dated July 2, 1974.

[13] Otmar Emminger, "The Evolving International Monetary System", June 1974.

7. Rambouillet Summit and Jamaica Conference

In summer 1975, it was finally decided to tackle both questions at the conference of the Interim Committee of the IMF planned for January 1976 in Jamaica. The aim was to achieve final agreement on the long overdue revision of the IMF Articles of Agreement. We had endless discussions on this, be it in the Monetary Committee of the EC or in the OECD or at the IMF. Again and again, the American and French viewpoints clashed irreconcilably. Some compared the inflexible stance of the French to the "Maginot Doctrine".

I had the opportunity to get the difficult decision-making process really rolling. At the beginning of November 1975 I was chairing a meeting of the Monetary Committee (Working Group III) of the OECD in Paris.[14] I had established the firm tradition that during the meeting the delegation heads would get together for an intimate dinner to discuss all pressing problems as freely and as openly as possible. At this dinner I deliberately played "agent provocateur" by raising the question of how we were going to handle the impending problems at the upcoming IMF conference in Jamaica if an end could not be put to the irreconcilable differences that still existed between the Americans and the French. I concluded by saying: "If the two of you cannot agree on a joint course of action soon, then there is absolutely no point in our going to Jamaica simply to hear the same old song again". I added: "If, however, the two of you were to reach a compromise, then we promise you that we will also adopt that compromise as the basis for further action". This plea, which found the support of other members, had astonishing results. The two committee members involved, Jacques de Larosière, at the time Directeur du Trésor at the French Ministry of Finance, and the American, Ed Yeo III, at the time Under-Secretary for monetary questions at the U.S. Treasury, then decided to meet as often and for as long as it took in the coming weeks to hammer out an agreement. After several bilateral talks they finally agreed on a joint memorandum ("Memorandum of Understanding") on November 15, 1975.

The Franco-American agreement came just in time for the beginning of the summit conference held in Rambouillet from November 15 to 17, 1975. This summit had been agreed on at the invitation of French President Giscard d'Estaing at the end of August 1975. However, the assertion[15] sometimes made that the Rambouillet summit was convened only or mainly to settle unresolved exchange rate questions is false. Quite the contrary. From the outset, the agenda contained a host of general questions about the economic recession at the time and how it could be overcome etc. The communiqué of the Rambouillet summit makes this clear. Monetary problems came 12th on a list of, in all, 17 points.

Above all, however, the monetary problems were not dealt with in any detail at the summit. Approving notice was merely taken of the Franco-American Memorandum of Understanding hammered out by de Larosière and Yeo. According to reports of those present, this is supposed to have taken less than an hour.

---

[14] I was chairman of this not unimportant OECD committee from 1969 until 1977.

[15] For example, by Reiner Hellmann in VWD Finanz- und Wirtschaftsspiegel" dated May 6, 1985.

In any event, the proposal remained a strictly bilateral Franco-American document and was treated as such until final agreement was reached in December 1975. The final wording was not even available for discussion at Rambouillet. It was only worked out later by the two partners and then circulated to the other countries concerned for further deliberation. Directly after the Rambouillet summit, Yeo and de Larosière visited the most important other countries concerned (including the Federal Republic) to acquaint them with the details of their memorandum. Understandably, some countries objected that the agreement had come about as a result of purely bilateral negotiations between the Americans and the French. But de Larosière and Yeo said they had received a "mandate" to do so from other countries, obviously referring to our talks in Paris on the fringe of the OECD meeting.

The summit communiqué is also quite clear on the fact that – at least with respect to the future exchange rate system – what was presented in Rambouillet was not an agreement reached by all concerned, but merely a Franco-American compromise presented at the conference. Point 12 of the communiqué states: "We welcome the rapprochement, reached at the request of many other countries, between the views of the United States and France on the need for stability that the reform of the international monetary system must promote. This rapprochement will facilitate agreement through the IMF at the next session of the Interim Committee in Jamaica on the outstanding issues of international monetary reform". And it did so. *In Jamaica,* agreement was reached swiftly in January 1976 on the future Article IV of the IMF Articles of Agreement concerning the international exchange rate system. Agreement was also reached on the gold question (which had been hardly touched on at the Rambouillet summit and had not been mentioned in the communiqué).

What form did the Franco-American agreement take? It consisted of two parts. The first part dealt with the principles governing the future exchange rate system, which – reformulated somewhat by the EC Monetary Committee, the Group of Ten and the IMF – were then reflected in the revised Article IV of the IMF Articles of Agreement. The main point was that every country could select its exchange rate system freely; they must, however, notify the IMF of the selection made and allow the IMF to monitor their exchange rate policy. Furthermore, Article IV of the IMF Articles of Agreement (like the Rambouillet communiqué) clearly states that the stability of any exchange rate system depends on the member countries pursuing a sound domestic policy. To this end, each member country was to "endeavour to direct its economic and financial policies toward the objective of fostering orderly economic growth with reasonable price stability". That is, by the way, the standard formulation to be found to this very day in all international monetary communiqués (sound, non-inflationary economic growth), like the communiqué of the recent economic summit in Tokyo. Finally, Article IV of the new IMF Articles of Agreement calls on the member countries to "avoid manipulating exchange rates or the international monetary system in order to prevent effective balance of payments adjustment or to gain an unfair competitive advantage over other members". All of this, and above all the free choice of exchange rate system, was completely in line with our German viewpoint. It also looked very much like a "victory" of the American position on the exchange rate system over the French.

In return, the Americans accommodated the French somewhat in the other part of the agreement dealing with the measures to prevent "erratic fluctuations in exchange rates". The same Point 12 of the Rambouillet communiqué stated here: "With regard to monetary problems, we affirm our intention to work for greater stability. ... At the same time, our monetary authorities will act to counter disorderly market conditions or erratic fluctuations in exchange rates". Specifically, the daily consultations which already existed between the central banks concerned were to be improved, and there was to be regular consultations between the finance ministers of the major countries. This, too, was taken up eleven years later in Tokyo.

Immediately after Rambouillet the Americans and the French, as was to be expected, gave varying interpretations of the compromise reached. It was no different seven years later after the second summit in France, the Versailles Conference. The French Finance Minister saw in the Franco-American agreement a three-stage plan for the establishment of fixed exchange rates; he believed that at the end of the road, "when conditions are right", the 85% majority provided for in the agreement (and later in Article IV of the IMF Articles of Agreement) would be achieved, allowing the creation of a general system of fixed but adjustable parities. As for intervention in the foreign exchange markets, the French hoped the Americans would always help support the dollar, at least in the event of "erratic" exchange rate fluctuations; the Americans were, they argued, now committed to do so, just as they were committed to constant consultation on foreign exchange market developments (which has existed for a long time anyway between central banks, including the Fed). The Americans, on the other hand, stressed the general freedom to select an exchange rate system; on the subject of intervention they stated their goodwill, but that the decision whether to intervene or not was theirs and theirs alone.

One aspect of some importance here was the definition of "*erratic exchange rate fluctuations*" mentioned in the Franco-American agreement and in the summit communiqué. This definition was understood as an extension of the expression "disorderly markets" used until then. When at the end of November 1975 Under-Secretary Ed Yeo III explained the Franco American compromise to us in greater detail, he defined "erratic" exchange rate fluctuations as "*such movements for which no explanation can be found in the underlying economic situation*". This is reminiscent of a similar passage in the Agreement of the *Group of Five* of September 22, 1985. Ten years later, the Americans realized that they could not simply stand by, exercising "benign neglect", and watch the dollar deviate substantially and persistently from the underlying economic fundamentals. In fact, they had already come very close to realizing this during the 1978/79 dollar crisis when – to use the words of an American spokesman – they went over to a "very activist definition of the fight against disorderly markets" and even wanted to win support for a sort of "target zone system" for the dollar. At the time, of course, U.S. exchange rate policy was activated to counter excessive *dollar* weakness. The latest bout of activity since 1985, on the other hand, was triggered off by an excessively strong dollar and its repercussions. In a nutshell: activity only in extreme situations.

Experience has taught us in the meantime that persistent upward distortions in the dollar rate – for years welcomed by the Americans as a "strong dollar" – can have unpleasant side effects: distortions in foreign trade structures and in the domestic economic structure, the accumulation of high foreign debt, protectionist dangers etc. But people have now also learned that such longer-term exchange rate distortions are not simply a result of floating, but reflect in reality structural faults in the economic and financial policies of major countries. An attempt is now being made to rectify the consequences of exchange rate distortion, in particular the huge disequilibria in world trade, through greater cooperation between the leading countries and through better "compatibility" of their economic and financial policies. The exchange rate, above all that of the dollar as the key currency, has become a "*signal for economic policy*" to be ignored at one's peril.

The Society for Business History: A Decade of Work

Hans Pohl

The Society for Business History was founded in 1976 by represen- tatives of business and scholarship. According to its articles of association it pursues the following aims: to stimulate and promote research of all kinds into business history; to engage in such research and publish the results; to organize scientific symposia and public lectures at which scholars, representatives of business and the public can meet; to propagate interest in business history and to preserve and make available the relevant historical material.[1] Over the past decade the Society has been able to realize these aims to differing degrees.

Ten years ago I pointed out that the institutional basis for the study of business history in the Federal Republic of Germany leaves much to be desired, in contrast, say, to the situation in Great Britain, the United States, and the GDR.[2] With the present level of public indebtedness and the cutbacks in expenditure in the university field that is still true today. Indeed, the whole field of economic and social history, which includes business history in the Federal Republic of Germany, is in a rather worse state today than it was ten years ago, for some professor's chairs have already been axed and others will be axed or changed when their present incumbants retire in a few years' time. This is not likely to be changed by the welcome fact that historians generally are showing a growing interest in questions of economy and society, even if usually only to trace the influence or repercussions of these on political events.

I.

Since its establishment the Society for Business History has held a public lecture and a research symposium every year. Both events help to realize one of the Society's main aims, namely to enable scholars and businessmen to meet and further mutual understanding, not least with regard to the need for more research into business history. The meetings are arranged so that speakers and participants from scholarship, mainly economic and social historians, economists and specialists in business management, meet with lawyers, sociologists and representatives of business, hear papers on a particular theme and join in a discussion. In selecting

[1] See Articles of Association, Para. 2, subpara. 1.

[2] Hans Pohl: Unternehmensgeschichte in der Bundesrepublik Deutschland – Stand der Forschung und Forschungsaufgaben für die Zukunft, in: Zeitschrift für Unternehmensgeschichte, Vol. 22, No. 1, 1977, pp. 26-41, here pp. 26f.

German Yearbook on Business History 1987

the subjects we have always chosen themes that are both historically relevant and of current concern. At the symposia a small group of representatives of business who have a particular interest in the theme discuss the subject with scholars who have specialized in it. The lectures are held before a larger audience and they are usually on a more general theme. There are two speakers, a scholar and a person with practical experience, one dealing with the historical aspects and the other with the current problems. This is followed by a panel discussion between scholars and representatives of business life, in which the subject can be considered in depth and the other participants have an opportunity to join in the discussion. The papers, most of which are detailed, and the contributions to the discussion, are published as supplements to the "Zeitschrift für Unternehmensgeschichte".

The papers and contributions to the discussion at the opening symposium on 18 November 1976 were published in the periodical itself.[3] It began with a general review. Peter von Siemens outlined the attitude to history of the man who heads a large company. He said: "From my own experience I can say that one can only stand firmly in the present, and help to shape the future, if one has a knowledge of the past, what has taken definite shape, its foundations, sources, motivation and contradictions. In present practice particularly, one has to recognize that without a living awareness of history there is no proper orientation, and so one cannot cope; inwardly or outwardly."

He saw the entrepreneur's awareness of history as part of the general attitude of the time, "which is just starting to break out of the current approach that is generally ahistorical, and in many cases actually anti-historical." Von Siemens rightly saw that the ahistorical attitude was breaking down. There has been a strong recovery of interest in history, particularly among young people, and the education authorities are responding by restoring history to a more prominent place in the curriculum. In the second part of his lecture von Siemens also said that companies need to be more aware of the role they play in history. He challenged them "to make clear the specific contribution business has made to general history ... and so to provide support and direction for action today ... and help us find the right decisions for the future."[4]

In the following years the Society's public lectures dealt with major themes in economic and social history that are still under discussion today, together with economic and social policy issues from the field of business history whose effects continue to be felt.

The group of themes on economic or political history began with a public lecture on concentration in the German economy since the 19th century.[5] Discussion on the possibilities of limiting the tendency to concentration is almost as old as concentration itself and still highly charged. In 1977 we dealt with the

---

[3] Zeitschrift für Unternehmensgeschichte, Vol. 22, No. 1, 1977.

[4] Peter von Siemens: Unternehmensführung und Geschichtsbewußtsein, in: loc. cit., pp. 3–8, here pp. 3 and 8.

[5] Hans Pohl, Wilhelm Treue (ed.): Die Konzentration in der deutschen Wirtschaft seit dem 19. Jahrhundert. The papers and contributions to the discussion at the second public lecture held by the Society for Business History on 28 June 1977 in Cologne, Zeitschrift für Unternehmensgeschichte, Supplement 11, Wiesbaden 1978.

question both in the historical context and as a matter of principle, such as all the different aspects of concentration, the difficulty of reaching a clear and satisfactory scientific definition of the process, from what degree and point in time cartels and company concentration become „a danger" to society as a whole and in how far concentration reduces or intensifies competition. Finally, the relation of the government, business and science to the process of concentration in Germany were examined.

Four years later we had a lively debate in Fürth on sales strategies of German companies in the past and today.[6] Fritz Blaich outlined the reactions from German businessmen to market changes from the second half of the nineteenth century to 1945. He divided his period into three phases (when businesses were oriented to production, sales and marketing). Hermann Sabel also identified three stages in the development since 1945 (sales strategy, marketing strategy and portfolio strategy), with first capacities, then the customer and since the end of the seventies the competitor being the main focus of attention. The discussion covered the different conditions for competition and the success or failure of strategies in German companies, together with the value companies place on marketing and the problems they face in the late 1980s.

In 1984, when a new wave of protectionism was threatening to break out in international trade, and politicians and businessmen throughout the world were demanding measures to protect their national economies, while others were warning against such steps, we organized a symposium in Düsseldorf to discuss the question of whether protectionism was progress or retrogression in business policy.[7] The absolutist rulers in the seventeenth century tried to protect their economies from foreign competition. After a brief interlude of free trade in the mid-nineteenth century, 1879 marked the beginning of three different phases of state foreign policy designed to protect domestic producers from foreign competition, in contrast to the system of free trade. The General Agreement on Tariffs and Trade (GATT, set up in 1947) was intended to create a new international system of trade with the objective of liberalising world trade as far as possible. Only since the oil crisis in 1973 has there been a resurgence of protectionist endeavours. At the symposium all the speakers and those who joined in the discussion basically agreed that the restoration of "an international trade system based on freedom and open competition" was urgently necessary, and that protectionism was not progress but retrogression.

General discussion on the social market economy and the question whether the concept needed to be changed or might even be obsolete caused the Society to hold a public lecture in 1985 on the establishment, development and features of the

---

[6] Hans Pohl (ed.): Absatzstrategien deutscher Unternehmen. Gestern – Heute – Morgen. Papers and contributions to the discussion at the sixth public lecture held by the Society for Business History on 13 May 1981 in Fürth, Zeitschrift für Unternehmensgeschichte, Supplement 23, Wiesbaden 1982, here pp. 12 and 66.

[7] Hans Pohl (ed.): Protektionismus. Fortschritt oder Rückschritt? Papers and contributions to the discussion at the 9th public lecture held by the Society for Business History on 18 May 1984 in Düsseldorf, Zeitschrift für Unternehmensgeschichte, Supplement 37, Stuttgart 1985.

social market economy.[8] In a paper dealing with the historical development Joachim Starbatty sketched out a huge canvas, tracing the idea from Antiquity through the classical British economists Adam Smith, David Ricardo and John Stuart Mill, the Pulpit Socialists and the Freiburg Ordo-liberals (Walter Eucken) to Alfred Müller-Armack, who had coined the term 'social market economy' from various historical sources and given it content and meaning. Starbatty also considered the misuse of the social market economy in practice, especially in state social policy and the group egoism that had been evident in the last few decades. Alfred Herrhausen took up the theme and demanded that the state should ensure economic freedom to enable private initiative to unfold on free markets stimulated by competition. This required clear framework conditions to be set by the government in its economic policy (a reduction of the tax burden on companies, and a reduction of subsidies) and its social policy (help to selfhelp). In short, we must return to the original concept of free competition and social protection. In the discussion there were complaints that the social network had become too wide, so that it was now unjust in some cases, and, mainly from Hans Tietmeyer, a demand for flexibility in wage policy and greater regional and sectoral differentiation, with more gradation of qualifications and intertemporal differentiation.

The question as to the optimal form of company has concerned entrepreneurs at all times, but particularly since the period of high industrialization began, with the increase it brought in the number of industrial firms. The question has been repeatedly raised and lawyers and economists have put forward answers. Apart from the foundation savings banks, experience with foundat- ions in a business context goes back about 100 years, in fact to Carl Zeiss. But as a form, the foundation related to a business, of whatever size structure and sector, has never been as popular as now, although there is no separate legislation on foundations and the bureaucratic difficulties in the way of setting one up are quite considerable. As an instrument for investment, the foundation has grown steadily in importance without displacing those that are of the nature of a service or promotional institution. There are many different reasons for setting up such foundations (to change the shareholdings by neutralising capital, provide earnings for social work and so on). This set of problems was considered by the Society for Business History in its third public lecture in 1978 in Frankfurt on the experience of foundations and their future prospects.[9]

There have been communal enterprises for more than two thousand years, but they have recently come under fierce criticism. Partly because the services provided were inadequate and the local authorities were suffering heavy losses, or for structural policy reasons, some cities have handed over some of their public services to private contractors. The discussion on the privatisation of communal

[8] Hans Pohl (ed.): Entstehung und Entwicklung der Sozialen Marktwirtschaft. Papers and discussions at the 10th public lecture held by the Society for Business History on 26 June 1985 in Frankfurt am Main, Zeitschrift für Unternehmensgeschichte, Supplement 45, Stuttgart 1986.

[9] Hans Pohl, Wilhelm Treue (ed.): Stiftung und Unternehmung. Erfahrungen und Zukunftsperspektiven. Papers and contributions to the discussion at the third public lecture held by the Society for Business History on 31 May 1978 in Frankfurt am Main, Zeitschrift für Unternehmensgeschichte, Supplement 14, also containing material from the Stiftungszentrum 12, Wiesbaden 1979.

supplies, waste removal and transport is in full swing. Against that background the Society held a meeting in Cologne in 1985, at which the objectives, meaning and achievements of communal enterprises since the Middle Ages were discussed, with attention focussing particularly on their great expansion in the age of industrialization and so their mass agglomeration, roughly since 1850.[10] The expansion in communal infrastructure investment, and the resultant expansion in communal enterprises, led after the last third of the nineteenth century to a gradual definition of the legal bases and tasks for communal enterprises, which changed from cooperative legal entities to police administrative units. The local authorities chose different legal and organizational forms for the enterprises they ran to provide general services, although the company owned by the local council is still the most frequent today. In addition to considering the lack of legitimation, the commercial success and the public purpose of communal enterprises, as well as the tension that has often marred cooperation with political bodies, administrations and associations, the speakers dealt with communal transport, gas, electricity and water enterprises, markets, trade fairs and slaughterhouses, savings banks and pawnshops over the last 130 years.

With public funds becoming scarcer, growing public borrowing and the education and research establishments in the Länder calling for more and more funds, there is growing demand for more private funding of education and research, while the requests to the private business foundations for promotion are becoming more numerous and more costly. Occasionally one has the impression that companies need to break new ground here. At a symposium held by the Society in Leverkusen in 1982[11] we learned that since the nineteenth century it has been mainly companies in the younger sectors (such as chemicals, electrical engineering and mechanical engineering), and in the iron and steel industry, that have promoted the training of junior scientific and technical staff and financed scientific research through various societies, particularly the Kaiser Wilhelm Society, now the Max Planck Society, and its institutes. After the First World War, when public funds for research and training were particularly scarce, leading German industrialists founded the Stifterverband der Notgemeinschaft der Deutschen Wissenschaft (Patrons Association for the Promotion of German Science) in 1920. Other promotional associations, like the Helmholtz-Gesellschaft zur Förderung der physikalisch-technischen Forschung (Helmholtz Society for the Promotion of Physical and Technical Research (1920)) and the Förderergemeinschaft der Deutschen Industrie (Association for the Promotion of German Industry (1942)) followed.[12] A large number of societies of friends and patrons of

[10] Hans Pohl (ed.): Kommunale Unternehmen, Geschichte und Gegenwart. Papers and contributions to the discussion at the 9th scientific symposium held by the Society for Business History on 17 and 18 January 1985 in Cologne, Zeitschrift für Unternehmensgeschichte, Supplement 42, Stuttgart 1986.

[11] Hans Pohl (ed.): Wirtschaft, Schule und Universität. Die Förderung schulischer Ausbildung und wissenschaftlicher Forschung durch deutsche Unternehmen seit dem 19. Jahrhundert. Papers and contributions to the discussion at the 7th Research Symposium held by the Society for Business History on 19 November 1982 in Leverkusen, Zeitschrift für Unternehmensgeschichte, Supplement 29, Wiesbaden 1983.

[12] Hans Pohl: Zur Zusammenarbeit von Wirtschaft und Wissenschaft im "Dritten Reich"; Die "Förderergemeinschaft der Deutschen Industrie" von 1942, in: Vierteljahrschrift für Sozial- und Wirtschaftsgeschichte 72, 1985, pp. 508–536.

universities and technical colleges were also set up in the regions, and industrial companies helped to set up and finance numerous university institutes and professors' chairs. The speakers showed that without the financial help from industry, German science would hardly have attained the international standard it has enjoyed in the twentieth century, and still does.

The meetings of the Society we have discussed so far were mainly concerned with questions of economic history and economic policy, and I should now like to turn to those lectures and symposia that dealt mainly with questions of social history or social policy. The following subjects were discussed: company social policy in general and occupational training and advanced training in particular, the legislation on labour disputes and co-determination, the legitimation of the management and problems of certain social groups, such as women and foreign workers, in business.

The growth in state social benefits after the Second World War, and especially since the 1970s, is increasingly causing politicians and the general public to ask whether and in how far the finance for this will be available in future, and whether a restructuring or reduction in some state benefits is not called for. In the last few decades various company benefits that used to be voluntary have been brought under legislation or collective agreements and so given a legal guarantee, and this has caused some talk of company social policy, which used to play a pioneering role for the state, being undermined. At a symposium in Hamburg in 1977 social historians, sociologists and the heads of social policy departments in German companies discussed questions of insurance against sickness, accident, invalidity and old age, contributions to lowering living costs (housing allowances, subsidised canteens), improving incomes (bonuses, gratuities, profit-sharing schemes), work structures and training conditions (training workshops), the assessment scales, means of ensuring performance and the groups who receive such benefits.[13]

The subject of the commercial and socio-political role played by company social benefits since the 19th century proved so big that three further meetings were held to discuss these questions. Each meeting was concerned with certain aspects of the general theme of company social policy, based on the wider issue.[14]

One of the main tasks and achievements of company social policy has been vocational training and advanced training in industry, the crafts and services companies since the phase of high industrialization. Basic and further vocational training also plays a major part in current discussion on company training and its future shape, so the Society held a symposium on this in Sindelfingen in 1978 with social historians, company trainers and educationalists.[15] As in other areas of

[13] Hans Pohl (ed.): Betriebliche Sozialpolitik deutscher Unternehmen seit dem 19. Jahrhundert. Papers and contributions to the Research Symposium held by the Society for Business History on 25 November 1977 in Hamburg, Zeitschrift für Unternehmensgeschichte, Supplement 12, Wiesbaden 1978.

[14] Hax recently described this as "social company policy" (in contrast to the narrow concept of social policy as "the policy of social benefits"). See Hans Pohl. Einführung in die Thematik, loc. cit., pp. 7–12, here p. 10.

[15] Hans Pohl (ed.): Berufliche Aus- und Weiterbildung in der deutschen Wirtschaft seit dem 19. Jahrhundert. Papers and contributions to the discussion at the 2nd Research Symposium held by the Society for Business History on 7 December 1978 in Sindelfingen, Zeitschrift für Unternehmensgeschichte, Supplement 15, Wiesbaden 1979.

social policy, companies have played a pioneering role here by building up on guild traditions, although these had lapsed so far in the 18th century that there was talk of a "crisis in occupational education". Craft and commercial enterprises provided training, and increasingly industrial firms followed suit (setting up training workshops and works schools). In some sectors special schools were opened (shipping, mining, trade and technical drawing schools). However, that was only the first and initially most important sector of occupational training within German industry, and in the twentieth century numerous other training measures have been instigated by German companies, associations and the trade unions after the dual system was given a firm legislative base in 1897. In 1978 about 60 to 70 per cent of young people in any one age year did "most of their first vocational training in a company".[16]

With its symposium in Hanover in 1979 covering legislation on labour disputes[17] the Society took up a theme that has been and still is almost more controversial than any other issue in public discussion on social policy. The main speakers were experts on labour legislation and economists. They dealt with the development of labour dispute legislation against the background of industrialization and the coalition legislation in Germany, but they also drew comparisons with conditions in Great Britain, France, Switzerland, Italy, the Netherlands, the Scandinavian countries and the United States, because agreements on working conditions in these countries are so often mentioned. There have been cases of strikes since the Middle Ages. So some elements in modern labour legislation date from earlier centuries or they are related to the transition to the division of labour in a modern industrial state (like state labour-protection legislation). Great Britain played a pioneering role in the intervention of the state in questions of working life (coalition and factory laws), and the continental European countries drew on this in the course of the 19th century.[18] The speakers gave differing views on the effects of the legislation on labour disputes and, for instance, the arbitration agreements between the unions and the employers with Walter Hamm demanding "effective protection for the general public from increasing labour disputes".[19]

Six months later we held a public lecture in Düsseldorf on the causes and development of co-determination in Germany.[20] If foreign states and institutions are now studying the co-determination regulations in the Federal Republic of

---

[16] Albin Gladen: Berufliche Bildung in der deutschen Wirtschaft 1918–1945, in: loc. cit., pp. 53-73, here p. 53.

[17] Hans Pohl (ed.): Die Entwicklung des Arbeitskampfrechts in Deutschland und in den westlichen Nachbarstaaten. Papers and contributions to the discussion at the 4th Research Symposium of the Society for Business History on 7 December 1979 in Hanover, Zeitschrift für Unternehmensgeschichte, Supplement 16, Wiesbaden 1980.

[18] Theo Mayer-Maly: Die Entwicklung des Arbeitskampfrechts in Deutschland und in den westlichen Industriestaaten vom Ausgang des 19. Jahrhunderts bis 1945, in: loc cit., pp. 11–17, here pp. 11f.

[19] Walter Hamm: Entwicklung des Arbeitskampfrechts in ihren Auswirkungen auf die westlichen Volkswirtschaften – unter besonderer Berücksichtigung der Entwicklung seit 1945, loc.cit., pp. 64–72, here p. 72.

[20] Hans Pohl (ed.): Mitbestimmung: Ursprünge und Entwicklung. Papers and contributions to the discussion at the 5th public lecture given by the Society for Business History, 7 May 1980 in Düsseldorf, Zeitschrift für Unternehmensgeschichte, Supplement 19, Wiesbaden 1981.

Germany with a view to adopting some of them, that is because over the roughly 140 years of the history of co-determination these rights have probably not been so comprehensively legislated in any other state. "As a general term for various forms of worker participation in will-formation within the business or company and the economy as a whole"[21] "co-determination" is a postwar term, but as early as the 1830s and 1840s philosophers and lawyers in Germany were demanding a right for workers to have a say in industry, following the lead of the West European states that had industrialized earlier, in other words, long before the trade union movements as such developed. While Hans-Jürgen Teuteberg described the beginnings and the fight for legislation on co-determination inside and outside the company up to the Central Association of Employers and Workers in Germany of 15 November 1918, the extension of co-determination in the Weimar Republic and its annullment in the Third Reich, together with the detailed provisions in the postwar period up to the Act on Co-determination for Workers of 4 May 1976, Harald Jürgensen concentrated mainly on the effects of co-determination, and certain problem areas, like the need for flexible adjustment, investment, competition, company social policy, free collective bargaining and labour disputes.

Management has played a growing, though changing role in industry and the services sector in the nineteenth and twentieth centuries. The problems of legitimation and company strategies, which have faced entrepreneurs since the beginning of industrialization, and the principle change in the problem of legitimation after 1945 were the subject of a public lecture held in Munich in 1982, which also aimed to provide a historical basis for the present discussion on company constitution.[22] Jürgen Kocka drew a distinction between two different phases, that of the ownerentrepreneur and that of the employed manager who is not a partner in the firm, which has been the increasingly predominant form since the end of the Kaiserzeit. In the first phase legitimation was through the use of economic and technical innovation, and public disinterest was overcome with high performance, demonstrations of success, a good style of living, improving the general level of prosperity and so on, as the head of the firm had to maintain his position in the contrast between capital and labour. In the second phase the possibilities for legitimation decreased as management functions were separated from the shareholders, and as companies grew in size the social gap also grew. Qualification and performance remained the main criteria of legitimation. There was approximation or integration of shareholders and top managers. After 1945 there was a change, not only in the legitimation of the management but also in the system of the social market economy itself, as Burghard Freudenfeld stressed. Business success alone was not enough, on the contrary, it greatly helped to change social values, and business activity had to take quite new factors into account in its legitimation. It could no longer be oriented only to "economic processes in the

---

[21] Hans-Jürgen Teuteberg: Ursprünge und Entwicklung der Mitbestimmung in Deutschland, loc. cit., pp. 7–73, here p. 7.

[22] Hans Pohl (ed.): Legitimation des Managements im Wandel. Zur Diskussion über Funktion und Auftrag der Unternehmensleitung während der letzten 150 Jahre. Papers and contributions to the discussion at the 7th public lecture held by the Society for Business History on 25 June 1982 in Munich, Zeitschrift für Unternehmensgeschichte, Supplement 28, Wiesbaden 1983.

narrower sense", it also needed to take into account "the adequate satisfaction of society, in material and ideal form".[23]

Of the different social groups in business, workers and their situation in and outside the company during the process of industrialization has repeatedly been the subject of scientific discussion and research in recent decades. The role of the sexes has also been considered, and the position of women at work, particularly since the nineteenth century, is relatively well researched. In several seminars I attempted to take a wider look at the question of women at work in the business world, both thematically and chronologically, by examining all the activities of women in German business life from the Middle Ages to the end of the Second World War. I felt that this was all the more necessary, since research and discussion on the subject of women always concentrate on their social position, that is, their past and present position in the family and society. These studies culminated in a research symposium on the role of woman in German business, which we held in December 1983 in Essen.[24] The response from scholars, the business world and the media was greater than at almost any other meeting of the Society. The discussion in Essen on this subject, which so often arouses strong public emotion, was, if often heated, on the whole factual and objective. We deliberately chose a wide historical framework, to clear up prejudices about the role of women in German business life in the Middle Ages and the early Modern Age, and above all to point out where there are large gaps in research. We also wanted to make it clear that it is not only in the twentieth century that women have made a noteworthy contribution to the national product, they have done so since the Middle Ages, working on the land, in trade and industry. It also became clear that the role of women at work and their position in the family and society are closely interlinked. The work done by women in past centuries was certainly not limited to dependent and inferior tasks, there were women who owned and ran businesses at a very early period, although there have only been women in professions like medicine and the public administration since the nineteenth century. We also dealt in detail with women as servants, and as blue-and white-collar workers. The position of women in business life has certainly not always received due recognition, it has been subject to upswings and downswings, as the papers on women at work from the 8th to the 20th centuries showed.

The "unresolved conflicts and controversies" over our foreign workers "arise outside the factory gates", while "the integration of the foreign worker into the factory and the adjustment to his functional needs has largely been achieved, or at least it appears to be practically within grasp". With those two sentences Josef Isensee summarized the results of the panel discussion he chaired at the public lecture in Cologne in 1983 on the integration of foreign workers.[25] Before that

---

[23] Burghard Freudenfeld: Perspektiven unternehmerischer Handlungsbedingungen, loc. cit., pp. 22–32, here p. 32.

[24] Hans Pohl (ed.): Die Frau in der deutschen Wirtschaft. Papers and contributions to the discussion at the 8th Research Symposium of the Society for Business History, 8 and 9 December 1983 in Essen, Zeitschrift für Unternehmensgeschichte, Supplement 35, Stuttgart 1985.

[25] Hans Pohl (ed.): Integration ausländischer Mitarbeiter. Papers and contributions to the discussion at the 8th public lecture held by the Society for Business History on 25 May 1983 in Cologne, Zeitschrift für Unternehmensgeschichte, Supplement 32, Wiesbaden 1984, quotation from p. 95.

Wolfgang Köllmann traced the historical trend in the migration of foreign workers (engineers, skilled, semi-skilled and unskilled workers) from the nineteenth century, particularly after the high industrialization phase, to the end of the Second World War.[26] Josef Stingl spoke on the inflow of foreign workers, particularly after 1961, the problem of integrating them into society as a whole, which was not a question of company policy, the recruitment freeze after 1973 and the difficult issues in policy on foreign workers, such as integration aids, family immigration, incentives to induce workers to return to their homelands, illegal entries and applicants for political asylum.[27]

II.

The Society for Business History has always sought to work together with other research societies and establishments, particularly since there are no institutes or chairs of business history in the Federal Republic of Germany. The Society has therefore always tried to maintain contact with university teachers, particularly younger scholars, and interest them in business history. As speakers from different academic disciplines have given papers or been present at the Society's meetings, the number of scholars who are interested in this subject and willing to work in it has gradually been built up.

In addition, the Society has taken up contact with the Society for Social and Economic History, the Association of German Business Archivists, the Institute for Bank-Historical Research, the Working Group on the History of the Savings Banks and the library of the German Business Institute (Institut der deutschen Wirtschaft), which has the best and most complete collection of German company Festschriften. The Society now publishes the German Yearbook on Business History together with the Institute for Bank-Historical Research and the directory of German business archives, "Deutsche Wirtschaftsarchive", together with archivists in the Association of German Business Archivists.

Since its inception the Society has also keenly fostered international cooperation between scholars and research institutions on business history. To that end it formed an editorial advisory council for the "Zeitschrift für Unternehmensgeschichte", consisting of 14 specialists teaching in nine countries at four German and ten foreign universities, while the Yearbook, which has been published since 1982, has an Editorial Board consisting of eight specialists, six of whom are colleagues abroad, from five different nations. We have also always invited guests from abroad to our lectures and particularly our symposia, welcoming scholars from neighbouring European states such as Austria, Switzerland, France, Britain, Belgium and Sweden, and from overseas countries like the United States and Japan, both as speakers and as participants.

---

[26] Wolfgang Köllmann: Ausländische Arbeitnehmer in Deutschland vor dem Beginn der Gastarbeiterzuwanderung, loc. cit., pp. 5–54.

[27] Josef Stingl: Arbeitsmarkt und ausländische Arbeitnehmer in der Bundesrepublik Deutschland, loc. cit., pp. 55–65.

To build up these relations we have held several international events, at which business historians from different countries discussed a theme using international comparisons. In Hamburg in 1981 we considered the interdependence of economic growth, technology and working time, a problem that has dominated discussion in nearly every country since the worldwide growth in unemployment.[28] The connection between technical progress and economic growth, and their repercussions on working time, the quality of work and possibilities for employment in Germany and the major industrialized states (Great Britain, France, Belgium, Switzerland and the United States) since the transition phase from the preand early industrialized society to the present were discussed by speakers from all the countries considered. The greater technical progress in the last 200 years has not only brought economic growth over the longer term, it has also improved the material standard of living, brought greater social achievements, provided better training possibilities and shortened working time; it has also brought changes in the economic structure. Conversely, the changes in working time have also affected economic growth and the labour market, since they constitute an aspect of the production factor labour.

The problem of "restrictions to competition" has increasingly concerned international discussion for a good century, as crisis symptoms appeared in the world economy and the national economies and the individual states moved increasingly from liberalism to protectionism. This has also led to measures to reduce international trade. In view of the lack of transparency on the restrictions to competition on international markets in the current and historical perspective scholars from nine nations discussed this subject in 15 papers at an international meeting in Lüneburg in 1985[29] They considered the effects of economic policy measures, such as customs and excise dues, policies on trade, exchange rates, subsidies, prices, raw materials and social policy, bilateral and multilateral agreements and cartels. They also discussed cartel policy, mergers and multinational companies on international markets in the three phases up to the First World War, the interwar years and after 1945. We heard some entirely new views, such as that cartels and multinational companies certainly do not always necessarily limit competition, they can act as a stimulant to it as well.

Some international meetings were held in cooperation with foreign societies. The Society has very close links with the Austrian Federation for Research into Entrepreneurs' Biographies and Company History in Vienna, whose chairman, Alois Brusatti, has been a member of the academic advisory council of our Society since its establishment. These links led to a joint event in 1984 at the Economics

---

[28] Hans Pohl (ed.): Wirtschaftswachstum, Technologie und Arbeitszeit im internationalen Vergleich. Papers and contributions to the discussion at the 6th Research Symposium of the Society for Business History on 15 and 16 December 1981 in Hamburg, Zeitschrift für Unternehmensgeschichte, Supplement 24, Wiesbaden 1983.

[29] Hans Pohl (ed.): Wettbewerbsbeschränkungen auf internationalen Märkten. Papers and contributions to the discussion at the 10th Research Symposium held by the Society for Business History on 25–27 September 1985 in Lüneburg, Zeitschrift für Unternehmensgeschichte, Supplement 46, Stuttgart 1988.

University in Vienna.[30] The subject, companies and the state since the Second World War in the Federal Republic of Germany and the Republic of Austria, is highly topical, because questions of reducing the high public share (of state-owned or quasi state-owned companies) and structural reform are being discussed in Austria, and in the Federal Republic of Germany the withdrawal of the public sector from companies through privatisation is under discussion. Since the framework for economic policy evolved very differently in Austria and the Federal Republic of Germany after the war, the relationship of the state to business also took a different path in the two countries. While in Austria as a result of the legislation on nationalization in 1946/47 large areas of industry (up to 30 to 40% of companies limited by shares) and the three major banks were taken over by the state and only 30 to 40% of companies, most of them small and medium-sized, remained in private ownership, all the governments in the Federal Republic of Germany decided in favour of continuing the social market economy set up by Ludwig Erhard. In his paper Alois Brusatti[31] described the possibilities for government intervention in the management of state-owned companies, the bureaucratic obstacles and the resistance on the part of the management. But he also discussed state promotion of small and medium-sized companies and the social partnership, that is, the organization of employers and workers to negotiate wage and price recommendations. Horst Albach stressed[32] that the state exercises supervision functions in the Federal Republic of Germany as well, intervening in business life with structural policy and process policy measures while there are state-owned enterprises in the utilities and transport sectors. He outlined the aims of state economic policy in the Federal Republic of Germany, pointing to the basic principles of the social market economy and identified some future problems in the relation between private businesses and the state.

The second foreign institute with which the Society for Business History established close links soon after it was set up was the Business History Society of Japan, whose President, Keiichiro Nakagawa of the University of Tokyo, and secretary, Hisashi Watanabe of the University of Kyoto, I had met. Over the years these relations brought closer contacts between the two societies, which yielded scientific fruit. The first was a joint public meeting followed by a research symposium in Berlin in 1978.[33] Three practitioners were the speakers at the public lecture. The Japanese Ambassador in the Federal Republic of Germany, Bunroku

[30] Alois Brusatti, Hans Pohl (ed.): Unternehmen und Staat nach dem Zweiten Weltkrieg. Ein deutsch-österreichischer Vergleich. Papers and contributions to the discussion at the meeting held by the Society for Business History, Cologne, and the Association for Research into Entrepreneurs' Biography and Company History, Vienna, on 11 October 1984 in Vienna, Zeitschrift für Unternehmensgeschichte, Supplement 39, Stuttgart 1986.

[31] Alois Brusatti: Unternehmen und Staat in Österreich nach dem Zweiten Weltkrieg, loc. cit., pp. 15–23.

[32] Horst Albach: Unternehmen und Staat in der Bundesrepublik Deutschland nach dem Zweiten Weltkrieg, loc. cit., pp. 24–45.

[33] Hans Pohl (ed.): Innovation, Know How, Rationalization and Investment in the German and Japanese Economies 1868/1871–1930/1980. Proceedings of the German-Japanese Symposion at the Siemens Training Centre in Berlin, 20–23 March 1979, Zeitschrift für Unternehmensgeschichte, Supplement 22, Wiesbaden 1982.

Yoshino, spoke on economic relations between Japan and the Federal Republic of Germany, discussing trade between the two countries and common points (e.g. a liberal economic policy) and differences (management structures, working conditions) in the development of business life in the two countries. Karl Otto Mittelstenscheid, member of the Management Board of Schering AG, Berlin, dealt with the significance of innovation and know-how for industry in the Federal Republic of Germany and how to finance it, and Shigiyoshi Kawakatsu, Managing Director of Matsushita Electric Sales Europa Verkauf GmbH, Hamburg, spoke on the sales conditions facing a Japanese firm wanting to sell technical products in Europe. The following symposium dealt with the subjects of innovation, know-how, rationalization and investment in the Japanese and German economies from 1868/71 to 1930, in other words, during a phase when Japan opened to the world, embarked on industrialization and became the leading industrial nation in Asia, while in Germany a national economy developed for the first time since the foundation of the Reich, the phase of high industrialization was concluded and Germany became the leading industrial power in Europe. In eight papers Japanese and German colleagues compared the development in the four problem areas in various industries in the two countries (iron and steel, textiles and automobiles, optical and electrical engineering, ship-building and shipping). This joint meeting in Berlin was followed by one in Tokyo in 1981, again with a general theme, this time organization and management from 1900 to 1930, on a comparison between Germany and Japan.[34] Specifically we discussed the development of the banks and their role in industrialization, the differences in occupational training and further training, the formation of a management in German and Japanese companies and the organization and management of large family businesses, the role of the middle management and the importance of small and medium-sized firms for the economy in the two countries.

Further international contacts are maintained with researchers in various universities abroad, such as Harvard, Yale and Berkeley in California, Paris-Nanterre, Leuven and Umea (Sweden), as well as with research establishments like the London School of Economics. With this and the Centre National de la Recherche Scientifique in Paris we intend to publish a bibliography listing publications on business history of recent years in France, Great Britain, Italy and the Federal Republic of Germany.

III.

Despite numerous other activities, relatively sparse funds and a correspondingly small staff, the Society has also stimulated research work, promoted this and engaged in it itself.

Entrepreneurs and companies are always in a field of tension between differing interests and in part conflicting values.

---

[34] Keiichiro Nakagawa , Tsunehiko Yui (ed.): Organization and Management 1900–1930. Proceedings of the Japan-Germany Conference on Business History, 1983.

There is a wide range of opinions on the functional integration of private enterprise in society as a whole, and the intellectual and political conflicts on the role of private enterprise in state and society are fought out in many areas, including our schools. Educational material can be used for this purpose, and the teachers have the difficult task of achieving sufficient objectivity when presenting the material. They need to have school text books which will provide them and their pupils with facts that are adequately sifted and presented. The situation differs in the various subjects, as well as in the different types of schools and grades. For us the historical component is the main focus of attention. The material is particularly complex in the humanities, in areas like social studies that lend themselves to ideological loading. Since the authors of the textbooks are not uninfluenced by their economic and sociopolitical environment, subjective value-judgements automatically flow into what they write, even if both publishers and authors endeavour to achieve an objective and accurate presentation and assessment. Hanne Braun, nee Michalak, examined the social studies textbooks for Secondary Stage I (grammar school, intermediary school and general school) and the senior classes in grammar school.[35] Her conclusions were: the concept of the entrepreneur and the manager are not shown as "problematical", and the various types of entrepreneur are not described for the pupils. In most of the books entrepreneurs and private enterprise are described in a one-sided, and sometimes actually false, way, although none of the books could be described as altogether unsuitable. What she criticised were rather "tendencies". "Most authors describe entrepreneurs in the secondary sector during industrialization, following Marx's doctrine, as wielders of power within the state, and in anonymous societies; finally the state is shown as entrepreneur in the various economic systems ... The negative image of the entrepreneur, private enterprise and the business world – which one certainly cannot simply dismiss as unrealistic – predominates in the accounts of the early phase of industrialization, the world of work, economic and political power and international trade. A positive view – which would be just as realistic – is relatively rare, and generally to be found where entrepreneurs or their associations themselves have the chance to speak in the source books."[36]

Other examinations of school books remain a future task for research and would be greatly desired, although only a few social historians are in a position to do such research, for a knowledge of at least one theoretical science like sociology or psychology is required to use the appropriate survey techniques and set up the necessary models.

Our aim to move from the general question of "Women in the German economy" and close a specific gap in research, namely women as entrepreneurs, by working through the source material, has so far not proved attainable, with two exceptions, and despite intensive research, owing to the lack of source material. Elke Hlawatschek's paper for the Essen conference on women in German business

[35] Hanne Michalak: Das Unternehmerbild in Schulbüchern. Eine Untersuchung der Sozialkunde-Lehrbücher für die Sekundarstufe I, Cologne 1978.

[36] Hanne Braun: Unternehmer und unternehmerische Wirtschaft im Schulbuch. Eine Untersuchung der Sozialkundebücher für die gymnasiale Oberstufe, Cologne 1981 (thesis, Bonn, 1980), quotations on pp. 543 and 546.

life[37] showed that this research field needs still greater methodological penetration. Elke Hlawatschek analysed about 60 women for her paper, on whose life and work we have more or less full information. She is currently preparing a thesis on this subject, and in Essen she drew a distinction between women who inherit a business, women who found one and "new beginnings" in the twentieth century, that is, women in permanent employment. Anke Probst chose one example, Helene Amalie Krupp, nee Ascherfeld (1732–1810), in Essen, the grandmother of Friedrich Krupp, to show how rewarding a biographical study can be if sufficient source material is available. Helene Amalie Krupp inherited a business, and after the death of her husband, Friedrich Jodocus Krupp, who was 26 years older than she, continued his trading company and administered the property she had inherited. "She stepped up her trade with Holland, established business ties with England and widened the range of goods". She even produced snuff. She invested most of the profits in land, bought mining shares and pits and took a share in the Gute Hoffnung iron smelter, which she finally bought and then sold again eight years later (in 1808). With her success as entrepreneur she laid the financial foundations for the emergence of the future Krupp concern.[38]

The big subject of voluntary social benefits provided by companies has been discussed, not only at conferences but also in various monographs printed by the Society.

Soon after the Society was founded its Advisory Council suggested that one important area of company social policy should be studied in a separate research project promoted by the Robert Bosch Foundation. Company social policy has undergone considerable changes and shifts in emphasis in the past 150 years. The main reasons were and are the attitude to the staff, the motivation for company measures in this field, changing objectives and not least the framework set by legislation and collective agreements.[39] On the other hand, company measures themselves actually seem to show a degree of continuity. As part of company social benefits participation in success, and above all wealth formation, have been topics since the early nineteenth century, and they have almost become slogans in current political discussion on social policy. The concept of participation in success has been used in economic literature since the 1950s, instead of the less clear concept of profit-sharing, and it has now largely become the general term for the various ways in which employees can benefit from the success of the firm that employs them. But there is as yet no generally accepted definition of the term "wealth", for once the concept is laid down a decision is also taken on the analysis of the existing distribution of profits.

---

[37] Elke Hlawatschek: Die Unternehmerin (1800–1945), in: Hans Pohl (ed.): Die Frau in der deutschen Wirtschaft, Zeitschrift für Unternehmensgeschichte, Supplement 35, Stuttgart 1985, pp. 127–146.

[38] Anke Probst: Helene Amalie Krupp, Eine Essener Unternehmerin um 1800, Zeitschrift für Unternehmensgeschichte, Supplement 33, Stuttgart 1985, see pp. 16ff., quotation p. 17.

[39] Hans Pohl, Horst A. Wessel: Einführung in das Forschungsprojekt: Erfolgsbeteiligung und Vermögensbildung von Arbeitnehmern ausgewählter deutscher Unternehmen von der Mitte des 19. Jahrhunderts bis zum Zweiten Weltkrieg, in: Christoph Conrad, Erfolgsbeteiligung und Vermögensbildung der Arbeitnehmer bei Siemens (1847–1945), Zeitschrift für Unternehmensgeschichte, Supplement 36, Stuttgart 1986.

In the research project "Success Participation and Wealth Formation for Workers in Selected German Companies from the Mid-Nineteenth Century to the Second World War" the concern is not to examine a firmly defined model using individual companies but to show the historical dimension of forms of success participation and wealth formation that have occurred in the past.

The following areas are examined:

In success participation:

- profit sharing schemes
- performance bonuses
- gratuities
- premiums
- commissions and
- pension and similar funds, if the payments into these funds made by the firm are dependent on the firm's performance and the benefits accruing to the individual workers were offsettable.

In wealth formation:

- funds for insurance against invalidity or sickness and provision for old age
- works savings funds
- staff shares and other forms of participation - measures and facilities to promote the purchase of housing or land
- premiums which were not piecework.

In many cases there may be overlapping between wealth formation and success participation. That applies to the above forms of insurance funds, works savings funds, if a higher interest rate was paid depending on the dividend paid by the firm, and premiums where the measurement threshold was a figure in the company's performance.

With so broad a subject we had to limit our examination to selected companies. Since the textile industry and coal mining are relatively well researched, we concentrated on the chemical industry and the metal industry, together with the electrical engineering and motor industries and plant construction. These sectors not only played a major part in the economy in the second half of the nineteenth and the first half of the twentieth century, they were also important because they include companies of all size categories and in all locations, some of which are major firms, while others are highly specialized companies. Some make mass products and others concentrate on high-quality individual goods. Accordingly, there are very different staff structures. The final selection was determined by the source situation, for unfortunately in many of the companies no material at all is available on this aspect of the activities. The research has so far yielded three published works and others are in the process of printing. The work by Elke Hamacher[40] deals with Paul Lechler (1849–1925), a Swabian wholesale merchant and manufacturer of sealing rings and nozzles, and covers a field seldom

[40] Elke Elisabeth Hamacher: Paul Lechler und die Wohnungsfrage um 1900, Zeitschrift für Unternehmensgeschichte, Supplement 31, Wiesbaden 1984.

researched to date, namely company initiatives on housing reform. Lechler was mainly concerned to ease the housing shortage for workers. In his writings he analysed the housing shortage at the end of the nineteenth century and then developed a basically cooperative concept for "national housing reform", as he called it. The state was to give guarantees for interest and capital payments, so making it easier to give loans for house construction. In her study Elke Hamacher examines the housing shortage and its repercussions around the turn of the century; she analyses Lechler's writings and subjects his concept to a critical examination.

The life and work of Robert Bosch have been duly honoured in the biography by Theodor Heuss,[41] but there is still no account of the company's social benefits. Jürgen Mulert undertook the difficult task of tracing success participation and wealth formation for the Bosch workers, and discovered that most of the best source material on this was lost in the Second World War. That is particularly regrettable since this Swabian major industrialist and patron, "a pragmatist with a strong humanitarian vein", had views on company wage and social policy which were certainly not general at the time. Bosch utilised "the link between the level of income and work motivation", and that is why he always maintained that it was not that he could pay high wages because he was rich, he was rich because he paid high wages. He also made intensive efforts to see that his workers had particularly good working conditions. They worked shorter hours than usual and had well lit, heated and ventilated workshops. "But apart from paying high wages and providing healthy working conditions Bosch did not want to offer further incentives to bind the workforce to the firm".[42] He wanted to leave his workers the maximum degree of independence, and that is why he refused for a long time to offer works-housing. Mulert examines wages and salaries, which were unusually high at Bosch, as instruments of success participation and wealth formation, inventor's fees and other remuneration, bonuses for performance and success, housing subsidies and the Bosch aid to provision for old age.

The situation regarding source material on this subject in Siemens is quite different from that in Bosch,[43] and Christoph Conrad had a wealth to draw on. He examines profit sharing and provision for old age in the context of the structure of the company, and discusses the concepts of success participation using extensive tables and calculations. In addition to such benefits as sickness and death funds, pension funds, savings and consumer associations, performance and profit-related income components have played a large part at Siemens since the 1850s. Success participation in the form of pure profit sharing was first limited to a small group of top managers. The considerable financial arrangements, particularly the pension fund, the opportunities offered for saving and the bonus system helped to prevent major labour disputes at the firm until 1918. The study also shows how closely the

---

[41] Theodor Heuss: Robert Bosch, Leben und Leistung, Tübingen 1946.

[42] Jürgen Mulert: Erfolgsbeteiligung und Vermögensbildung der Arbeitnehmer bei der Firma Robert Bosch zwischen 1886 und 1945, in: Zeitschrift für Unternehmensgeschichte, Vol. 30, 1985, pp. 1–29, quotations p. 5.

[43] Christoph Conrad: Erfolgsbeteiligung und Vermögensbildung der Arbeitnehmer bei Siemens (1847–1945), Zeitschrift für Unternehmensgeschichte, Supplement 36, Stuttgart 1986.

individual facilities and payments were bound up with the wage and salary structure, the hierarchy within the firm and the social differentiation among the workers.

The only research project concluded by the Society so far which deals with only one company is the documentation on Daimler-Benz AG from 1933 to 1945.[44] Marion Hüchtermann and Stephanie Habeth carried out extensive studies in the Daimler-Benz archives and in public archives. The documentation consists of three parts: a text, notes and an appendix of hitherto unpublished sources. It deals with the following subjects: management (the management board and the supervisory board), production and products, including the distribution between the different works, research and development, sales and finance, personnel promotion and social benefits.

IV.

From the start the Society for Business History aimed to provide aids for research into business history and services to research workers. The bibliography of independent writings on the history of companies and associations and the biographies of entrepreneurs[45] already published in the periodical "Tradition" was compiled for this purpose by the managers of the Society, from 1976 to 1983 by Horst A. Wessel[46] and since then by Beate Brüninghaus.[47] The bibliography has been computerised since 1984 and researchable according to various criteria, and provides a continuous central list of titles on business history which is maintained as fully as possible.

The Yearbook also includes a bibliography[48], but this is mainly intended for researchers abroad, and so it is not simply a list of titles but a more detailed account of publications in German, giving a brief description and evaluation of selected works, and arranging these according to themes (general works and individual sectors).

In cooperation with business archivists and under the direction of Klara van Eyll a questionnaire was sent to more than 4000 companies and associations in the Federal Republic of Germany to establish what source material they have on business, social and technical history. The result appeared in 1978 in the form of a catalogue of more than 400 archives or places where material was to be found with altogether 700 items.[49] The publication was well received by research workers and

---

44 Hans Pohl, Stephanie Habeth, Beate Brüninghaus: Die Daimler-Benz AG in den Jahren 1933–1945, Zeitschrift für Unternehmensgeschichte, Supplement 47, Stuttgart [1]1987.

45 Ina Neumann: Bibliographie zur Firmengeschichte und Unternehmerbiographie, in: Tradition 12 (1967) - 21 (1976).

46 Horst A. Wessel: Bibliographie zur Unternehmensgeschichte und Unternehmerbiographie, in: Zeitschrift für Unternehmensgeschichte 22 (1977) - 29 (1984).

47 Beate Brüninghaus: A Review of the New Literature on Business History, in: Wolfram Engels, Hans Pohl (ed.): German Yearbook on Business History, Berlin, Heidelberg, New York.

48 Beate Brüninghaus: Bibliographie zur Unternehmensgeschichte und Unternehmerbiographie, in: Zeitschrift für Unternehmensgeschichte since 29 (1984).

49 Klara van Eyll et al. (ed): Deutsche Wirtschaftsarchive. Nachweis historischer Quellen in Unternehmen, Kammern und Verbänden der Bundesrepublik Deutschland, Vol. 1, Wiesbaden 1978.

the companies, chambers and associations themselves, and so in 1983 a companion list of more than 320 archives or sources of material in German credit institutions was published, containing more than 640 items.[50] A second edition of both is now in preparation.

In that connection it should also be mentioned that through the mediation of the Society or individual members researchers have often been given access to archives which would otherwise have remained closed to them or which they would not have known about. But much remains to be done in this field to break down the mistrust which often exists on both sides, companies and research workers. Regrettably, one-sided views by journalists often tend to put up further barriers to understanding here. But it is easily overlooked that company archives are private, and that even in public archives family and company material is not always necessarily available to the public. Moreover, the usual initial periods before which material is opened to the public, and which are very short in the Federal Republic of Germany in comparison with some other countries, must be observed, as must the need to protect personal and business data. Foreign research workers frequently confirm that altogether German companies are more willing to make their archive material available to research workers than companies in other countries. German research workers also easily overlook that even major companies often do not keep systematised archives, so that the material is stored in different places in the premises, moreover, that there is no staff or room to set up an archive and above all provide the necessary advice on how to use the material. In public archives the users naturally accept the fact that some items cannot be viewed or that lack of space often entails waiting periods. But if this happens in a company it is too readily assumed that the company is on principle averse to giving permission for the material to be used because it has something to hide.

On every occasion the Society has attempted to convince companies of the importance of collecting archive material and making it available in an ordered collection, or it has tried to encourage companies to open up existing collections. The managers of the Society have been engaged in this work for years, and they still are, in cooperation with qualified social and economic historians and specialists from the companies concerned, and the Society has put forward proposals to various companies on organizing and building up an archive.

But the advisory service and other aids to research provided by the Society's secretariat go further. In consultation and correspondence with research workers, generally younger scholars abroad and especially those engaged in preparing a doctoral thesis, the Secretariat will take up contact with company archives and put forward suggestions on themes for doctoral theses from the entire field of business history. Often the knowledge that certain archive material exists, or the desire on the part of individual companies for certain themes to be studied, facilitates the work. For example, the wish by the Cologne gas, electricity and water works for their available archive material to be sifted yielded a subject for a thesis by Mariele Schulze Berndt.

---

[50] Ibid. Vol. 2: Kreditwirtschaft, Wiesbaden 1983.

V.

In addition to publishing the papers given at its symposia, the contributions to the discussions and the results of the Society's research and providing aids to research workers, the Society has also published several books in the supplements to its periodical "Zeitschrift für Unternehmensgeschichte". The manuscripts of these were offered to the Society for publication and in some cases it was able to finance the printing.

Most important are the results of research carried out at various universities on business history themes. The monographs, habilitation and other these which were the result of very intensive work in archives deserve special mention. In publishing such research work the Society is fulfilling one of its main objectives and helping younger research workers and junior academic staff in particular by promoting business history at universities.

In this way work has been published on the following sectors: a study by Fritz Blaich of the Department of Economic and Social History in Regensburg on US direct investment in the German mechanical engineering sector between 1890 and 1914[51], and by Reinhardt Hanf on Daimler-Motoren Gesellschaft,[52] from the Department of History in Bonn the history of the dyes industry in the Rhineland during the Industrial Revolution by Ralf Schaumann, Frauke Schönert-Röhlk and myself[53], Wilfried Feldenkirchen's habilitation thesis on the iron and steel industry in the Ruhr area from 1879 to 1914[54] and the collection of essays by Gerhard Adelmann on regional economic and social history.[55]

In the case of the theses the Board held the view that if the funds for normal publication could not be raised a cheaper printing process was acceptable. That enabled two modern history theses on economic policy from the Department for Political Science in Göttingen to be printed, the first by Friedrich Stratmann on state influence on the chemical industry from 1933–1945[56] and the other by Alexander Drexler on the regulations in the textile industry in the British zone and

[51] Fritz Blaich: Amerikanische Firmen in Deutschland 1890–1918. US-Direktinvestitionen im deutschen Maschinenbau, Zeitschrift für Unternehmensgeschichte, Supplement 30, Wiesbaden 1984.

[52] Reinhardt Hanf: Im Spannungsfeld zwischen Technik und Markt. Zielkonflikte bei der Daimler-Motoren-Gesellschaft im ersten Dezennium ihres Bestehens, Zeitschrift für Unternehmensgeschichte, Supplement 17, Wiesbaden 1980.

[53] Hans Pohl, Ralf Schaumann, Frauke Schönert-Röhlk: Die chemische Industrie in den Rheinlanden während der industriellen Revolution, Vol. 1: Die Farbenindustrie, Zeitschrift für Unternehmensgeschichte, Supplement 18, Wiesbaden 1983.

[54] Wilfried Feldenkirchen: Die Eisen- und Stahlindustrie des Ruhrgebiets 1879–1914. Wachstum, Finanzierung und Struktur ihrer Großunternehmen, Zeitschrift für Unternehmensgeschichte, Supplement 20, Wiesbaden 1982.

[55] Gerhard Adelmann: Vom Gewerbe zur Industrie im kontinentalen Nordwesteuropa. Gesammelte Aufsätze zur regionalen Wirtschafts- und Sozialgeschichte, Zeitschrift für Unternehmensgeschichte, Supplement 38, Stuttgart 1986.

[56] Friedrich Stratmann: Chemische Industrie unter Zwang? Staatliche Einflußnahme am Beispiel der chemischen Industrie Deutschlands 1933-1949, Zeitschrift für Unternehmensgeschichte, Supplement 43, Stuttgart 1985.

the Bizone from 1945–1948[57]. Both were directed by Walter Euchner. In addition, three theses on economic, technical and regional aspects of business history were printed: one on bankruptcies and settlements in Siegerland from 1951-1980 by Axel Gösche[58] from the Department of History in Siegen, directed by Harald Witthöft, the second on the Württemberg iron industry in the nineteenth century by Gottfried Plumpe[59] of the Department of History in Marburg, directed by Akos Paulinyi, and the third on the electrical communications sector and industry in the Rhineland up to the First World War by Horst A. Wessel of the History Department in Bonn.[60]

Three theses dealt with questions of company social history: Wolfgang Muth of the Department of History in Münster studied vocational training during the Weimar Republic[61] under Hans J. Teuteberg, Hisashi Yano dealt with working conditions and the social situation of smelter workers at Aktienverein Gutehoffnungsshütte and Fried. Krupp AG from 1936 to 1939[62] under Dietmar Petzina of the Department of History in Bochum, and Günther Schulz of the Department of History in Bonn studied blue- and white-collar workers at the Cologne firm of Felten & Guilleaume up to 1914.[63]

In addition, we published some accounts of individual companies: three on Siemens, by Herbert Goetzeler and Lothar Schoen[64], Sigfrid von Weiher[65], and Horst A. Wessel[66] and three by Wilhelm Treue on Gothaer Lebensversicherung[67],

---

57 Alexander Drexler: Planwirtschaft in Westdeutschland 1945–1948. Eine Fallstudie über die Textilbewirtschaftung in der britischen und Bizone, Zeitschrift für Unternehmensgeschichte, Supplement 44, Stuttgart 1985.

58 Axel Gösche: Insolvenzen und wirtschaftlicher Wandel. Eine wirtschaftsgeschichtliche Analyse der Konkurse und Vergleiche im Siegerland 1951–1980, Zeitschrift für Unternehmensgeschichte, Supplement 40, Stuttgart 1985.

59 Gottfried Plumpe: Die württembergische Eisenindustrie im 19. Jahrhundert. Eine Fallstudie zur Geschichte der industriellen Revolution in Deutschland, Zeitschrift für Unternehmensgeschichte, Supplement 26, Wiesbaden 1982.

60 Horst A. Wessel: Die Entwicklung des elektrischen Nachrichtenwesens in Deutschland und die rheinische Industrie, Zeitschrift für Unternehmensgeschichte, Supplement 25, Wiesbaden 1983.

61 Wolfgang Muth: Berufsausbildung in der Weimarer Republik, Zeitschrift für Unternehmensgeschichte, Supplement 41, Stuttgart 1985.

62 Hisashi Yano: Hüttenarbeiter im Dritten Reich. Die Betriebsverhältnisse und soziale Lage bei der Gutehoffnungshütte Aktienverein und der Fried. Krupp AG 1936 bis 1939, Zeitschrift für Unternehmensgeschichte, Supplement 34, Stuttgart 1986.

63 Günther Schulz: Die Arbeiter und Angestellten bei Felten & Guilleaume. Sozialgeschichtliche Untersuchung eines Kölner Industrieunternehmens im 19. und beginnenden 20. Jahrhundert, Zeitschrift für Unternehmensgeschichte, Supplement 13, Wiesbaden 1979.

64 Herbert Goetzeler, Lothar Schoen: Wilhelm und Carl Friedrich von Siemens. Die zweite Unternehmergeneration, Stuttgart 1985.

65 Sigfrid von Weiher, Herbert Goetzeler: Weg und Wirken der Siemens-Werke im Fortschritt der Elektrotechnik 1847–1980. Ein Beitrag zur Geschichte der Elektroindustrie, Zeitschrift für Unternehmensgeschichte, Supplement 21, Wiesbaden 1981.

66 Horst A. Wessel: Emil Guilleaume und Siemens Brothers in London, Cologne 1982.

67 Wilhelm Treue: Dreimal 50 Jahre Gothaer Lebensversicherung. Ein Bericht über die letzten 50 Jahre 1927–1977, Zeitschrift für Unternehmensgeschichte, Supplement 10, Wiesbaden 1977.

the Bankhaus Sal. Oppenheim jr. & Cie during the Third Reich[68], and the firm of lawyers Deuchler, Krauel & Commichau.[69]

In cooperation with the Federation of German Plant and Machinery Construction Firms Wolfgang Fach and Horst A. Wessel published a volume of essays on finance for industry in the "Gründerzeit"[70], which more than two dozen writers contributed articles on the general economic trend, on management structures, questions of finance and art, information technology and special areas of the mechanical engineering industry. The volume is distinguished by its appearance, with numerous illustrations, many in colour, and it is designed for a broader public. It is also a guide for visitors to an exhibition on the history of mechanical engineering, which the two authors also organized, and which will be shown in a number of German cities.

The Society's publications, the "Zeitschrift für Unternehmensgeschichte", the successor to "Tradition" and the "German Yearbook on Business History" have all become major publications. The "Zeitschrift für Unternehmensgeschichte" is the Society's official scholarly periodical. Like the Anglo-American Business History Review and Business History it publishes the results of research into business history themes on regional, national and international basis, and comparative analytical studies. The articles cover macro-economic problems, like the role of companies in business and society, as well as micro-economic aspects, such as studies of companies or plants as single economic units. The periodical is open to contributions on business history research in the broadest sense, in other words studies on questions of concentration, finance strategies, the change in motivation, new businesses and mergers, forms of organization, management, workforce structure, social and training policy, and the role of companies and entrepreneurs in politics, to give only a few examples. It also aims to stimulate representatives of various academic disciplines, particularly economic and social historians, political scientists, economists and lawyers to undertake work on business history and especially to provide younger scholars with an opportunity to publish and a forum for discussion on their work. We also hope to arouse interest in business history among representatives of the business world and promote the dialogue between business and scholarship.

A consideration of the 76 articles and miscellaneous items in the issues of the periodical from 1976 to 1985 showed that more attention had focussed on studies of companies (39 articles)[71] than entrepreneurs (23) or associations (five articles). In recent years particularly a trend away from the biographical approach has become evident. Twelve articles dealt with theoretical and methodological problems. Then there was the bibliography, which covered the years 1972 to 1979

---

[68] Ibid: Das Schicksal des Bankhauses Sal. Oppenheim jr. & Cie. und seiner Inhaber im Dritten Reich, Zeitschrift für Unternehmensgeschichte, Supplement 27, Wiesbaden 1983.

[69] Ibid: Geschichte einer Hamburgischen Anwaltssozietät. Von der Gründung der Kanzlei im Jahre 1822 bis zur Gegenwart, Zeitschrift für Unternehmensgeschichte, Supplement 48, Stuttgart 1986.

[70] Wolfgang Fach, Horst A. Wessel (ed.): Hundert Thaler Preussisch Courant. Industriefinanzierung in der Gründerzeit, Vienna 1981.

[71] Since some articles deal both with enterprises and their entrepreneurs, and covered both the nineteenth and the twentieth centuries, they amount to a higher number than 76.

and was published from 1977 to 1985. The 76 articles are by 58 authors, among them nine from other countries, Great Britain, the USA, Sweden, Austria, Belgium and Czechoslovakia. The essays were on the following subjects: heavy industry (13), the electrical industry (5), trade (5), banking (4), the chemical industry (3), mechanical engineering (2), the crafts (2), agriculture (1), foodstuffs (1), textiles (1), insurance (1). In time most dealt with the nineteenth century (40), and the twentieth (34); only six were on the period before the nineteenth century.

The German Yearbook on Business History[72] was born in a discussion in Munich between the board of trustees and the management board of the Society on the state of research and the possibilities of publishing the results of research by German business historians abroad. It became evident – as we already knew from the natural sciences and congresses – that German business historians would only have a chance of international recognition in an English-language publication. That was fully confirmed by the reviewers of the first issue[73], who gratefully acknowledged its appearance, and our colleagues in Japan, who followed our example in their first Japanese Yearbook on Business History.[74] Although the costs are high and no public subsidy was forthcoming, the Society decided to continue to publish the Yearbook in conjunction with the Institute for Bank-Historical Research in Frankfurt. The book is based on the following concept: it provides a collection of articles, translated into English, that have been published by German scholars in German language periodicals. Each volume also contains an article by a wellknown entrepreneur and/or theoretician (economist or lawyer). The Yearbook has the following objectives: "This Yearbook is to help German research in keeping contact and in cooperating with scholars and enterprises from abroad, by making available some select articles on business history from German periodicals to the English-speaking world. Thus we want to promote the international dialogue between business historians and arouse more consciousness of history among representatives of the economy around the world."[75]

---

[72] Wolfram Engels, Hans Pohl (ed.): German Yearbook on Business History 1981, Berlin, Heidelberg, New York 1981.

[73] Leslie Hannah, in: Economic History Review 35, No. 4, p. 638.

[74] Hidemasa Morikawa: Editor's Note, in: Keiichiro Nakagawa, Hidemasa Morikawa: Japanese Yearbook on Business History, 1984, p. III.

[75] Wolfram Engels, Hans Pohl, Introductory Remarks, in: ibid (ed.): German Yearbook on Business History 1981, Berlin, Heidelberg, New York 1982, pp. Vf., here p. VI.

The Bankers Simon and Abraham Oppenheim 1812–1880 The Private Background to Their Professional Activity, Their Role in Politics and Ennoblement

Wilhelm Treue

Various accounts have been written of the business history of the Bankhaus Sal. Oppenheim jr. & Cie in the generation of Simon, Abraham and Dagobert Oppenheim, that is, between 1828 and 1880 and later, using the sources in the bank's archives.[1] Recently the main focus of attention has shifted from the immediate biography to the cooperation and parallel work of the three brothers.

This article draws on contracts, correspondence, wills and the records of the ennoblement of the two banker brothers, Simon and Abraham', and some of Simon's letters to his sons, Eduard and Albert, later his partners and successors, to look rather more into the family relations on which the joint banking activity was based. We find very close understanding between the brothers but some tension and friction as well; this was kept so close a secret that the outside world, from the bank's customers and business colleagues in Cologne and Paris, Berlin and Dresden right up to Bismarck and the King and Kaiser William I, all saw only an extraordinarily successful large German private bank. A consideration of the process leading up to the ennoblement of the two brothers will also give us a glimpse into the courtly circles in which the two moved as easily as in their bourgeois professional world.[2]

So the aim of this essay, which draws on source material of great rarity value, is not to penetrate the private or intimate sphere, on the contrary, it is solely to show how complex entrepreneurial activity is, and what difficulties can lie behind great success and close cooperation in local, provincial, national and European business, difficulties that make themselves felt only occasionally but can virtually jeopardise the enterprise.

To clarify the background to the following remarks we should briefly show how the two brothers experienced the economic side of the revolution of 1848.

They were extremely successful in business, and together with their brother Dagobert had played a leading part up to 1847 in the development of steam shipping, the railways, insurance, mining and industry, mainly in the Western part of the Kingdom of Prussia and its Customs Union. From childhood there had been

[1] Most recently in the Festschrift "Köln und das rheinische Judentum", Cologne 1984, and Wilhelm Treue: Das Schicksal des Bankhauses Sal. Oppenheim jr. & Cie im Dritten Reich, Zeitschrift für Unternehmensgeschichte, Supplement 27, Wiesbaden 1983, which also lists the older literature; ibid: Die Kölner Bankiers Oppenheim, in: Rheinisch-Westfälische Wirtschaftsbiographien, Vol. 13, Munich 1986, pp. 171ff.

[2] Almost all the material for this study is in the archives of Bankhaus Sal. Oppenheim jr. & Cie in Cologne and very little secondary literature was needed.

German Yearbook on Business History 1987

a very close bond between them, and they enjoyed a happy family life, living after the death of their father in the same harmony with their mother, with whom they also took the business decisions after 1828. All three brothers enjoyed good health and were industrious and ambitious for their family.

The investment by Cologne banks in industry had been the decisive factor in the industrial expansion of the Rhineland, putting it ahead of Berlin/Brandenburg and Silesia, where Rother's long obsolete late mercantilist policy in state finance, which influenced business development through both the Königliche Bank and public debt administration and the Seehandlung, continued to have a negative effect until his resignation in April 1848. Perhaps understandably, therefore, it was in Berlin industry that the first signs of crisis appeared, but after the autumn of 1847 the economic recession and social unrest were being felt in Cologne as well, and after the beginning of March 1848 there could be no doubt that this was a crisis: well established businesses were collapsing, balances were being withdrawn from the banks and loans requested far beyond the usual extent, while the inflow of funds had virtually dried up. The highly respected bank run by Abraham Schaaffhausen was suffering worst, and to preserve jobs in a wide vicinity it was being changed into a joint stock bank with the help of the state – the first in Prussia.[3]

When the Rothschilds were "burned out" in Paris, Laffitte and D'Eichthal went bankrupt, Hottinger, Mallet, Delessert and even Fould, a relative of the Oppenheims, "could not take on any further business" and Haber in Karlsruhe closed its doors, the bank run by the brothers Simon and Abraham Oppenheim also found itself in difficulties, and by the end of March 1848 the brothers had no doubt that they would be in trouble without state assistance.

In this situation Ahraham Oppenheim went to Berlin on 1 April 1848 to see the Aachen entrepreneur David Hansemann, with whom he had enjoyed close and good business relations for years. Only three days before, Hansemann, now Minister of Finance, had formed the Camphausen-Hansemann cabinet together with the Cologne banker Gottfried L. Camphausen[4] at the request of the King, and Oppenheim came with an urgent request for a state loan of half a million thalers. As security he offered mortgages and shares, although their value was dropping. Six letters written by Simon, who was fighting to save the bank at home, in the eleven days between 3 and 13 April to Abraham have survived. They give a very dramatic picture – the answers are lost – of how the two brothers worked out the arguments, indeed the very words to be used, together during these weeks in full accord.

[3] On the general development in Cologne, see Klara van Eyll, Wirtschaftsgeschichte Kölns vom Beginn der preußischen Zeit bis zur Reichsgründung, in: Hermann Kellenbenz (ed.): Zwei Jahrtausende Kölner Wirtschaft, Vol. 2, Cologne 1975, pp. 163ff.; Schaaffhausen had invested heavily in property, the value of which was falling; E. Kleinertz, Die Bau- und Bodenspekulation in Köln 1837–1847, in: Kölner Unternehmer und die Frühindustrialisierung im Rheinland und Westfalen (1835–1871), display volume, Cologne 1984, p. 163. On the other hand, Schaaffhauscn also owed more than 1200 creditors, most of whom were living in Cologne and working in the Prussian Rhineland, around 5.8 million thalers at the beginning of 1848, Verzeichnis der Gläubiger von A. Schaaffhausen, Historisches Archiv der Stadt Köln, Bestand 1096 B35, Schaaffhausen family archive.

[4] B. Poll (ed.) David Hansemann 1790–1864–1964, Cologne 1964.

The two railway companies, Rheinische Eisenbahn and Köln-Mindener-Eisenbahngesellschaft, run by their brother Dagobert, were withdrawing thousands of thalers every day and when the Rheinische finally asked for 40,000 thalers in the middle of the month, Simon wrote to his brother on 6 April: "All my hopes now rest in you. Your understanding and prudence will, I am sure, find the right way to help us out of all embarrassment. 500 M/Th ... would be enough, but that is what we need ... if the government trusts the bankers and gives them advances they will be able to help the manufacturers, but not otherwise, and then there will be no end to the calamities. It is most fortunate that Camphausen & Hansemann are at the helm, they understand business matters and will help, if you advise them accordingly ..."

But Abraham does not appear to have been able to see Hansemann, and Simon wrote more and more pressingly on 8 and particularly 10 April: "Our position is quite different from all the others, as Hansemann will see. We are the foremost, almost the only bank in the Rhine province, and it must be of great concern to the state, for its future loans as well, to keep a bank like ours, with so much intelligence, as all admit we have, going ..." On 10 April Hansemann invited Abraham Oppenheim to a discussion. Simon, restless and worried, wrote the next day: "I hope that the expected decision was given yesterday, with God's gracious assistance, ... and Hansemann has given us the loan of 500 M/Th, which is the least we need, for one year ... Pray be convinced, my dear Abraham, that we really need this sum if we are to sleep with any ease in our beds ..." Finally, when Abraham was still unable to report success, he wrote on 13 April: "... the government must have the greatest interest in keeping banks like ours going. Hansemann knows your ability, and he will need us for future government business. It is time the Rhineland Ministers did something for their province as well." A few days later Hansemann agreed to grant the desired half million; the Oppenheim brothers and their bank had survived the crisis. They had also become even more attached to each other than they had been in the two preceding decades of their responsibility for the business. That business conditions in Cologne and the Rhineland really were as bad as the two Oppenheim brothers judged them to be from the affairs of their bank, is very evident from a letter from Mevissen to his family, written on 2 April 1848 from Berlin: "Financial matters are pushing politics into the background. If credit cannot be restored the existing order is hopelessly lost. The Ministry is of good will but apart from Hansemann and Camphausen lacks the necessary insight."[5]

As in Paris, where the inflow of Californian and Australian gold was a great stimulus after 1849/50, the economic situation improved in Cologne with astonishing rapidity, and in the new boom in mining and industry, trade and transport the Oppenheim brothers' bank enjoyed a powerful upswing as well. But after the experience of the 1848 "storm" both the brothers tended occasionally to melancholy and to a gloomy view of things, for all their business success and a happy family life. This inclination to pessimism increased as they grew older, and it was frequently mentioned between them.

---

[5] Joseph Hansen, Gustav von Mevissen, Vol. 2, Berlin 1906, p. 362.

When the Oppenheim bank participated in the establishment of the Crédit Mobilier in Paris in 1850/51, – it was the only German bank to do so and took 500 shares for a total of 250,000 francs – and immediately set about preparing the establishment of similar institutions in Germany, Western Europe was not only enjoying a boom, in the government of the Prussian monarchy the Elberfeld banker and confidant of the King, August von der Heydt, as Minister of Trade[6], was working to ensure, like his predecessor Hansemann, that in the economic development of the state as a whole the lead enjoyed by the west over the east and the south east was growing ever greater. The Rhineland was on the borderline, so to speak, between this western part of the monarchy and the empire of Napoleon III, which was now being rapidly consolidated after the coup of 2 December 1852, and with their relations in the powerful business class in the Rhineland, and more friends and relations in Brussels and Amsterdam, bankers and entrepreneurs like Simon, Abraham and Dagobert Oppenheim, industrious and with strong ties of brotherly affection, could look with confidence to the future.

Were these three brothers, so closely bound in business life and among the most prominent business men and industrialists in Cologne and the Rhineland, satisfied in their private lives, were they "happy", did they form a family community? Enough material has survived to answer this question for the two older brothers, and we may find some surprises. On the private life of the youngest brother, Dagobert, however, nothing is known after he changed from publishing a newspaper to a leading position with two of the biggest West German transport companies. Neither letters nor diaries from his hand have survived, and he is hardly ever mentioned in the correspondence of the two older brothers – at most occasionally as an efficient business man, with whom one could work well.

And the two bankers? After the death of their mother, whose "partners" they had been since 1828, with 10% each, and after 1833 25% each in the profit and loss of the bank, they concluded a company contract for six years on 11 May 1842, to be "tacitly" prolonged: the business was to be continued "to joint account", both retained the management of the business and had a 50% share each in profit and loss. On the death of one of the brothers "the survivor remains sole head of the business". Abraham Oppenheim's marriage was childless in 1842 (and it was to remain so), and Article 9 of the contract states: "It is the will of Abraham Oppenheim that the bank founded by his late father of blessed memory and operated to date with great renown should be maintained in the distant future as well solely by the direct descendants and heirs of good father Oppenheim."

A decade later, in the summer of 1852, Abraham Oppenheim suddenly announced his intention of "giving notice of termination of the contract before the end of the year, so that this may cease to apply on 31 December 1853". To explain this at first sight very surprising decision one really needs to go back to the "storm year 1848" as Simon often called it later.

On 12 May 1848 Abraham Oppenheim left the Cologne city council, of which he had been a very active member for several years, on the grounds that the

---

[6] Alexander Bergengrün, Staatsminister August Freiherr von der Heydt, Leipzig 1908; M.-L. Baum, Die v. d. Heydt aus Elberfeld, Elberfeld 1964.

"turbulence of the time" necessitated his frequent absence on business, and he would "shortly have to undertake a journey of extended duration". That was presumably not the only reason. Other members of the council undertook "extended" journeys from time to time and for a variety of reasons, and so had to interrupt their work for the council, but they always came back on their return to Cologne. The main reason for Abraham's resignation was no doubt that the bank was in difficulties at the time and the two brothers needed all their time and exertions to get it through the crisis.

Four weeks later, on 5 June 1848, when the economic and social consequences of the revolution were becoming fairly clear, Simon Oppenheim drew up his third will. He wrote in it: "A reversal of all our social and political conditions has unfortunately so shaken and jeopardised my fortune, which was very large until the outbreak of the revolution, that I must not and will not place any burden upon my heirs after my death."

How great Simon Oppenheim's "great fortune" was before March 1848 we do not know, but we do have a statement of the bank's assets and liabilities 14 months after the outbreak of the revolution, which had been preceded by a considerable period of social unrest and economic depression in agriculture, industry and trade. On 15 May 1849 the Bankhaus Sal. Oppenheim jr. & Cie had altogether 376 accounts with assets totalling 496,000 thalers, while its liabilities were 2.1 million thalers, 279,000 francs (to one creditor) and 95 guilders. Three weeks later, on 10 June 1849, when Simon Oppenheim drew up his next will, he said: "The revolution last year has had a terrible effect on my assets, and the greater part is still in jeopardy today."

We do not have the corresponding information for Abraham Oppenheim and his financial position, and the first will by him that has survived is from 1853. But as we know, he had a 50% share in the profit and loss of the bank. So in mid-1849 the two brothers had hardly more than a respected name. But within a few weeks the situation appears to have changed radically, for reasons that can no longer be reconstructed, for on 25 August 1849 Simon Oppenheim was given a passport, which he presumably had applied for *after* drawing up his will on 10 June that year, in other words, *after* the above statement of the assets and liabilities of the bank, "to travel for pleasure from Cologne through the German Federal states to Sardinia, Tuscany, Rome, Naples and back". We do not know exactly when he embarked on this "journey for pleasure", nor which cities he visited, we only know that he returned to Cologne on 22 April 1850. So for months, at a time when business was far from easy, he left the direction of the bank entirely in his brother's hands. Was this really only a "journey for pleasure"?

From the spring of 1850 Simon Oppenheim set about stabilising the bank's business in Germany from his location in Cologne and expanding it. One example of the latter activity is the relation to Krupp. The bank – in this case presumably Abraham alone, without being able to consult his brother – gave Krupp the first major loan at the end of 1849, and after 1850 the Essen industrialist needed and was given larger and larger amounts in rapid succession (we have evidence of this on both sides), some in connection with supplies to the Köln-Mindener railway company run by Dagobert Oppenheim. In 1852/53 he caused the bank such concern by overdrawing his credit that on one occasion it demanded "immediate and full settlement of the account", threatening serious measures should this not be done; another time Dagobert Oppenheim had to threaten measures by the railway company he directed. On 11 March 1854 Simon wrote from Cologne to Abraham in Paris: "I have sent Krupp a sharp reminder, since he has still not sent the remittance for the Köln-Mindener ..." This annoying state of affairs went on, indeed it continued to grow up to 1856, when Krupp, irritated by the Oppenheim's concern for their money, loosened his ties with the bank. Oppenheim was also intensely occupied for a long time on clearing up the difficulties caused by the political events of 1848 - several bankruptcies, for instance, and the collapse of the Haber bank in Karlsruhe. And finally new business was being planned, among other things, participations in several future railway lines. All this appears to have been highly successful, for Simon's next will, drawn up exactly five years to the day after that of the summer of 1848, on 5 June 1853, begins: "God the Father has blessed our enterprise and my property is restored to the level of before the revolution."

Abraham Oppenheim's life in these years was quite different from his brother's. He was almost constantly travelling, and when he was in Cologne, busy with the appropriately voluminous correspondence. His itinerary, on which we do not have all the details, was roughly as follows: In August 1849 he was doing business with Mevissen in Paris and Berlin; in January 1850 he was corresponding and negotiating with David Hansemann, now head of the Königliche Bank, in Berlin on the establishment of a newspaper and a Cologne trade fair. In November and December 1850 he appears to have spent an extended period in the French capital, judging from letters from his wife and brother, from whence he paid several visits to Brussels, where, among other things, he attempted to obtain the post of a Belgian consul. In Paris he was looking into the possibility of a participation in a bill agency, and observing the capital market through the general and particular financial conditions. In the course of these visits to Paris and Brussels, which lasted altogether more than five months in 1849–51, he spent periods of several weeks at a time in the French capital and became accustomed to its society. The French way of life had become a habit with Abraham, as is very evident in letters written in June, August and October 1851, while his brother spent most of his time in Cologne, seeing him briefly in Paris on his return from London at the beginning of August 1851, rather than having Abraham at his side for any greater length of time in his own city.

So Abraham Oppenheim spent several periods of some weeks in Paris while the preparations for the Crédit Mobilier were being made. The edict on the establishment of the bank was published on 18 November 1852, and it was thanks to him that the Bankhaus Oppenheim had a participation, the only German bank to do so, in this joint stock bank, which aroused so much excitement and was soon to be so successful. Abraham wrote to Cologne that the possibilities for capital investment in Paris and Brussels were far better than in Cologne, and from January to April 1852 he followed the preparations for the establishment of the Crédit Foncier, in which Sal. Oppenheim jr. & Cie again took a share, this time 75,000 francs, and at the same time conducted legal procedings in Paris.

Probably it was these varied and successful periods of activity, lasting for months at a time, mainly in connection with the establishment of the two Crédits, which proved immensely stimulating to French business life, which were the main reason why Abraham Oppenheim contemplated a major change in his life. For it was in the middle of these events, in the summer of 1852, as we have already seen, that he announced his intention of terminating the bank contract with his brother. He then did actually give notification on 9 November 1852 that the contract would be terminated with effect from 31 December 1853. He went even further. On his last visit to Paris on private and business matters, together with his wife, who often did accompany him to that city, he had been looking at houses, and he decided to buy a "hôtel" that was apparently a bargain, although we do not know its size and location, and move to Paris altogether in due course.

From Simon Oppenheim's letters to his "dearly beloved", "most amiable" brother it is very evident how unexpected Abraham's announcement was. Simon was horrified, indeed, he wept for days and nights, but he was unable to persuade his brother to change his mind. He then entreated him at least to arrange mutual visits of several weeks a year, every year, either in Paris or Cologne. Finally, he went further. He became "convinced" that he literally could not live without his brother. That finally became clear to him in the winter of 1852/53. So if Abraham absolutely had to move to Paris he, Simon, would go with him. They would sell up the business in Cologne or move it to Paris. He himself was in Paris when he wrote to Abraham in Cologne on 10 March 1853: "We should seriously set about building up a bank here, and it would certainly immediately take its place among the foremost in the capital". But the proposal to set up a major bank together in Paris was clearly not what Abraham and his wife had in mind. It was not mentioned again, and Simon had to be content with remaining alone in Cologne. Abraham Oppenheim wanted to stop being a banker, once and for all. So Simon wrote to him on 21 December 1853, ten days before his brother intended to leave the business: "Painful as it is for me to continue to conduct the business without you, I could not in responsibility to my children follow your example and leave the bank". Moreover, for the first time, he was having difficulties with his own sons. His letter goes on: "So my duty requires me to continue, and only to take the decision to end the business if I am not convinced, after a number of years, that my sons are capable of honorably maintaining the business founded by our beloved father of blessed memory, and, praise be to God, continued by ourselves with such success". He intended to give his eldest son Eduard 2% share in the "profit" of the bank from 1 January 1854 "to arouse his interest", and his second son Albert went "to New York for a year" on 1 January 1854.[7]

[7] In the United States he worked for a time at least with the firm of Marcuse & Baltzer, of which we know that it had close links with the Darmstädter Bank in 1859. Abraham (so Albert's uncle, not his father) wrote to Marcuse from Cologne on 4 August 1854: "From your last kind letter to my brother I believe I can read between the lines that you are satisfied with my nephew Albert and that he himself is very industrious. He was sent for no other purpose than to work extremely hard and advance his knowledge of business. It is therefore my most urgent request to you not to treat him as a voluntary assistant but let him work really hard, and keep an eye on him outside office hours as you would your own son. My brother has entrusted his son to you on my recommendation, and I therefore feel a great responsibility in this. So I ask you not to be lenient with my nephew in any way, and always to tell me the truth about him, should you have any complaints about him or his industry ...".

Finally Simon asked his brother "to remain in the business with me until the end of 1855, and since, thanks be to God, you are wealthy enough, to be content with a share of one quarter for the last year, which would be the crown of thy brotherly love ..." He himself would then give his two sons procuration when Abraham left, after himself "spending four months with my wife and daughters in Paris or Italy" in the winter of 1854. For after Abraham left he would "always be on a chain ... Your ever most affectionate brother".

Abraham remained insistent that he wanted to leave the bank at the latest by the end of 1854, which, as Simon wrote to Paris from Cologne on 9 March, was "vexatious, very vexatious". Two days later Abraham gave in. He not only stayed in Cologne in 1855, an equal partner with his brother in the bank, he also, for what reason is no longer clear, stayed there in the next few years as well. But he did not give up his dream of life in big and beautiful Paris, and this was no doubt partly because the old division of the work, that had proved its worth over a quarter of a century, was retained, in practice if not on principle: the elder brother remained in Cologne, from inclination and on account of his large family, dealing mainly with the business in the Rhineland and so maintaining the relationship with brother Dagobert and his railway and steamship enterprises, while Abraham was mainly responsible for the foreign business, which necessitated frequent travelling in the large area between Vienna, Basle and Berne, Paris, Brussels and Luxembourg. Since Abraham's marriage remained childless, and his wife clearly liked travelling as well – at least to Paris, Switzerland and in great old age to the German spas – she often went with him. His letters, not only those to members of the family but also to Gerson Bleichröder in Berlin, with whom the brothers had worked closely on various occasions since the 1850s and after 1863, clearly show how happy and content the couple were on these business trips, with the opportunities they gave to enjoy the social life in the top international circles in Western Europe.

The division of the business between the two brothers, that had grown up gradually and become established as years went on, did not, however, prevent Simon as well, sometimes accompanied by his wife, from spending several weeks in Paris or London and other major commercial cities from time to time. A brief glance at the itinerary of the two brothers in 1852 and (for a special reason) 1859 will illustrate this.

Since 1852 Simon Oppenheim had been intensively preoccupied with the rapid development of the mining and industrial area around Aachen, which also brought many disappointments and problems. We need only mention the establishment and development of Phönix AG, Eschweiler, of whose supervisory council he was a member for a long time, on behalf of his bank, which had a considerable financial involvement in the company. With his brother Dagobert, who apparently did not often have to undertake extended journeys, he also played a major part in the decision of 9 June 1853 to combine the two major steamship companies in Cologne and Düsseldorf into a "joint operation" that would eliminate the disdavantages of excessive competition.

Abraham Oppenheim, on the other hand, was in Paris at the time, where he was successful in persuading the Crédit Mobilier and the Bankhaus Fould & Fould-Oppenheim to take a participation in the Darmstädter Bank, founded on 2 April 1853 with considerable impetus from Cologne, and so forging even closer links with these two major Paris banks. But his work in the French capital did not prevent him, like his brother Simon, from joining the supervisory board of the Concordia, a Cologne life assurance company which received its concession that year.

During the early months of 1854 Abraham spent almost his entire time in Paris - and possibly in Brussels as well - *almost,* for we know that in other years as well he sometimes only went to Cologne for a few days, soon returning to Paris again. The following year a brilliant season and the World Exhibition drew the two brothers and their wives back to the French capital. Simon was actually there from 3 February to 23 May, and Abraham was there at least from 10 to 28 May. They attended the opening of the exhibition together on 15 May.

Paris offered another international highlight in 1856 as well, in which Abraham Oppenheim and his wife took part. Abraham was mainly busy that year with G. Mevissen and R. Erlanger establishing the International Bank in Luxembourg,[8] which was organisationally not entirely easy and entailed numerous visits to that city, Paris and Brussels. But apart from that he and his wife also went to Paris for the conclusion of the peace treaty after the Crimean War on 30 March 1856, which was also a great social event. On 16 April one of the Prussian diplomats in Paris gave Abraham's wife a group photo of all the signatories to the treaty, with their signatures. Three days later the couple left the French capital, but by 21 April Abraham was back, this time alone. He and his wife spent the whole of July and the first half of August in Wildbad, where Simon and his family were also staying, as well as visiting Baden-Baden and several places in Switzerland.

Simon Oppenheim, on the other hand, was busy that year with major participations the bank was taking in new railway companies and banks, such as the Berliner Handelsgesellschaft. He increasingly involved his son Eduard in the business, and actually sent him to St. Petersburg from May to July, to "initiate" the establishment of a railway company and a bank. Eduard executed the commission satisfactorily and was made a holder of procuration on 30 June the following year. But his father always remained at the centre of *all* these activities, from Paris to Petersburg, and coordinated them all, which was not only a major organisational achievement but also brought and secured significant business success.

The wealth of both brothers grew rapidly and strongly in these years, if at different rates. Abraham's may have increased by as much as 50% between 1853 and the second of his wills that has survived, that dated 8 July 1857. Again, as in the first will, he makes his wife sole heir, after bequeathing no less than 900,000 thalers in capital sums and several annuities to the amount of 3,000 thalers each per year (2,000 in 1843) to his brothers and sisters and a foster daughter. Simon, on the other hand, in his will dated 29 June 1856, increased "the dowry for my children to 100,000 thalers each, since my remaining fortune will be more than sufficient to ensure that my beloved wife need make not the slightest change in her way of life and, on the contrary, will have sufficient funds to live in the greatest luxury and satisfy her needs in every respect." This growing wealth was due not only to personal ability and energy but also in no small part to a development which

[8] Wilhelm Treue, Die Gründung der Internationalen Bank in Luxemburg vor 125 Jahren, in: Bankhistorisches Archiv, Vol. 7, No. 1/1981, pp. 3–15.

caused Mevissen to remark in a lecture in 1856 that the Rhineland bankers, far more than those in Western Europe, had to work as industrial entrepreneurs as well, "because not so many personalities with proven experience in the management of industrial undertakings and the appropriate spirit of enterprise are available as in France and Britain".

In the summer of 1858 two events occurred which give us a very clear picture of the different characters of the brothers. On 6 June 1858 Simon once more drew up a new will. Materially it was the same as that of 1856, but it contains an additional clause on business policy, the immediate occasion for which is no longer apparent, but which on principle is striking both in regard his relation to his sons and his assessment of business prospects after the experience of recent years. Perhaps it was the trouble with Krupp, perhaps the developments in mining and industry in the Inde and Wurm area, but whatever the reason, Simon wrote: "I desire and most earnestly request my sons never after my death to participate in an industrial enterprise, however distinguished the name may be (!), and to avoid all business in mining like the plague; I further entreat my beloved wife, should my dear brother no longer be in the business, to have the balance sheets checked most carefully each year by our dear son-in-law, Felix Kaskel (since 1857), in whose caution and trustworthiness I have full confidence, and if a transaction forbidden by myself has been undertaken, I request my beloved wife to leave the business immediately and only leave that sum as limited-liability participation which can pass to my sons as inheritance after her death." His "private capital, which is not in the business" was "never, under any conditions, to be put back into the business again". He hoped that his sons would "honour the principle of conservation and act with great caution", but he added immediately "I make these conditions because they do not at present inspire me with confidence ..."

At the same time Abraham, who had spent most of April in Paris, some of it with Mevissen, and had to go to Switzerland in the second half of September for the International Bank in Luxembourg, was busy on a new and major undertaking: he was in Vienna in August, arranging a participation for the bank in the merger of the South Austrian railway with the Kärntner railway. So one of the brothers was cautiously concentrating the bank's activities on banking business pure and simple, avoiding any participation in mining and industrial establishments or mergers in West Germany, while the other was constantly travelling, and working in an increasingly wide and significant international context.

1859 was the year of the Italian War of Liberation, in which Napoleon III involved France against Austria, and in which Prussia threatened to become involved. Abraham Oppenheim, who spent February at least in Paris carefully observing political and financial developments, wrote to Bleichröder on 5 June: "It will depend entirely on the attitude taken by our government whether we are spared the trials of war". He spent the whole of September and the first half of October travelling in Switzerland. Then between 24 October and 1 November he and Bleichröder exchanged three letters and answers each (proof of the speed of the postal service) on the difficult financial situation in Austria and the general confusion of the political scene.

Perhaps these turbulent autumn weeks made him more than ever convinced that in Paris one was not only in the centre of Europe but in the most comfortable and secure circumstances as well. For suddenly, around 5 November, he told his brother that he wanted to leave the bank on 31 December that year, to enable Simon to take his sons in as "Associés". Simon answered that "after the greatest possible consideration he had reached the conclusion that we must not part ... what God has put together let no man put asunder. We have worked together for 40 years now, and are so bound together in true brotherly love that it would be the greatest possible misfortune for both of us if we were to part now, and probably one of us (he could only mean himself) would not long survive. My most earnest entreaty to you, my dearly beloved brother, is therefore that we should remain together until God our Father be pleased to separate us, and then I hope you in your brotherly love will protect and guard my loved ones."

Simon had another, no less difficult request. "Beloved Abraham, give me peace of mind, give me peace at home ... I know of no true answer to the arguments repeatedly put forward by my sons, Eduard and Albert, generally in the presence of their mother as well, and most earnestly entreat you, therefore, to help me. What can I say when Eduard says: We are no worse than others, we are as intelligent as other sons – v. Rath, Stein, Schnitzler, Herstatt were all taken into the business by their fathers as Associes straightaway and empowered to sign. It was only with the greatest possible difficulty that we persuaded Uncle Abraham to make us holders of procuration (Eduard in 1857, Albert in 1858)... have you had any cause to regret that so far? Have we misused the authorisation, or caused you any harm? We are both married, Albert already has a child, and I shall soon have one, and I am nearly thirty years of age. The honorary commercial posts are closed to us. We can become neither members of the Chamber of Commerce nor Commercial Judges as long as we are not independent businessmen. It is your duty as a father to further us and not undermine our position. If Uncle Abraham had sons you would long since have accepted them as partners. You must prevail upon Uncle Abraham to give us power to sign, or accept the resignation he has now offered, all the more since he assures us most earnestly that he will always stand by us in the bank after his departure with advice and active cooperation, and actually himself wanted to take procuration ..."

"Put yourself in my position", Simon concluded his letter, "and consider the matter carefully." He was firmly convinced "that you will accede to my urgent request and permit my two sons, Eduard and Albert, to be taken into our business as partners on 1 January". He even enclosed a draft contract with his letter, making his two sons partners in the bank from 1 January 1860, each with a share of 10% in the proft and loss. He drew up a "circular on the partnerships given to Eduard and Albert Oppenheim", which he also enclosed with the letter.

But Abraham would not give way, and Simon's sons did not become partners in the bank in 1860, indeed they had to wait another twenty years, until Abraham died. Simon was close to collapse. In the last days of 1859 he wrote to his brother: "Permit me, my good and dearly beloved brother, to pour out my heart to you in this letter, since I do not have the strength to do so verbally, without being choked by tears. You err greatly in assuming that I do not know you. I know you through and through, and have had time enough to study you. I know you love me extraordinarily, but I believe I have earned that, since I would always gladly have sacrificed my life for you. I know you are far superior to me in understanding and strength of mind, and that your views are much more often right than mine. But precisely because I know you so well, through and through, and because recently you have shown yourself so totally different to me than you usually are, I am beginning to be confused. A deep rage gnaws within me, and I feel that I cannot stand this for long. With your heated temperament you often do not know what bitter wounds you cause in your brother's heart. But more than that makes me unhappy: to see you always under pressure of cares and fear. You deserve to be the happiest person alive but are now unfortunately not so at all, you live in constant sorrow and care. You know, beloved brother, how I have asked you to remain in the business when you wanted to leave. I was motivated in that entirely by my love for you. I believed you would be unhappy if you were to leave the business. I see that I was wrong, and that my greatest wish, to be associated with you until the end of my days, will cause my unhappiness. Your beloved wife is of the same view and has told me that she will not rest until you have left the business. Your fearfulness has come to dominate your mind to such an extent recently that I am beginning to believe your wife was right. I will gladly make any sacrifice to add to your happiness. For you may be firmly convinced that I love you more than myself. You must also bear witness, if you are honest, that I have subordinated myself totally to you, and if I did not always approve your "sell at any price business" it was because I regarded this as countervening my duty to my children, and I would have agreed to all the sacrifices, unconditionally, if my wealth were not so much smaller than yours. With your great generosity in all things and on all occasions I expected you to understand that, when for your own peace of mind you mobilised more money than necessary. You seem to see it differently, but you are wrong. Basically you may be proved right, since sadly nothing but misfortune seems to be visited upon the world; but then I have to take the rap and should the money ever be needed, which God forbid, I shall have to pay at any price what you spent willingly and at a higher price.

I cannot tell you often enough that your peace and happiness are more to me than anything, and I know what burdens and sorrows I myself shall have to endure, how I shall be bound like a slave, if you leave the business. But I am ready to make any sacrifice, and I therefore propose to you that you should leave the business on a trial basis at the end of this year. I say, on a trial basis, for you should try it out for one year, and see if you are more at peace and more satisfied when you are not burdened with the weight and cares of business. You shall be free to state in December 1860 that you want to come back, and you shall have the right to your usual share in the 1860 results. I have nothing in mind but your peace and happiness. After so many years of work you should enjoy the fruits. If you find, in the course of the year or later, that you prefer to be in the business, I shall always welcome you with open arms, as I expect of your brotherly love that your wise counsel will always be given and that you will not leave your place of residence in Cologne. I would not survive if you were to do that ..."

But Abraham did not leave the business, not even on a trial basis, and consequently Simon tried again at the end of 1861 to get his brother to agree to his sons being made partners – but again he failed. More than three years passed without any changes outwardly or in the relations within the family that had grown up in the old Jewish traditions of community, authority and obedience and for the last fifteen years had on occasions been in danger of breaking apart.

When Simon Oppenheim wrote his long eighth will on 24 June 1863, in which he was able to bequeath very large capital sums and annuities, he included the sentence: "My (!) bank is one of the foremost in Europe and, if properly managed, should show a very sizable profit each year." He again thought it right to "warn his sons not to participate in any industrial enterprise, however brilliant its prospects might appear." Again he also stressed that he trusted his son-in-law Kaskel far more than his own sons.

Why Abraham Oppenheim wrote a farewell letter to his brother Simon on 25 October 1865, which he was only to read (and did read?) after Abraham's death is not clear. The letter says:

"My dearly beloved brother Simon,

In this letter I state that next to my most loved and excellent wife Charlotte I cling to you, my dearest brother, with a love as only my heart is capable of. Could my heart speak as it can love, feel, suffer and delight, it would tell you in every hour that it has always beat for you with such feeling. I have also prayed daily that heaven may protect you, and begged that in His mercy God might take *me* away from here before you, brother.

When you read these lines Almighty God in heaven will have heard my prayer, and then I ask all my beloved brothers and sisters to thank heaven most sincerely, for this is proof that my daily prayers have not been in vain.

Thank God you, beloved brother, are in the same fortunate financial circumstances as myself, and I need therefore give you no other sign of my love than my other dear brothers. I ask you, brother, to be so good as to use the 10,000 thalers which my beloved wife will put at your disposal for a fitting memorial to me. Then I ask you from now on to be the true and loving counsellor to my beloved Charlotte, and to express on my behalf my most sincere thanks to all my dear brothers and sisters for the many signs of love and affection they have always shown me. Your ever loving brother, Abraham Oppenheim, Cologne, 25 October 1865.

When the brothers were working with Bleichröder in 1865/66 on the big project of privatising the shares in the Saar held by the state of Prussia[9] and had to devote all their attention to the correspondence and discussions with Bismarck, the latent friction between Simon and Abraham, between the nephews and the uncle and between the wives as well, one of whom wanted to advance her sons, while the other wanted to have her "hôtel" in Paris and enjoy French high society at the peak of its imperial power, became more marked than ever.

Emma Charlotte Emilie, born in Cologne in 1837 the daughter of Simon Oppenheim, had married the young banker Felix Kaskel in Dresden in 1857, where his father was President of the State Bank of Saxony. In the spring of 1866 Abraham Oppenheim again decided to leave the bank; and equally surprisingly Simon this time wanted his son-in-law Kaskel to take a partnership to replace

[9] Wilhelm Treue, Wirtschafts- und Technikgeschichte Preußens, Berlin 1984, pp. 476ff.

Abraham – not his own sons. Kaskel accordingly wrote to him on this subject from Dresden on 5 June 1866: "Dear, beloved Papa, Your kind letter of the day before yesterday reached me this morning, and I was greatly distressed to learn that your excellent brother wants to leave the business. I find it only too understandable that the present state of things has soured Secret Government Councillor Abraham's taste for business life, and I know your love for him too well not to understand that you will put his peace of mind and welfare above all things.

But I must say that in my view there is no connection between his departure and the entry of an Associé who could never be compared with him in any way. The first question was raised many years ago, but the second was never aired in any way. So I should ask you to keep the two matters quite separate and assure me that you will not make one dependent on the other, before I can answer the proposal you have had the goodness to make me.

You put this proposal as your own, and as dear Mama's wish. I cannot do otherwise than assume you have ascertained that it is also your sons' desire. If I accept, it can, as I give you my word, only be on the one condition, that I am permitted, dearly beloved parents, to fulfil your wishes, for you yourselves esteem the relation between child and parents too highly not to understand and accept my reservation that I can only accept if this does not meet with too much objection from my own good father. I do not have the courage to approach him immediately on an idea that will uproot our entire existence and finds me quite unprepared. He would have to give up his business, since he could not continue it without me. What combination could be found to make that bearable to him, is something I need to think about. I shall use the coming weeks to prepare him for the matter, and if possible familiarise him with the idea. Assuming I succeed, I cannot admittedly at present say anything about the point in time when I might be able to place myself at your disposal, the only thing that is certain is that it cannot be soon. For first we must fight our way through the present bad times, and then we can start thinking about winding up a business which is dearer to me than I can say, and to which we owe a loyal obligation. That can only be done in a quiet, normal time, to avoid any suspicion that we are in financial difficulties and that is why you are drawing me to you.

The many important questions in this regard will have to be kept for verbal discussion; with God's help we will soon embrace you here, for you cannot fail to visit Karlsbad.

In the meantime my willingness shows you how great my devotion to you is, for with my lack of ambition (for great wealth), as I have often admitted to you, a smaller business is preferable to me than a large one ..."

But only five days later the matter no longer appeared so urgent to the father and father-in-law. In a letter dated 10 June 1866, written from Cologne, but of which only part has survived, Simon thanked his son-in-law and daughter "for the readiness you have shown", but added "the more I have talked the matter over with your dear mother in the last few days, the more I see that it needs to be very carefully considered and examined in all respects". The move to Cologne must not be "a sacrifice" for the children; they should think very carefully and consider "what you would be losing and what you would gain". The balance would have very much to their advantage". "I know, dear Felix, how you love Dresden and know that Cologne cannot offer the same". He also knew "how you, dear Emma, are flattered to be able to move in high society, which you would have to do without altogether here". So it all needed very careful thought, and of course Felix Kaskel could not leave his own father's business in Dresden "until the present bad times (the German war of 1866) are over". After a few more lines of hesitation and consideration Simon suddenly says, in this letter of 10 June 1866: "It must be decided by 1 July whether Abraham will stand by his resolve, and you have until then to think about it" – so only two weeks after they would have received the letter. And to cap it all Simon thought that his son-in-law, if he did decide in that short time to move to Cologne, should be ready "to be here by the end of November and stay until the end of March, to see whether life in Cologne and the business suits you". He would not formally join the bank until 1 July 1867 or 1 January 1868 "... I shall suffer my sons for one year."

So trouble with his brother and with his sons, presumably with their mother as well, who was pressing for their advancement. Felix Kaskel's entry as partner into the bank of Sal. Oppenheim jr. & Cie remained for more than a decade a possibility laid down in a contract, but he never made use of it.

It is no longer possible to say whether Abraham Oppenheim had decided formally to resign on 1 July 1866, but an "agreement" concluded between him, Simon and Simon's sons on 7 November that year has survived. Article 1 states: "On 1 January 1868 Abraham 0. will leave the bank ..." – with "40% of all the assets on that day", while "all the property belonging to the bank" was to be sold during the course of 1867 and the proceeds duly divided, for on principle Abraham wanted to take 40% of the bank with him.

Did Simon accept such a contract, that would deal the bank, now *his* bank, a heavy blow that would set it back for many years, without raising any objection? Yes and no. On the same day, 7 November 1866, he wrote to Abraham what can almost be called an answer to his letter of 25 October 1865: a "letter, not to be opened until after my death". In this letter, very brief for his customary style, he told his brother "after 46 years of working together" what he thought of their mutual relationship. The letter reads:

"Cologne, 7 November 1866

Dearly beloved brother,

On the day on which with a bleeding heart I have signed the contract dissolving our partnership, and which can separate me from you in business, I feel urged to express to you the innermost feelings of my heart. God Almighty will witness that I am only saying the pure truth. For a long, long time I struggled with myself, I wept for many nights, before I reached this decision. I was not moved by love of money, as you seem to believe, but interest in your own welfare. I have always felt with deep pain that your melancholy and foreboding over events of the utmost triviality made you unhappy, and if after 46 years working together with you I am separating from you, it is only to give you peace and rest in your old age.

You have great and excellent qualities, which no-one sees more clearly than myself, who have followed your work for so many years. But no-one is perfect, and you have the great fault of not letting anyone else rise beside you. In the long years of our work together I have had to bear with much from you, but on mature reflection you must see that I have suffered greatly from your treatment of me.

On the edge of the grave I forgive you everything and thank you as well for the many tokens of love you have given me. May God grant you from now on rest, peace and blessing into a ripe old age, that is my most sincere and earnest wish!

And now on the edge of the grave I have an urgent request to make to you, that, if I should die in 1867, you will continue the business with my sons and if possible take my son-in-law, Felix Kaskel, in whom you have full confidence, into the business as well. Should I die later and you really not have changed your mind and have left the business at the end of 1867, I ask you earnestly to stand by my heirs with advice and deed. Although you have not treated me in a brotherly fashion in the contract we have just signed today, I dare to count on your regret in this regard and appeal to your great brotherly love.

Thy ever most tenderly loving brother extends to you his blessing on his deathbed

Simon Oppenheim"

Abraham Oppenheim never read this letter. He died two years before his brother Simon, on 9 October 1878 in Cologne. After the death of his brother Simon naturally concluded a new company contract with his two sons – we shall discuss this later – and no doubt on this occasion the old contracts were read through again very carefully. But the letter to his brother Abraham, now meaningless, was not destroyed. His widow and sons may have read it after his death, and remembered all the tension, hopes and disappointments of around a quarter of a century.

Abraham Oppenheim did not leave the Bankhaus Sal. Oppenheim jr. & Cie in 1867, on the contrary, on 18 November 1867, more than a year after the "resignation agreement", a new company contract was signed. It began with the sentence: "After Herr Abraham Oppenheim has declared, at the request of Simon, Eduard and Albert Oppenheim, that he wishes to withdraw from the contract to dissolve the business concluded on 7 November 1866, under which he was to leave the business and the firm of Sal. Oppenheim jr & Cie on 31 December 1867, the following new contract has been drawn up and concluded between Abraham, Simon, Eduard and Albert Oppenheim: Para. 1: Simon and Abraham 0 remain joint heads of the business and as such retain control of the entire bank ..." So Abraham would still not let Simon's sons have partnerships. He only permitted an increase in their share of the profit from 1 January 1867 to $12^1/_2$% each and from 1 January 1870 to $16^2/_3$%, "if ... Abraham Oppenheim has not left the business under Para. 6 of this agreement ..." For "each of the two heads can terminate this contract at any time ..." The period of notice was 6 months. Felix Kaskel was given the possibility of joining the business as partner "at any time", so Emma's husband was in a better position than her brothers.

But in fact it all remained as ever before. Just as Simon and Abraham had been fighting their family and brotherly feuds since 1852, while at the same time successfully concluding major business transactions and preparing for the future, they continued to work against the same background after 18 November 1867 –

leaving written comments on another in their papers. Over the next ten years they also enjoyed great success in business and no less in society, all under the constant threat that Abraham could declare any day that six months later he no longer wanted to be joint "head" of this business.

At this point we must deal with an issue which acquired particular significance in 1867/68 in several respects – for the relationship between the two brothers, for Abraham Oppenheim's position at the Prussian court and finally for the attitude of this court and court society to the Jewish question. It was the award of title and orders to the two brothers, and finally their ennoblement.

Salomon Oppenheim received the title of "Senior Court Agent in our Most Gracious Confidence" on 22 January 1822, probably at the instigation of Hardenberg, who died in December that year, "in regard for his good qualities, of which We have the very highest report... that he may remain a true and industrious servant of Ourselves and Our Royal House and at all times be assiduous in his endeavours for the well-being of the Fatherland and Our Royal House". The Christian Cologne bankers Abraham Schaaffhausen and Friedrich Herstatt were decorated at the same time, with the Red Order of the Eagle, 3rd Class and the General Medal, Class 1 respectively, and by about 20 years later Sal. Oppenheim's two eldest sons had joined the ranks of successful bankers and industrialists and reached the age when such men were generally decorated or given titles.[10]

In what follows we are concerned solely with the events surrounding the elevation of Simon and Abraham Oppenheim into the Austrian and Prussian nobility, but for various reasons at least a brief outline should be given of the preliminary stages which led to this.

Simon Oppenheim, born in Cologne in 1803, received his first medal in 1844. It was the Knight's Cross of the Belgian Order of Leopold, and it was given for services rendered in March 1839, when during a crisis of the Rhine Railway Company, of which he was one of the founders and shareholders, he had gone to Brussels and initiated negotiations with the Ministry of Home Affairs there which culminated in the Belgian government taking 4000 shares in the company. Simon Oppenheim used the occasion of the application he had to make to the King of Prussia to be allowed to accept the decoration to thank the King once more for the "most gracious honour" he had shown in 1842 "in visiting my house" on the laying of the foundation stone for the building work on Cologne cathedral. In 1845 Frederick William IV made Simon Oppenheim a Commercial Councillor for his services in promoting industry in the Rhineland by founding the AG für Bergbau und Zinkfabrikation (a mining and zinc production company) in Stolberg, and it was not until 1865 that William I elevated him to the rank of Privy Commercial Councillor, after correspondence and suggestions to this end since 1859. At the beginning of 1859 a Lieutenant General von Schack, on whose relations to the Oppenheim family no more is known, had suggested that Simon Oppenheim should be made Privy Commercial Councillor for his services in extending the Rhineland railway down to Koblenz, after his younger brother Abraham had already been awarded this title in another context. The Chief Executive of Cologne,

---

[10] When Salomon Oppenheim died in 1828 he was the richest Jew in Cologne.

von Möller, expressed his opposition to the idea very forcibly on 4 April 1859: Simon Oppenheim was not a member of the board of directors of the railway company, he was only a member of the supervisory council of various companies, "as which he, as is well known, only draws the fees and other advantages but does not bear any real responsibility for the business". Appointing him Privy Commercial Councillor would "solely be to grant distinction to wealth". Möller must have made this remark against his better knowledge, for the Chief Executive of Cologne in 1859 must have known that the supervisory council fulfilled the functions exercised by the supervisory board, and certainly did not only draw a fee. But he went even further: he wrote of the banker, who was extremely cautious in his politics and very devoted to the Hohenzollerns: "His attitude is certainly not anti-governmental, but he has his own views on government measures, like others too. If he is said to have shown *particular* patriotism in 1848 it was no doubt because he expected greater benefit to himself from the soldiers than the democrats. I do not mean to say that Simon Oppenheim could not be acknowledged to be a very useful citizen; but I cannot bring myself to speak in favour of giving him and his bank so exceptional a distinction as to make the two heads Privy Commercial Councillors without any particular occasion. It would only be generally acknowledged as a reverence to the wealthy Jews and that, in my view, could not be of service to the state."

The latent anti-Semitism and the envy of the Cologne entrepreneurs, which was evident in other Chief Executives as well, are very plain in this letter from a highly intelligent senior official. But almost half a century after the Rhineland was incorporated into the Prussian monarchy he still does not seem to have recognised the importance of the province for the state as a whole and the modernisation of the old nobility and bourgeois society, or if he did, he was unwilling to admit it. Möller may have believed that he was representing the majority of the government in taking this stance against the rich industrialists and bankers and the wealthy Jews in Cologne, but he was not really, for his report was not, as usual, prepared by a clerk, it was written entirely in his own hand and copied in his own hand as well.

A week later, on 11 April 1859, the Senior Executive von Pommer-Esche in Koblenz not only echoed Möller's view but actually went further by adding: "Even in his banking business, which for the rest scarcely pursues other aims than to make a very good profit, his personal influence is said to be of slight significance." Like Möller he opposed the award – "all the more since the award of such a title to *both* brothers ... would be to show exceptional preference to the Oppenheims and their banking business, which would no doubt be interpreted only as reverence to wealth, since there are no services to justify it."

When the proposal was once more put forward in April 1861 on the occasion of the succession to the throne it was turned down in May without any reason being given at all. The same happened again in September and in December 1862, particularly since no new arguments were put forward in favour of Simon Oppenheim. When a further application was addressed to the Senior Executive in the autumn of 1863, he requested Möller "to be so good as to provide information on the attitude of the person named and the other persons named elsewhere during the last elections" – these were the elections in connection with the controversy over the Prussian army. Möller, who had in the meantime swung round to support

Simon Oppenheim's appointment,[11] declared on 27 November 1863 that he could not abide by his "earlier proposal, after the person in question signed the well-known address of the socalled Rhineland Potents last year ... Moreover, one of his sons, it is said, has for some time publicly aligned himself among the founders of the Progressive Party." The Senior Executive supported this argument in his report to the Minister of Trade on 29 December 1863.

A brief explanation is necessary here. The three Oppenheim brothers, like Hansemann, Camphausen, Mevissen and many other successful, "potent" entrepreneurs were Rhineland liberals. They had not hesitated to state this repeatedly in public, and the legal state, which Prussia embodied after 1850 even more than before the revolution, had accepted this without reprisals – Hansemann and Camphausen had actually been given ministerial posts in 1848. But in 1862/63 this liberal movement had become politically active for the first time. In the controversy over the constitutionality of the reform and expansion of the army Dagobert Oppenheim, who a quarter of a century before had been the main founder and shareholder in the oppositional Rheinische Zeitung, and his brother Simon signed the "address" by the socalled Rhineland potents (not petitioners) on 6 January 1863. They were a group of wealthy and influential men and they stated in their address that Minister President von Bismarck was pushing through the "submission on the army ..." despite the refusal of the Land parliament to ratify the budget and so was acting "unconstitutionally".[12]

Dagobert Oppenheim, moreover, was one of the initiators of the address, which was displayed for signature in the head office of the Köln-Mindener Railway Company,[13] and on 14 January 1863 it was also printed in the Kölnische Zeitung. It stated: "The foundation of constitutional monarchy is the law, and the law is infringed if the government of the state conducts its finances without the basis of a constitutionally established state budget". At this time Simon Oppenheim could call his bank "one of the foremost in Europe", and his name under an address to the King, accusing the Minister President of acting unconstitutionally, would have weight.

So the Chief Executive's statement that he could not "abide by" his former proposal is quite understandable. After all, the Cologne banker had clearly spoken out against the government by which he wished to be decorated. And his sons were really among the "founders" of the German Progressive Party on 6 June 1861 – the Chief Executive commented that "as one might say, to keep the family count – one in each of the parties ..." That was not kind, but quite possibly true.

Then came the proposals from the Oppenheims and Bleichröder to privatise the state holdings in the Saarland, and for the first time the King's attention was really drawn to the Oppenheims on a political issue. He asked for information on them and on 14 February 1865 the Minister of Trade, von Itzenplitz, stated in a letter to Pommer-Esche: "The fact that His Majesty himself is inclined to give the proposed award directly to S. Oppenheim induces me to request Your Excellency to be so

[11] The relevant letters have not survived.

[12] Hermann Aubin, Geschichte des Rheinlandes, Vol. 1, Essen 1922, p. 324.

[13] Joseph Hansen, Gustav Mevissen, Vol. 1, pp. 738f.

kind as to express an opinion on whether since making that (unfavourable) report you have become aware of anything that has caused you to change the views expressed therein."

Pommer-Esche and Möller stuck stubbornly to their negative opinion, and Pommer-Esche was challengingly ironic. Moreover, during these very weeks a memorandum "File Note on the Proceedings concerning the AG für Bergbau, Blei- und Zinkfabrikation zu Stolberg" appeared, in which, as Möller reported to the Senior Executive on 4 March 1865, "a report was made on the modus acquerandi of Herr Simon Oppenheim, which is sufficient to show that it would be quite inopportune to give him a major decoration". Proceedings were pending "at the appeal court here". The brochure is lost and no more is known of the legal proceedings either.

But Möller was just two days too late. On 6 March the Senior Executive informed him of an order from the Minister dated 3 March "under which His Majesty the King on 2nd inst. was pleased to complete the decree making Commercial Councillor Simon Oppenheim Privy Commercial Councillor, and I saw no reason not to communicate the same to the said Oppenheim". He also had to convey the congratulations of Minister von Itzenplitz; and he actually added his own. But Möller himself remained silent. Simon Oppenheim expressed his thanks on 10 March 1865 from Paris - perhaps not entirely without political considerations.

Since 1858 he had acquired a number of foreign decorations, which we do not need to discuss in detail here. By far the most important was the honour shown to him on 18 March 1867 by the Emperor Franz Josef, when he decided to award Simon Oppenheim the Imperial Austrian Order of the Iron Cross, Class II "with the stipulation that by way of exception the statutes of the Order which apply to nationals and under which the title is hereditary apply with this award". Simon Oppenheim was informed that this had been "executed" by the Imperial and Royal Minister President on 2 April 1867, but contrary to other unconfirmed reports, it was not actually executed in all formality in April 1867 but, strangely enough, not until 4 January 1868 in Vienna, with reference to the decision of March 1867. On 10, and according to other reports, on 8 January 1868 the Imperial and Royal Ambassador in Dresden, Werner - Saxony had fought on Austria's side in 1866 - presented Simon Oppenheim with the medal[14].

We no longer know who made the application, which is now lost, to help Simon Oppenheim to the peerage in this way, or when (it was not Simon himself, although, as we shall see, this would have been possible). It certainly need not have been Simon Oppenheim himself, the application could have come from a business friend in Vienna or been made by a Minister - although this could hardly have been without the knowledge of the Cologne banker. "The announcement of this ennoblement in the Wiener Zeitung was held back for the present, in consideration

[14] The Gotha genealogy handbook of the peerage, Gothaisches Genealogisches Taschenbuch der Freiherrlichen Häuser 24/1874 p. 491f., the first to show the line of "Freiherr von Oppenheim, does not give a date for his ennoblement, it only states that Simon Oppenheim had been elevated to the ranks of the Austrian nobility "as a knight of the Imperial Austrian Order of the Iron Cross Class II, with the supreme decision of His Majesty the Emperor Franz Joseph I of Vienna of 18 March 1867".

of the indication given in the estimable communication of ... March this year, Z 3093/6", as a letter from the Austrian Home Ministry to the Foreign Ministry of April 1868 states. The enclosed text for the newspaper announcement is crossed out. It states in the usual official terminology simply that "the elevation to the ranks of the Austrian hereditary nobility" had been executed "by way of exception with the application of the statutes of the Order". The text is eleven lines long, and it was already crossed out in the draft of the letter. So the general public, and with them the Austrian nobility, did not find out that a Jewish Prussian banker had become an Austrian nobleman - and of course the Prussian press did not find out either.

When Oppenheim was given the award he had first to ascertain "for the purposes of the due and proper execution of the elevation to noble rank proposed in the above Royal decision" that this would receive the approval of the Royal Prussian government, whose citizen he was. Simon Oppenheim fulfilled that condition before 2 March 1868 "together with all the attendant obligations" and requested "the execution of the said ennoblement". Thereupon the diploma was executed and delivered on 20 April 1868, "by order of His Imperial and Royal Majesty himself", and the ennoblement was duly entered into the Ministerial Directory of the Nobility, Vol I, p. 250, by the appropriate official.

The diploma states: "We were pleased to note that Simon Oppenheim, banker in Cologne, Knight of our Order of the Iron Cross, Class II, ... Royal Prussian Privy Commercial Councillor, has performed a number of excellent services for us and our Imperial House."

Then follows a kind of brief biography, after which the text of the diploma continues: "Distinguished by great knowledge of business, of proven reliability and untarnished honour, the said person has been appointed Director and Member of the Supervisory Council of various commercial and railway companies, and for many years, at the head of numerous charitable enterprises and institutions, has shown an industry that is as pleasing as it is worthy of recognition. The above-named devotes particular interest to the railways and finances of our Imperial Realm, he played an outstanding part in the establishment and construction of several major railway lines and provided strong and successful support for our government in various financial operations, in that his bank took major amounts of all our loan issues and also invested considerable sums in Austrian securities.

In recognition of the many years of devotion and wide-ranging excellent services shown to Us We have in Our Imperial decision of 18 March 1867 awarded the said person Our Order of the Iron Cross, Second Class, and, applying by way of exception the statutes of that Order, We have with Our Imperial and Royal powers of disposition been moved to raise

Simon Oppenheim

together with all his legitimate descendants of both sexes for all future times to the ranks of the nobility of Our Empire of Austria ... "

Kaiser Franz Josef signed the diploma "in his own hand" and the newly ennobled Simon von Oppenheim confirmed receipt of the same on 6 July 1868, after having evidently hastened to "deposit" 185 gulden through his Viennese representative, the banker Sina, with the "Head of Protocol" in Vienna, and "to send a description of the services that should be mentioned in the diploma, curriculum vitae, and a sketch in colour of the proposed coat of arms together with a description of the same" to Vienna.

So altogether it took 13 months from the Imperial decision on 18 March 1867 that the award should be given, until the actual ennoblement on 20 April 1868, and a further 11 weeks until the diploma was handed over.[15] We may take it that Simon informed his brother Abraham from time to time of the progress of the protracted affair.

So Simon, the elder of the two Jewish brothers (his son Eduard had become a Christian in 1859 at the age of 28, when he married Amalie Heuser, the daughter of a Cologne merchant) was the first to be ennobled – in Austria. But Abraham was the first to endeavour to obtain elevation to noble rank – and his efforts were made in Prussia. For widely as he travelled, and numerous as his international connections, which he also cultivated assiduously, were, they mainly concerned Europe to the left of the Rhine, while Austria-Hungary was largely Simon's field of operations. He never appears to have considered applying for ennoblement in France or Belgium, and probably he wanted a Prussian title on account of his close relations with the Prussian monarchy.

But Abraham Oppenheim also had to take some initial disappointments in his attempts to obtain title and order. On 28 July 1854 the Minister of Trade, A.v.d. Heydt, informed the Minister President, von Manteuffel, that following his verbal suggestion he had "believed he should" approach the Senior Executive, von Kleist-Retzow, and through him the Chief Executive, von Möller, "with a request for a report on the award of the title of Privy (!) Commercial Councillor" to Abraham Oppenheim. "Both are against such an award, because there is no reason for such distinction of the said A. Oppenheim".

On 28 September 1855 Möller made a proposal regarding the award to the Minister of Trade, suggesting "most respectfully" that Mevissen and Abraham Oppenheim should be made Commercial Councillors. He described Oppenheim as "known to be one of the leading bankers in the Province", praising in particular his services to the Rhineland railway company, especially the construction of its

---

[15] There is an interesting parallel in time and persons to Simon Oppenheim's ennoblement, and it also throws a light on the social history of the period. The Dresden banker Karl Kaskel, born on 6 October 1797 in Dresden, the son of a Saxon court agent and banker, whose son, as we have seen, married Simon Oppenheim's daughter Emma in 1857, made an application in Vienna for the award of a hereditary noble title on 28 June 1867 (he was the richest man in Dresden, as Simon was held to be in Cologne). In his application Kaskel listed all his services to the Austrian monarchy and not least his work for the property and dowries of members of the Imperial family. The Viennese government enquired of the Saxon government whether it agreed with the ennoblement. In Dresden the opinion was held that a non-hereditary Austrian title was more suited to the social standing of banker and Counsellor Kaskel and would be more appropriate, and thereupon Karl Kaskel was awarded the title on 28 October 1867 but not elevated to the hereditary peerage (the award was tax-free). He immediately set about making further applications on his own behalf in Vienna. On 31 March 1868 he apparently renewed his request for an hereditary title, and on 19 May 1868 was awarded this for himself and all his descendants. The Austrian Ambassador in Dresden, Werner, also informed him of his ennoblement. But this was not published in the Wiener Zeitung either, and so not made generally known. Joachim E. Kaskel, Vom Hoffaktor zur Dresdner Bank. Die Unternehmerfamilie Kaskel im 18. und 19. Jahrhundert, in: Zeitschrift für Unternehmensgeschichte, Vol. 28.

bridges. On 1 October 1855 Frederick William IV made this award to Abraham Oppenheim, with v.d. Heydt's counter signature, "trusting that as Commercial Councillor he will remain a true and loyal servant of Ourselves and Our Royal House and will continue to contribute to the general welfare to the best of his ability."

When on 11 November 1858, a date long celebrated in the history of the railways in the Rhineland, the strategically important railway bridge at Koblenz was opened, several senior officials, engineers and so on were decorated, but not the banker Oppenheim. The following day v. d. Heydt wrote to Otto von Manteuffel, who had retired as Minister President a week before, "No application has been made for Abraham Oppenheim, and I thought that might be possible when the line is opened as far as Bingen, which, I hope, may be in a year. But it gives me particular pleasure to make most respectful application at this point in time for the use of the title as suggested by Your Excellency without recourse to the authorities, and you may be sure I shall inform you of our success."

By 15 November 1858 v. d. Heydt was able to inform the Senior Executive, von Pommer-Esche, following another recommendation from von Manteuffel, that the Prince Regent had been pleased to appoint Abraham Oppenheim Privy Commercial Councillor, and "Citissime" Möller had been sent a copy of the document. Möller, who was evidently not well disposed towards the Oppenheim brothers, had reported to Pommer-Esche a few months later, on 4 April 1859, that Abraham Oppenheim had not been decorated in Prussia for his services as banker and promoter of the railways in that state on a recommendation from v. d. Heydt, but at the instigation of von Manteuffel, "to whom he was of service in an important foreign affair". What this consisted of, Möller could not say, since v. d. Heydt had only written to him on 25 November 1858 to say that Manteuffel had given him some indications of Oppenheim's "good services elsewhere a few years ago". However, at the same time he expressly stressed Oppenheim's "services to the railways in the Rhineland, especially the major extensions to these".

In December 1859 and May 1864 Abraham Oppenheim was awarded further honours, again with express reference to his services to the railways. Then he was also ennobled. The process is of great interest for social history. When efforts were being made in Vienna to obtain a decoration for Simon Oppenheim, the award of which would very probably entail an application for elevation to the nobility, there was never any mention or even indication – at any rate in the records – of whether he belonged to the Jewish or Christian faith. But it is possible, although it cannot be proved and is not even probable, that this is the reason why the ennoblement was not publicly announced in the Wiener Zeitung, as was the usual practice.

Brother Abraham fared quite differently in Berlin, and here, it must be stressed, the initiative came from King William I, who expressed his intention to raise Abraham Oppenheim to the ranks of the nobility. Whether the King in turn had received the appropriate suggestion from elsewhere, and from whence this might have come, cannot be established. But it is known[16] that William I and Queen Augusta had remained in "close personal contact" with four Rhinelanders from his

---

[16] Hansen, Mevissen, loc. cit., Vol. I, p. 723.

period as Governor of Koblenz (1849–1857), L. Camphausen, F. Diergardt, whom he appointed to the Prussian upper chamber, Abraham Oppenheim and G. Mevissen.

In connection with the opening of the railway line from Rolandseck to Koblenz on 11 November 1858 Abraham Oppenheim corresponded with the lady-in-waiting Gräfin Hacke on the travel arrangements for the Princess of Prussia, and it is clear from the letters that personal relations already existed between himself and the Princess. On 10 November 1858 Oppenheim arrived in Koblenz, "to attend the evening reception in the Royal Residence upon receipt of the invitation to the same", as the Coblenzer Zeitung reported on 13 November 1858. All three Oppenheim brothers attended the dedication of the bridge over the Rhine at Cologne on 3 October 1859, and on 12 November 1859 Abraham and Dagobert Oppenheim were invited to Koblenz to celebrate the event of 11 November the preceding year. At least after 1863 Abraham Oppenheim always attended the annual banquet to celebrate 11 November in the residence in Koblenz, and he of course met the Minister of the Royal Household, Freiherr von Schleinitz there, confidant of Queen Augusta (and also of Princess Victoria), whom Bismarck called the "Minister of the Harem". At the celebrations of the building of Cologne cathedral in 1863 Abraham Oppenheim invited the royal couple to a "luncheon" on 15 October through Schleinitz, on 10 September 1863, and Schleinitz recommended that they accept. On 20 September 1863, however, he feared demonstrations in Cologne against Bismarck, and added: "It is certainly not necessary for Herr von Bismarck to go to Cologne, at most the Minister of Culture". At the end of September Abraham Oppenheim and his wife invited Mevissen, among others, saying that "their Majesties have been pleased to agree to take luncheon with us".

But on 12 October Oppenheim was informed that the King would not attend the celebration in Cologne on 15 October. Ten days later, on 22, Schleinitz wrote, clearly having received a letter from Oppenheim, not to William I but to the Queen, and as we shall see later, this was characteristic of Abraham Oppenheim's relation to the royal couple: "Permit me to express ex post my most respectful thanks for all Your Majesty did to lessen the pain of the cancelled luncheon for Herr Oppenheim. The poor man was really to be pitied. Of in the main good, indeed excellent qualities, he is not entirely free of a very sensitive vanity and he can see in the cancellation of the Royal visit to Cologne nothing but the work of a low intrigue directed mainly against his person. And so he is still hoping for the satisfaction of a demonstration of the Royal favour that will be evident in wide circles. He would see such above all in the award of a title, which he has long desired with all his heart, but should this not be deemed appropriate, in the award of the Hohenzollern order Class 2. I will try to obtain one or the other for him, but I am afraid that insurmountable obstacles will appear in the way of either wish being fulfilled."

This letter is interesting for what it tells us about the relations at court. Schleinitz, whose wife maintained "the foremost house" in Berlin in the sixties[17], is firstly showing that he could count on considerable sympathy for A. Oppenheim on the part of the Queen. He then tells us that Oppenheim was of a "sensitive

---

[17] Gert Heinrich, Geschichte Preußens, Staat und Dynastie, Berlin 1981, p. 392.

vanity" that was apparently not usual at court, and that he was not familiar with politics on a wider scale. That might perhaps be somewhat to his disadvantage with Her Majesty. He was also warning the Queen discreetly not to take Oppenheim's side too openly: probably opposition to the decoration of Oppenheim personally or a Jew generally – which could only come from the King or the Cabinet – would be the "insurmountable obstacle". But of course Schleinitz also wanted to serve his Queen, whose influence on William I and through him on the political scene, had been felt every day for years. And so five days later, on 27 October, he wrote again: "If Your Majesty could do something in the direction indicated (no longer clear, but probably the King) for Oppenheim, I would be very pleased. I will also do my best."

So the Queen clearly wanted to see Oppenheim receive his decoration, and Schleinitz was working to fulfil her wish. But the resistance must have been stronger, although no evidence of it has survived. Although Oppenheim sent the Queen a magnificently bound volume of 12 original watercolours in November 1863 "in memory of the celebration to mark the building of the cathedral in Cologne on 15 October 1863, with the greatest respect, for Her Majesty Queen Augusta", to remind her of himself, his services and his wishes, no further progress was made. In Mevissen's papers[18] there is a note: "3 February 1864. Her Majesty the Queen will receive Privy Commercial Councillors A. Oppenheim and Mevissen today at eleven. Berlin, 3 February 1864, Graf Boos-Waldeck, Comptroller of the Royal Household."

At the beginning of April 1864 Oppenheim travelled to Paris from Berlin, where von Schleinitz had asked him to take a letter to the Prussian Ambassador in the French capital. On 5 April Schleinitz informed Goltz that "Oppenheim, the rich banker from Cologne" would visit him, adding that Oppenheim would return direct to Berlin on 11 or 12. "Perhaps you would like to make use of this occasion, which is absolutely confidential". Mevissen and Abraham Oppenheim were in Berlin on 14 April 1864, for on that day the Queen again received the two Privy Commercial Councillors, at twelve.[19]

So Oppenheim (and probably Mevissen as well, who was already dreaming of building railways in Schleswig and Holstein) was engaged in the political struggle over the two duchies, in other words, he was now involved in the great political arena. For on the same day Schleinitz wrote to Goltz: "Oppenheim will probably have told you what I answered when he told me of his idea of a visit from the Emperor (Napoleon III) to calm things down."

On 18 April 1864 Schleinitz told the Queen: "The occasion to decorate the excellent Oppenheim would probably not have come until the dedication ceremony (sic) and I hope on my part that I can find an occasion before that to recall the matter to the King's mind." On the same day he wrote to Goltz, to whom Oppenheim was again taking a letter, that Oppenheim "will for the rest be able to tell you more about conditions and the moods here than I can, for I am still tied to my room, all the more as he has been received repeatedly, not only by the King and

---

[18] Mevissen papers, Cologne City Archive.
[19] Loc. cit.

the Queen but even the Prime Minister, and honoured with a political conversation".

So Abraham Oppenheim was playing an active part in Franco-Prussian politics. It was also during this period that he was able to initiate the relations with Bismarck which were to involve him in major economic and political considerations in the following year. In 1871 (with Bleichröder) he was also involved in the discussion on the level and method of payment of the French war reparations and finally, some years later, through his brother Dagobert, in the nationalisation of the Köln-Mindener railway company in the context of the Reich railway problems and Bismarck's Reich intervention policy. One of the most interesting strands in Bismarck's cooperation with bankers and industrialists, therefore, began during these days in Berlin. Abraham Oppenheim was clearly aware of what was developing - or seemed to be developing - for him. Schleinitz told the Queen that Oppenheim had visited him before leaving for Cologne, he "was most deeply moved and delighted by the grace with which Your Majesty had overwhelmed him".

Soon after that Oppenheim was back in Paris. On 20 May 1864 he wrote to Mevissen in Cologne: "Yesterday evening I returned safely from Paris ..." and then the Schleswig-Holstein question was settled for the time, and Oppenheim appears to have seen rather less of Schleinitz and the royal couple. When the Queen travelled to Koblenz in October 1865 from Münster, where she had been inspecting charity institutions, via Essen, where she visited the Krupp works and Cologne, Abraham Oppenheim organised a reception for her on 21 October on Cologne railway station, which was mentioned in the Cologne press.

On 9 May 1866 the King dissolved the Land parliament in preparation for new elections. The following day A. Oppenheim was in Berlin, "while troops were being mobilised everywhere ... with others to speak for peace ... as the representative of 17 Rhineland Chambers of Commerce". He was received by Bismarck, whom he told that if a war was unavoidable Bismarck should first make his peace with the Land parliament. The Prime Minister told him that he had offered the King his resignation but it had been refused. Oppenheim, as Bismarck's assistant Keudell remembered later, "recounted this conversation the same evening to his friend Bleichröder, with the expressions of the utmost admiration, as Bleichröder told me the next morning".[20]

This courageous representation of the political attitude of a large section of the Rhineland bourgeoisie did not influence the government's policy, but it probably did as much harm to Oppenheim himself, as we shall see, as his signature three years before under the address by his brother Simon against Bismarck's "deficit theory", although the banker, who, of course was also mindful of the effects a war would have on his business, bowed to the inevitable and continued to serve the government well. William I, for the rest, knew that the Archbishop of Cologne, Paul Melchers, and so the Catholic Rhineland, shared the view taken by the Chambers of Commerce. The King had already written to Melchers on 4 June:

[20] Robert von Keudell, Fürst und Fürstin Bismarck, Erinnerungen 1846–1872, Berlin 1901, pp. 264ff.

"I know that many fail to grasp the reasons for the war which is probably coming."[21]

It was at this time that Bleichröder and Abraham Oppenheim were recommending to the Prussian government that the Prussian state holdings in the Saar should be privatised, and this entailed many visits to Berlin. The Saarbrücker Zeitung, which of course was intensively preoccupied with this question, actually expressly reported on 17 March 1866 that the "elder Oppenheim", in other words, Simon, was, "as everyone in Berlin knows, the intellectual initiator of the project" and had "negotiated" with Bismarck, v. d. Heydt and Roon on it. But that was not correct. Abraham Oppenheim was often in the capital at this time. Crown Prince Frederick, for instance, entered in his diary on 11 March 1866: "Oppenheim, the red-haired banker from Cologne, came to see me".[22] The red-haired banker was Abraham. On 19 May 1866 Schleinitz wrote to the Queen: "The excellent Oppenheim, who was in Paris during the last few weeks where his connections have given him many an insight, has been here since yesterday, to inform the King of what he has learned." Then came the war, the course of which made the further consideration of the Saar question superfluous, and after Königgrätz the King forbade it as well. But when the Queen was in Baden-Baden in the autumn of 1866 she wrote to the King on 13 October: "Oppenheim of Cologne is here, and interests me greatly. He says that the Emperor (Napoleon) is (touch wood!) better now, but does not spare himself enough. By his account there is a kind of stagnation in political life at present, that is, a very desirable and important turning point has occurred, although one does not know how long it will last."

A few days later the Queen went to Koblenz, where the lady-in waiting, Gräfin Hacke, immediately extended an invitation to Oppenheim and Mevissen on her behalf. When Oppenheim handed on the invitation to Mevissen on 30 October 1866 he added a long letter from himself, saying, i.a.: "I still have not had a cable from my friend Schleinitz to tell me when he will be here". So he was close enough to the Minister to invite him to lunch, and Oppenheim invited Mevissen and his wife to join them.

The war was over, the time of rewards in the form of endowments, titles, promotions and ennoblements began, and thoughts once more turned to Abraham Oppenheim in this connection. On 10 November 1866 – on the previous day the traditional celebration of the opening of the railway had been held in Koblenz and Oppenheim had as usual attended – Schleinitz wrote to Graf Eulenburg, the Minister of the Interior: "As Your Excellency will probably know, Privy Commercial Councillor Abraham Oppenheim of Cologne/Rhine so excelled himself by his intense and voluntary activities during the course of the war of 1864 and last summer in support of the families and surviving dependents of the troops in the field, and His Majesty the King has already verbally declared himself inclined, in consideration of this, to accord him ennoblement as an appropriate acknowledgement of the patriotic attitude shown by him in this and on other occasions as well."

---

[21] Ernst Berner (ed.): Kaiser Wilhelm der Große, Briefe, Reden und Schriften, Vol. II, 1861–1888, Berlin 1906, pp. 125f.

[22] Heinrich Otto Meisner (ed.): Kaiser Friedrich III. Tagebücher von 1848–1866, Leipzig 1929, p. 413.

The King himself had "said he was inclined". Did he say so to the Queen, or the Hausminister? Schleinitz left that open, as he did the question of who initiated the idea. In fact, the Minister whom Oppenheim had called his friend, went on, cautious to the point of insincerity: "Oppenheim, however, (as far as I know) is of the Jewish faith, and even if this need not be regarded as an absolute obstacle under current legislation, the Prussian monarchy has never yet conferred a noble title upon a Jew, so far as we have been able to ascertain."

So Schleinitz had already made some investigations. He went on: "With the fundamental significance this case would then assume for the view of the nature of the nobility in general and the further treatment of related matters, I therefore believe I should reach closer agreement with Your Excellency, before instigating any further action in what I understand to be His Majesty's intentions, on whether and what doubts there may be in your department against the envisaged most gracious act with regard to the religious persuasion of the person in question. To that end I therefore make so bold as to request you most humbly to be pleased to let me have your comment on the matter, and would be extremely grateful if this could be as soon as possible, since His Majesty the King wishes to have the award to Oppenheim set in some relation to the coming Christmas celebration." So the King did indeed have "intentions" and the gracious act was to take place in the immediate future.

Eulenberg read the letter two days later, on 12 November, but he appears to have believed that the gracious act could be delayed, and perhaps prevented altogether, if he delayed in answering it beyond the date in question. For on 3 February 1867 Schleinitz had to admit he still had not received Eulenburg's reply, and "beg most humbly for a response as soon as possible". But Eulenburg did not reply in the next four weeks either. On 5 March 1867 Schleinitz became more insistent. "In the matter of the ennoblement of Privy Commercial Councillor A. Oppenheim in Cologne, which His Most Gracious Majesty has been pleased to consider, His Majesty the King has asked me personally to remind you of the report which we still await". Again "your most obedient servant" Schleinitz begged the Home Minister to let him have his reply "as soon as possible, if you would be so good".

But Eulenburg's draft answer to Schleinitz's letter of 10 November 1866 – the reminder of 3 February was tacitly ignored – was only dated 26 April 1867. So the Minister had taken five and a half months to think about the matter and enquire as to the opinions of others. The result was interesting. He was honoured "to answer, as your most obedient, that I personally would not recall to mind any objection to the ennoblement of ... the person named, in consideration of the fact that he is childless and that now (1866) Baron Rothschild, also of the Jewish faith, has become a Prussian citizen (he lived in Frankfurt and his father had already been ennobled in Austria). Graf Bismarck, the Prime Minister, is of the same opinion, but the other Ministers of State have considerable reservations concerning the ennoblement of a Jew, and it might perhaps be appropriate to bring this divergence of views to the notice of His Majesty".

So Bismarck, and following him Eulenburg, thought they had found a solution by pointing out that the ennoblement would be limited to a few years, which in effect made such a mockery of it that the King would have to renounce his gracious act – without expressly taking into consideration the doubts held apparently by virtually all his ministers. Once more the matter got stuck somewhere for several months – but not this time to the advantage of those who opposed the ennoblement of a Jewish banker. On the contrary, during this period complications that could never have been foreseen arose. Even before Eulenburg had cautiously pointed out that a Jewish Imperial Austrian Baron living in Frankfurt (and who was not childless) had automatically acquired the right to use his title in Prussia through the annexation of the City of Frankfurt (and not been permitted to do so by way of exception) Simon Oppenheim was ennobled by the Austrian Emperor on 18 March/2 April 1867. So while some were trying to prevent Abraham's elevation to the nobility, his brother was given his diploma at the beginning of July. Sure that he would be granted Prussian recognition of his title, he immediately ordered from "F. L. Möhring, formerly Baron von Hackewitz" in Berlin "a solid silver seal skippet" for the Imperial seal on the diploma, paying 31 thalers for it on 6 November 1867. But why Simon Oppenheim did not put in his application for Prussian recognition of his ennoblement – it has not survived – until 20 December 1867, is not clear.

But by 25 January and 4 February 1868 reports were with the King on the matter, although these are now lost too. And now, after years of "intentions" and "reminders" from the Queen and von Schleinitz, with evasions and semi-doubts or references to Abraham's childless marriage, the King suddenly tired of this way of treating an honourable and useful subject. On 14 February 1868 he wrote to Schleinitz: "On these reports I intend to grant Privy Commercial Councillor Simon Oppenheim of Cologne the permission he requests to accept and use the order given to him by His Majesty, the Emperor of Austria ... and the hereditary title which this also confers, but at the same time I intend to raise Privy Commercial Councillor Abraham Oppenheim to noble rank and look to the presentation of the diploma which needs to be drawn up for my execution of the same. Berlin, 14 February 1868." In Prussia, and since 1871 the German Reich, the two brothers were therefore united as noblemen by an elegant act of the King that was as generous as it was independent (influenced by the Queen?).

Of course news of Abraham's ennoblement spread rapidly, and a flood of congratulatory letters began to arrive. Only two of his answers have survived – both to his trusted friend Bleichröder. On 24 February he thanked Bleichröder, on behalf of his wife as well, for his congratulations of the previous day. This had given him so much pleasure "because we know it comes from the heart. The news that our excellent monarch has raised me to the ranks of the nobility came as a delightful surprise to me because I had not the least idea of it. I only found out on 15 inst. from the Cabinet, that the King had just confirmed the approval for my brother and been pleased to raise me to the ranks of the nobility on entirely his own initiative. It is a triumph for all of our faith".

The following day he added a post script, so to speak, in another letter. "And now I assure you by all that is holy to me that I was only informed on 15 inst. by the Home Ministry (so by Schleinitz) that His Majesty yesterday, in the moment when he was signing the cabinet order permitting my brother to wear the order awarded him by Austria and use the noble title in the Prussian states, raised me to the nobility also. I was most pleasantly surprised by the news, and I attach all the more value to the great and gracious act as it comes direct and *only* from the King himself." So Schleinitz had presumably given him exactly the same account of how the Royal decision had come about as is to be found in the surviving sources as well.

On 19 February Schleinitz instructed the Heralds Office to "make the appropriate contact" with A. Freiherr von Oppenheim regarding the text of the diploma. All the rest, such as "the official notification of this most gracious act", he had already dealt with himself. We see from this remark that the Minister himself, who had done so much to bring the affair to a satisfactory conclusion, in fact made sure that the notification was not given. The Kreuzzeitung, for instance, has no reference at all to A. Oppenheim's ennoblement, so that the public in Prussia and the Prussian nobility learned of it no more than the Austrians had of the ennoblement of his brother Simon some time before.

On 3 March 1868 the Heralds Office informed A. Freiherr von Oppenheim that he had to pay "1121 thalers 20 groschen in taxes, stamp duty and fees to the Heralds Cash Office in the Ministry of the Royal Household, and about 60 thalers for cash expenditure, not determinable in advance, altogether therefore praeterpropter 1281 thalers 20 groschen". He should also send a coloured sketch of the coat of arms "which you wish in future to be your own". So the title cost a great deal more in Prussia than in Austria. Oppenheim paid on 7 March and informed the Heralds Office that "in a few days" he would "wait upon" the Master of Ceremonies, Count Stillfried, and intended "on that occasion to discuss the further details of the coat of arms in question with that honourable gentleman himself".

But the Heralds Office still had a delicate matter to raise with von Schleinitz after all this, and on 23 March it wrote that the Royal Cabinet Order contained "no decree on whether and in what way the title should be hereditary. The question in itself is hardly likely to be of practical importance, since the marriage of the said Oppenheim is childless, and likely to remain so at such an advanced age, but it must be raised in view of the diploma that needs to be drawn up. Before drafting the same, we therefore take the liberty of humbly asking Your Excellency for a most gracious decision on whether we should regard the ennoblement of the said Oppenheim solely as concerning himself alone, or whether it is hereditary, and according to what principle?" So someone in the Ministry was still trying to create obstacles, and perhaps even now discriminate against the Jewish nobleman.

But Schleinitz was not going to give in and on 15 April he stated "that the Order of 14 February stipulates ennoblement without adding any restriction in regard to the hereditary nature of the title" and "under the general legal regulations of Para ... of the General Law of the Land there can be no doubt that this is to pass to any children of the same and his further descendants. The rank is therefore not intended for his person alone, it must be regarded as hereditary without any restrictions whatever".

Abraham von Oppenheim had to wait a long time for his document and coat of arms. At the end of October 1868 he wrote to Schleinitz from Paris: "May I be so bold as to remind Your Excellency of my diploma? I would be extremely grateful if this could be despatched without delay. Nor have I to date received the various sketches". Suddenly it all happened very quickly. On 3 November the "draft and clean copy" of the diploma were ready "for the most gracious Royal assent" and on 11 November 1868 King William executed the diploma.

However, on 21 December 1868 the Heralds Office established that the 1282 thalers paid by A. Freiherr von Oppenheim on 9 March (he appears to have rounded the sum up) were not enough. He had a further 725 thalers and 12 groschen to pay, so his ennoblement cost altogether no less than 2007 thalers and 12 gr. According to the sums listed by the Office the largest amount was taxes (680 thalers), followed by "clean copy of the diploma" (566 thalers 20 gr.), the "grace stamp" (400 thalers) and the "decoration of the edges of the text pages" (195 thalers). But even before Abraham Oppenheim had sent the money the Heralds Office posted the diploma, on 21 December. On Christmas Eve, 24 December 1868, Freiherr Abraham von Oppenheim sent the remaining sum and was honoured "most humbly to acknowledge receipt of the diploma".

More than five eventful years, in which A. Oppenheim had performed many a valuable service for the state of Prussia, had passed since Schleinitz, on 22 October 1863, first drew the attention of the Queen to his "most earnest wish". The documents on the ennoblement of Simon Oppenheim corresponding to these files on the ennoblement of Abraham, and from which this account is drawn, are not to be found, either in Vienna or in the archives of the bank in Cologne. Nevertheless, the historian will gain the impression that, as the Kaskel case suggests, the Viennese were less long-winded and bureaucratic than the Prussians. Moreover, there appear to have been persons in the Home Ministry in Prussia, unlike Vienna, presumably members of the Christian Prussian nobility, who would gladly have prevented the ennoblement of even a childless Jewish banker. It is now hardly likely that these persons can be identified individually, apart from some Ministers and their staff in Berlin. Keudell later recalled the weeks before the outbreak of war in 1866: "At the time currents of soft, entirely unPrussian feeling were flowing through the land. Outstanding members of the Conservative party were setting all possible levers in motion to prevent war. Not only did 17 Rhineland Chambers of Commerce and a Cologne assembly petition for the maintenance of peace, four constituencies in Berlin and the municipal authorities of Stettin, Köslin and Königsberg did the same. The deputies in Frankfurt and the Committee of the National Assembly declared unanimously that the only solution to the difficulties was a German parliament ... Only two sensible statements were made during that period: an address from the Old Liberals in Halle and one from the Municipal Authority in Berlin".

So in 1866 Abraham Oppenheim, like his brother Simon four years before, had spoken out in an "entirely unPrussian" affair. One or the other loyal Prussian in court circles may actually have recalled that around a quarter of a century before the third brother, Dagobert, had helped to found an oppositional newspaper, and had tried to prevent this being banned in Berlin, or at least to delay the order, and perhaps they did not want all this to go unpunished now.[23] In such an atmosphere

[23] Dagobert Oppenheim, who had become a Christian to be able to take the office of Government Assistant, and was unmarried, with no heirs, was for the rest never ennobled. Since he had shown good service in the financing of the war of 1866 the King, no doubt on a recommendation from one of his Ministers, probably v. d. Heydt, appointed him Secret Government Councillor in the great wave of entitlements and decorations in connection with a great peace festival in 1866, since he was a retired government official and not a banker or industrialist.

the personality of Queen Augusta stands out all the more strongly. After the Prussian victory at Sedan around two years later, on 30 September 1870, the Finance Minister, Otto von Camphausen, wrote to his brother Ludolf, whose relations to the Royal family have already been mentioned, that he wanted spontaneously "to offer the Queen, with whom I have enjoyed close relations for more than two decades, my congratulations as Queen and woman". "The unusual request encountered no obstacles, the Queen was visibly pleased to see me and thanked me most warmly". Since her time in Koblenz this great lady, of outstanding character and intelligence in the Prussian Royal house, and long deserving a detailed scholarly biography, had maintained relations with the Rhineland liberals, be they Catholic, Protestant or Jewish, and she influenced her husband accordingly – although there was much resistance to this at the court and, as Keudell's memories show, in Bismarck's circles as well.

After his ennoblement it would appear that Abraham Oppenheim never again contemplated "leaving" the bank and certainly never declared this to be his intention, only to draw back later. But that did not mean the end of all family cares for his ageing brother Simon. The brief excitement in the early months of 1873, when at the height of the "Gründerjahre" the bankers were urged to change their business into a joint stock corporation, a transaction which would yield great profit to the owners, is an episode which we cannot discuss in detail here, because the source material would not suffice. But it is clear that Simon, who had to think of his sons and their future, hesitated over his decision – as, apparently, Abraham did as well. He wrote from Berlin on 16 March to Simon, who was with Kaskels in Dresden: "I only want to give you my honest opinion. If we could get three million thalers for the business now, straight down on the table, without further ado, and without letting them have an insight into the business, I would agree to the proposal, because I think it would greatly benefit your sons to have a supervisory board and not have to bear the responsibility alone for our extensive business, since it is also very probable that this will expand further, and so I would agree to the sale."[24]

But it was possible that the bank would be ill managed and do badly in business and the shareholders might lose their money. "There would be a huge outcry against us if the dividends were low and we had sold the shares at such a high price. I have deliberately put down all the pros and cons here, and conclude that we should resist the temptation, for it would create an enormous stir if we were to sell our flourishing business ..." Simon wrote the following day, on 17 March, to his son Eduard, who, together with his brother, had apparently initiated the whole affair, in Cologne, that "we should want at least 4.5 million thalers ... I am curious to see what happens. We would not be doing badly if we got 4.5 million, since, as you rightly say, you would still be in the business and would certainly retain a leading position ..."

But the next disappointment was already at the door. If Simon's sons had not succeeded in all these years in becoming partners in the bank, they now, on its conversion to a joint stock corporation, wanted "equal shares", that is, the 3 or 4.5

[24] The handwritten text of the letter.

million thalers should be divided into four equal parts. Outraged, Simon wrote to his sons on 19 March from Dresden that he found their "claim totally unjustified... for precisely because you would enter the new business with certain profit and prospects of large shares of all the good deals, you truly have no ground to expect a larger share on the liquidation, and you are forgetting that the business can be liquidated without your help". He wrote again the following day: "My opinion on your totally unjustified, truly ridiculous demands ... You are so bold as to regard the business as your own property now, you forget that you have only a subordinate position in it. I am entirely of Abraham's opinion... if the affair comes to nothing I see nothing for us all in future but sad, very sad prospects, which could end in a terrible breach".

But this time the sons were not prepared to give in, and the result was really virtually a breach. Simon wrote on 23 March 1873, still from Dresden: "I cannot tell you both how deeply pained I am by your strife with Abraham. And as Felix (Kaskel) tells me from Aunt Charlotte (Abraham's wife) you, dear Eduard, will deeply regret letting yourself be carried away to overstep all bounds in this way. I shall do my utmost to pacify Abaraham... but do not forget that he is an old man, and you owe him respect ... had there been no strife with you, and did I not fear that this will cause us constant annoyance and vexation, I would never agree to sell our business ... for it is not quite honourable, and even at 4 million it would be underpriced." That was the end of that affair: the Bankhaus Sal. Oppenheim jr. & Cie remained as it was, but the friction in the Oppenheim family had certainly not grown less, and the two members of the younger generation were more dissatisfied than ever. Nearly three years later, on 24 February 1876, Freiherren Simon, Abraham, Eduard and Albert Oppenheim concluded a new company contract. Simon and Abraham remained "heads of the business and as such retained the top management of the whole". Eduard and Albert received all in all very modest powers of attorney and the above increase in their share of the profits.

More than twenty years after he conceived his plan to spend the rest of his life with his wife in Paris court society, the motives for abandoning which are not quite clear, Abraham found a certain substitute after 1874 in numerous business or private visits to Berlin, where he could move in the very highest circles. However, this now had to be without his wife, who, as he wrote to his brother on 14 March 1874, "was occasionally vexed" because he worried too much over business. Simon had suffered for years from Abraham's tendency to over-excitement in business matters. The brothers were now growing older, one or the other frequently suffered from one complaint or another, and they tired more quickly. But since 1873/74 relations between them had clearly been very harmonious. Abraham sent his "dearly beloved brother Simon" long letters from Berlin, often containing detailed descriptions of invitations and visits to the King and Queen to take tea or dine. He gives information on the health or indispositions of the royal couple and recounts conversations with them and persons in their circle. Ennobled, honoured with invitations, orders and autographs, Abraham was clearly a welcome guest, not only a leading banker who was always ready to give donations, and in addition to attending to his business affairs, which he always pursued with the greatest care, he spent many weeks of pleasure and diversion in 1873/75 in the social atmosphere of Berlin, which was quickly becoming the business centre of the German Reich. A few dates will suffice to illustrate this. On 17 March 1874 he saw the Kaiser in the afternoon; the following day he dined "very pleasantly" with the Kaiserin. On 22 March 1874 the Kaiser and the Kaiserin gave a party to which he was invited. On 12 March 1875 he had an audience with "our beloved Kaiserin", but he was not able to see the Kaiser because he was suffering from a sore throat. On 19 March 1875 he sent his brother a long report of an evening party given by the Kaiser and his consort.

But after mid-1875 his painful complaints worsened rapidly, and he was able to travel less and less. In the summer of 1878 in his residence Schloss Bassenheim he was so tired and weak that he had to tell the Kaiserin, who wanted to visit him there on 3 September, that he could not receive her. She asked Abraham's wife to telegraph two or three times a day: "Her Majesty wanted to be kept constantly informed"; on 4 she sent him a cup with her portrait, instructing him to take his medicine as prescribed from it. On 7 September she did visit him and "behaved to me as a close relative". After tea on the terrace with the family she asked Abraham von Oppenheim "to conduct her to my study, where we sat together alone for a full hour, while the Kaiserin gave me proof of her devotion and trust". A few days later he was ill again, and again the Kaiserin wanted to be kept informed of how he fared. "Her Majesty gives me constant proof of her affection", he wrote to his brother in Cologne on 14 September 1878. On 15 September she sent him a doctor, who was instructed to bring her "exact information". A week later the celebrated Professor Johann F. A. Esmarch operated on his bladder. Then Abraham returned to Cologne, but he died there on 9 October 1878. Clearly the friendship with the intelligent Kaiserin, who together with her daughter-in-law Victoria favoured liberalism over the "spirit" of the court in Berlin, was not only an honour to Abraham but a great source of happiness as well.

And what did she feel on his death? Presumably she wrote a letter of condolence in her own hand to Abraham's widow and addressed this to her private residence, but neither the original nor a copy is to be found in the bank's archives. She instructed her lady-in-waiting, Countess Hacke, who usually accompanied the Queen and also saw how she had asked Abraham von Oppenheim to take her to his study in Bassenheim, to write a long and very personal letter to his brother Simon, whom she also knew, in which she said that she was "losing more than one should believe or guess in his dearly beloved brother". She also instructed the lady-in-waiting to write to Gustav Mevissen, who had been a close friend of Abraham Oppenheim for many decades, on the "loss which Cologne has suffered in one of its noblest citizens".

After 1875 Simon von Oppenheim derived more and more joy from his sons, although, as he believed, they still lacked the experience and insight he thought necessary. He still clung particularly to his daughter Emma von Kaskel, whose husband had become chairman of the supervisory board of the Dresdner Bank in 1872, founded that year by his father, and he liked to be in Dresden, where he actually built himself a house. Abraham visited him here in 1875, coming from Berlin. "We are enjoying ourselves here greatly", he wrote to his "dear sons" on 24 February 1876 from Dresden. "Society here is quite different from Cologne". Together with his wife, and Emma and Felix, he was often invited to court. "We stole away immediately supper was over, towards midnight", he went on to say in the same letter, "but the children stayed till about two". "The King at the head was very amiable ... Now there is only the court ball on Shrove Tuesday, but I shall not go, as I hate wearing uniform. I shall let my dear wife go with Emma ...". And so in the smaller but very sophisticated Saxon capital – the father of his son-in-law was banker to the King and to many noble families and, himself a composer, had corresponded with Robert Schumann[25], Simon enjoyed, together with his family, what Abraham had to and could partake of alone in high society in Berlin.

Nor did Simon have so happy a disposition as he – unlike Abraham – liked to believe. From one of the ever more frequent trips to leading spas which she undertook from 1875 his wife wrote from Karlsbad on 2 June 1875 to her eldest son: "The black thoughts are unfortunately uppermost with both brothers". He was now 73, and had never spared himself. Pains of all kinds, especially fevers, plagued him with increasing frequency after 1875. After the spring of 1876 he was constantly concerned for "dear Abraham", who was liable to chills. On 18 March 1876 he wrote to his sons from Dresden: "If I were not so worried about dear Abraham I would be quite cheerful, despite the low share prices and other problems".

After Abraham von Oppenheim's death Simon concluded a new company contract with his sons, on 2 November 1878, with effect from 1 January 1879. In Paragraph 1 the sons were designated partners in the business; the father, however, remained the true "head of the firm", with a share of 50% in the profit and loss, while the sons had 25% each. Felix von Kaskel still had the right to join as partner "whenever he wishes, but at the latest immediately after the death of Freiherr Simon von Oppenheim" on 1 January of the following year.

Age and pain forced Simon, as noted, to travel for recuperation ever more frequently. On one of these trips, towards the end of his life, he again met Kaiser William I. As he wrote to his son Eduard from Bad Ems on 11 July 1879: "I eat well and sleep passably. The Kaiser was extremely gracious to me yesterday, and spoke to me at length before and after the meal". On 7 August he was "again invited to dine with the Kaiser ... I enjoyed myself greatly ... the Kaiser was very kind, he has recuperated well here but much of his strength has gone, he has aged greatly". In mid-August 1879 he asked his son Albert not to send him the Cölner Nachrichten any more "since we do not read the paper". A year later he was back in Karlsbad, and in June felt "very tired all the time, it is increasingly difficult to think". On 18 June he wrote "We lead a very quiet life here, retiring to bed at nine, when the others are going to supper". On 19 October 1880 he and his wife Henriette were able to celebrate their golden wedding anniversary in Cologne, where he died on Christmas Eve that year.

Thus far our attempt to answer the questions raised at the beginning of this article. There are three aspects to these: the first is the family, in the real, closest, and most intimate sense, and it has only been outlined here. The second is a piece of business history, part of the "history of entrepreneurial pyschology", and so a part

[25] R. Martin, Jahrbuch des Vermögens und Einkommens der Millionäre im Königreich Sachsen, Berlin 1912, pp. 206ff.; Heinrich Schnee, Die Hoffinanz und der moderne Staat, Vol. 2, Berlin 1954, pp. 252ff.

of general economic history as well. Finally, the third aspect is political, especially social political history. The two brothers, as Rhineland liberals and bankers, played a role in Prussia's internal and foreign policy. Abraham Oppenheim's ennoblement in connection with his services to the state, as important documents preserved in the bank's archive show, revealed the attitude of some of the Prussian ministerial bureaucracy more than half a century after the emancipation edict, probably not only to the rich Jews in the Rhineland but Jews in general.

Life is complicated. And the lives of these two brothers were made up of so many successful business deals, so many surprises and chance occurrences, as well as so much vexation, so many tears, hopes, disappointments, new hopes and new disappointments, so many fulfillable, but unfulfilled wishes, combinations carefully considered and yet not realised, right up to letters only to be opened after the death of the writer. They certainly loved each other dearly, and their lives and mutual relations were held up as a model in public and envied. Was childless Abraham satisfied with his life, did Simon die happily two years later, at peace of mind in regard to his sons, Felix Kaskel and the bank? These questions were not discussed, of course, in the published obituaries or the speeches at the graveside, and business history has not so far concerned itself with issues such as these.

Russian Business in the Brüning Era

Hans-Werner Niemann

The Russo-German friendship pact signed on 24 April 1926 in Berlin led to the development of brisk trade between Germany and the Soviet Union, which was seen by German politicians as a counterweight to the pressure of the Western powers and Poland, to which they were hostile. The German Government had said it was prepared to give a 33% guarantee for supplies of German industrial goods to the USSR to a total value of RM 300 million up to the end of 1930. The loan was given by a bank consortium headed by the Deutsche Bank, while the Reich rediscounted the credits and provided a guarantee against default. The Soviet Union used the RM 300 million loan to buy machines and equipment for the industry it was building up, and German exports to the Soviet Union (consisting mostly of finished products) rose by four and a half times between 1924 and 1928, while German imports from the Soviet Union trebled. The following table shows the development in Russo-German trade before the 1929 slump:[1]

German Trade with the Soviet Union 1924 to 1928 (in RM million)

Year	Imports	In % of total imports	Exports	In % of total exports
1913	1470	13.6	978	9.7
1924	126	1.4	89	1.4
1925	205	1.6	250	2.9
1926	302	3.0	265	2.7
1927	433	3.1	339	3.1
1928	379	2.7	403	3.3

In 1928 the Soviet Union was 12th on the list of importers of German goods, but the volume was still far below the pre-war level, and in February 1928 new trade negotiations with the Soviet Union began with the aim of increasing German exports. To provide some counterweight to the Soviet monopoly in foreign trade the Reichsverband der Deutschen Industrie (Reich Federation of German Industry - RDI), the Federation of German Chambers of Industry and Commerce (Deutscher Industrie- und Handelstag), the Central Association of German Banks

[1] Kuczynski, Jürgen/Wittkowski, Grete: Die deutsch-russischen Handelsbeziehungen in den letzten 150 Jahren. 2nd edition, Berlin 1947, p. 59.

German Yearbook on Business History 1987

and Bankers (Zentralverband des deutschen Bank- und Bankiergewerbes) and the Russo-German Association for the Promotion of Trade (Deutsch-russischer Verein zur Pflege und Förderung der gegenseitigen Handelsbeziehungen) formed a Russian Committee with Director Hans Krämer as Chairman. The Committee was to handle all Soviet orders for German industrial goods to prevent German suppliers undercutting each other. However, the Soviet Union would not agree to purchase goods through the Committee and in the end it functioned only as an information office.[2]

On 21 December 1928 a German-Soviet trade agreement was signed to improve trade between the two countries. Then as the world slump set in the Soviet Union became very much more important as an importer of German goods, both in relative and in absolute terms, for while production in the capitalist countries shrank to a hitherto unknown degree, the forced industrialisation in the Soviet Union under the five-year plan brought a rapid upswing, with industrial production doubling between 1928 and 1932 alone.[3] During these years the Soviet Union was buying large quantities of high quality investment goods abroad and so it became a major trading partner for Germany at a time when world trade was rapidly declining. When Britain left the gold standard in 1931 and as other countries increasingly imposed customs duties and import restrictions only the Soviet Union still seemed to offer a promising market for exports.

Maintaining and increasing the level of exports was not only an economic necessity for the German Government, it was a political imperative as well, since Brüning was hoping by fulfilling the reparation demands to the letter, which could only be done with a trade surplus now that the foreign credits had been withdrawn, to convince Germany's creditors of its good will and at the same time show them that it was objectively impossible to transfer the reparation amounts. He was also hoping that stepping up German exports expressly during the worldwide economic crisis would demonstrate to the recipients how much damage further insistence on German payments could inflict on their own weakened economies.[4] So the Russian market was welcome, not only to the industrialists, who were concerned for the future of their companies, but to the Reich Government as well, and this article examines just what the considerations and motives were that finally moved the industrialists and the Brüning Government to such an enormous increase in German-Soviet trade in the middle of the slump.

There was no lack of political fears of the possibly destabilising effects of an expansion of German-Soviet trade in industrial circles. Carl Duisberg, for instance, Chairman of the RDI and of the Supervisory Board of IG Farben, said in May 1930 "Bolshevism ... is a new philosophy that has colossal attraction in some circles and it is something we must watch very closely if we are not to be overcome by it. At present we are still the bulwark. But if the Bolshevik wave rolls over us as

[2] This is the term used by a well-informed American journalist, H.R. Knickerbocker, whose book "Der rote Handel lockt" appeared in 1931 and created a sensation. It is still worth reading today (p. 58).

[3] Kuczynski, see Note 1, p. 65.

[4] According to his Memoirs, Brüning told Hitler on 6 October 1930 that his objective was "to pay the reparations next year solely from our trade surplus and so tear the whole world market apart." (Heinrich Brüning: Memoiren 1918–1934, Stuttgart 1970, p. 193).

well the rest of Europe will be lost, there can be no doubt of that."[5] Duisberg told the same RDI meeting that "Communist agitators" had distributed questionnaires to workers in the IG Farben factories to find out as much as possible about various chemical processes. They had got what they wanted for "to their astonishment" senior staff from the concern had then seen their own processes working in the Soviet Union. Duisberg issued a serious warning to his colleagues not to underestimate the Soviet five-year plan and the pace of industrialisation in that country. He was particularly concerned at the sale of whole plant to the Soviets, since this would enable them to make products and machines of all kinds with German, British or American methods. Although production costs for chemical products were twice as high in the Soviet Union as in Germany the Soviets had put these products on the German market at half the German price. In Duisberg's view they were engaging in "dumping in such a mean way that one should really take note and ask how much longer we can stand by and watch this."[6] In fact, the USSR had to step up its exports to earn the money for more equipment to accelerate the pace of its industrialisation. Duisberg thought there was a tendency "to dump goods at any price on the European market, and maybe the American market as well", which he interpreted as an attempt to "cause unemployment and so stir up unrest ... to create a fertile ground for Bolshevik propaganda."[7]

But political fears of this kind could not stop the upsurge in German exports to the USSR, and fears of damage to the German economy from the expansion of Russian industry diminished as the economic crisis deepened, since the Germans were not prepared to stand back and let other countries take the Russian market without a struggle. The minutes of the RDI Board meeting of 19 September 1930 contain the comment: "If we don't do it the others will! It is certainly better for us to provide the equipment than other countries that are competing with us on world markets and will only grow stronger if they export to Russia!"[8]

In mid-1930 the Soviet Government and the Soviet Trade Commissariat asked for the German loan to be increased from the present RM 300 million to at least RM 1 billion.[9] One of the German industrialists involved in trade with Russia wrote to the Russian Committee, also asking for an additional loan for the Soviet Union to the amount of RM 750 million, while the head of a private bank asked for a credit of RM 1.5 billion for Russian business, pointing out that this would bring Russian orders that would provide jobs for 750,000 people for a year.[10] But the majority of the members of the Russian Committee were sceptical as regards approving a further global loan to Russia, preferring to secure the "Russian business" with Reich and Land guarantees, and leave the German firms or groups of firms to negotiate the conditions independently. The earlier global loan for RM 300 million and the speed with which it had been granted had tempted German

---

[5] Minutes of the RDI Board meeting on 22 May 1930, p. 9; Bayer AG Leverkusen, works archives, RDI (BL RDI), microfilm 42.4.

[6] Loc. cit., p. 11.

[7] Loc. cit.

[8] Minutes of the RDI Board meeting on 19 September 1930, 69 BL RDI, microfilm 31.8.

[9] Loc. cit.

[10] Loc. cit., p. 70. The names of the senders are not given.

firms to play each other off in a race for Soviet orders. But the Soviets were also playing one firm off against another, as we see from the minutes of one of the RDI Board meetings: "If the Russians are now rather bold in their demands (Quite right!) this is because the antechambers of the Russian trade office are thronged not only with agents but with managing directors as well."[11]

But there did seem to be considerable risks attached to further loans to the USSR. The Chairman of the Russian Committee, Director Krämer, expressed his fears that the Soviets would not be able to supply their domestic market adequately because of the high reject rate (of more than 40% in some cases) from Soviet factories built with the help of foreign technicians, due to the lack of managers, foremen and masters in the works, which in turn would lead to demands for more loans. So there was a risk "that the last to lend to the Soviet Union will either lose his money or be forced to convert it into long-term government stock."[12]

The Soviet need for credit was largely due to the big deficit on its trade balance, for while the few products the Soviet Union could export had suffered a drop in price on the world market of 20, 30 or even 40%, more imports were needed to carry out the five-year plan. The deficit was RM 400 million, and it could only be reduced by stepping up exports, which in turn was the prerequisite for further imports from industrial countries. Measures by European and other countries to counteract Russian dumping would only have jeopardised repayment of the loans.

The high level of unemployment was another factor in the German Government's consideratons on further loans to the USSR, even if not a decisive one, and it was expected that the jobs the Russian orders would create would soften the financial risk of the business. But the main factor was to be foreign policy. The Board of the RDI had the impression that it was not not so much the Reich Chancellor, nor the Reich Economics or Finance Ministries who were pressing for an increase in the loan to Russia but the Foreign Office – "admittedly for political reasons".[13]

Krämer, the Chairman of the Russian Committee, felt there were some inconsistencies in the policy pursued by Curtius, the Foreign Minister: "The ways of Herr Curtius are mysterious (laughter). They are doubly so, because the same Foreign Office, or rather its present head, take the stand that Russian dumping in Germany constitutes an enormous danger to the German economy (here, here!). I must admit that in my tiny brain I cannot quite see how the two can be reconciled."[14]

In the summer of 1930 the RDI itself applied for an increase of the Reich guarantee from RM 175 million to RM 350 million. At 35% cover this would mean a volume of business of RM 1 billion. Since the Länder were guaranteeing a further 25%, 60% of the purchase price would be covered. But the industrialists were pressing for an increase in this percentage. Some in the Rhineland were actually asking for full state cover for Russian business, suggesting that the Soviets should pay 15% down, while the Reich and the Länder guaranteed 80%. But a risk as low

---

[11] Loc cit. p. 76.
[12] Loc. cit., p. 74.
[13] Loc. cit.
[14] Loc cit.

as this (5%) would have led to further price undercutting or maybe an increase in higher-risk business and there had already been cases of this. One North German firm, for instance, had done a deal with the USSR, outbidding two major Rhineland concerns. It had been able to undercut their prices because it had not only a 60% guarantee from the Reich and the Länder governments but also a municipal guarantee for 30% given on account of the high level of local unemployment. The RDI regarded it as particularly deplorable that the firm had then bought the iron for the Russian order from Czechoslovakia, so that despite the state guarantees it had not actually primarily employed German workers.[15] If such a cumulation of public guarantees became the usual practice there was a danger that all the risk would ultimately be passed to the state.

In the summer of 1930 the Soviets indicated that orders for a further RM 100 million might be given but asked for a revision of conditions for existing orders, mainly an extension of the terms of the loans from 18 to 36, and 24 to 48 months on average. For one major order to the German machine industry for RM 15 million this would have meant a 5-year loan. The Russian Committee regarded terms of this length as unacceptable and warned the Reich Government against acceding to requests of this kind.[16] The Reich Government then also refused to prolong the loans, particularly since the number of cases where Russian bills failed to reach German firms on time were mounting.

German-Soviet trade received a major boost when the Supreme Economic Council of the USSR invited a delegation of prominent German industrialists from the heavy industry, electrical and mechanical engineering sectors to visit the Soviet Union in January 1931. The RDI saw the purpose of the visit as to establish personal contacts between German industrialists and the leaders of Russian industry, gain an insight into the state of industrial development in the Soviet Union and see how the five-year plan was progressing. As the RDI interpreted the invitation there was no intention of discussing concrete details of trade or political relations between the two countries or the size of German loans.[17] But, as Kastl, Manager of the RDI remarked, the question should be discussed in how far German industry could play a part in future Soviet industrialisation by supplying the necessary imports.

The RDI put great emphasis on the fact that the invitations had been sent to individual industrialists, this was not an official delegation or a visit by the RDI. Efforts were also made not to let the press hear of the visit too soon, evidently to avoid giving the wrong impression abroad. Kastl stressed that in that sense this was "no different than all the other visits by industrialists from Britain, North America and Italy at the invitation of the Russian Government; it is not a special initiative to intensify German-Russian trade."[18] It is striking that Kastl said this at an RDI Board meeting, although it is not possible to say whether he was trying to dispel the fears of other Board members or only prevent the visit from arousing too much attention in public.

---

15 Loc. cit. p. 78.
16 Loc. cit., p. 80.
17 Minutes of the RDI Board meeting of 20 February 1931, BL RDI 32.1.
18 Loc. cit.

Kastl stressed that whether Germany would supply more goods to the Soviet Union would depend on details that should be settled after the visit, especially whether Germany was prepared to take on further risks by increasing the Russian debt. But the Presidium of the RDI was unanimous that in view of the economic situation in Germany the RDI should not change the policy it had been pursuing for years of taking as big a share of the Russian market as possible; on the contrary, German industry depended on a continuance of business with Russia. However, it stressed the need to ensure that the business did not cause major damage to the German economy one day.

The German industrialists went to the Soviet Union from 26 February to 11 March 1931. Klöckner asked Reich Chancellor Brüning for an interview immediately upon their return through the German embassy while he was still in Moscow, and this took place on 11 March in the Chancellor's office. In addition to Brüning himself, the Ministers Dietrich, Curtius and Stegerwald, together with the President of the Reichsbank, Luther, were present. Klöckner first gave an account of his impressions of the visit. The industrialists had been convinced "that the Russians will fulfil their plans and maintain their system. The extraordinary energy of the top men and the excellent condition of the army will guarantee that."[19] The Russians had assured him that imports of machines from Germany would still be needed after the fiveyear plan had been fulfilled. Klöckner said that the Soviets wanted further deliveries to the amount of RM 500 million in addition to the RM 200 million still outstanding on existing contracts. At first the industrialists had wanted 10% cash down payment but finally agreed to a 20% advance payment in the form of bills, so the Soviets were not to make any cash payment at all. According to Klöckner no further commitments had been made and the industrialists had merely agreed to work towards a deal worth RM 300 million. What was envisaged were 12 months contracts for light, 18 months for medium and 24 months for heavy machines; the average term of the bills was to be 14 to 28 months, while the earlier bills had been for 12 to 24 months. The rate was to be 2% above the Reichsbank discount rate.

Klöckner then asked for a Reich guarantee for 70% of the RM 300 million, pointing out that the order situation in German industry was very unsatisfactory and the Russian business would be needed to enable firms to keep on workers and employ more. Deliveries totalling RM 300 million would enable a further 100,000 workers to be taken on and it would then be possible to negotiate on deliveries for a further RM 200 million. The main benefit of the Russian business would go to processing plant, but heavy industry would profit as well; however, Klöckner raised a crucial point when he stressed that the Soviet Union would only be able to raise the foreign exchange needed for the purchases if the industrial states did not try to block imports of Russian goods.

General Director Reuter set about dispelling any fears that might have been held on Russian dumping, saying that as he had been informed by leading personalities on the Russian side the dumping had been due to the urgent need for

[19] Discussion with representatives of industry on business with Russia on 11 March 1931, in: Akten der Reichskanzlei (AR). Die Kabinette Brüning I and II, Vol. 2, Boppard 1982, pp. 935f.

foreign exchange while the major investment was going on, but once Soviet industry was established and functioning the factories would be fully occupied meeting domestic needs and there need be no further fears that manufactured goods would be dumped.

Dietrich, the Reich Finance Minister, thought there was a danger in massing orders from the Soviet Union and felt it would be better to spread the risk through several countries.

Curtius, Reich Foreign Minister, expressly thanked the industrialists for "keeping the matter private" and asked them not to "turn it into a political affair".[20] Like the RDI he was concerned to avoid any misinterpretation of the transactions abroad.

A further discussion took place between members of the Government and representatives of industry on 16 March 1931. Trendelenburg, Secretary of State in the Reich Economics Ministry, put the Russian debt at about RM 1 billion if the envisaged deals went through (RM 500 million from existing contracts, RM 300 million now under discussion and a further RM 200 million sometime in the future). He held the view that a state guarantee (40% from the Reich, 30% from the Länder) would be needed and was justified because the firms in the private sector were dealing with a country in which the state held a monopoly and could not take the risk this entailed themselves. Trendelenburg mentioned two crucial points that still needed to be considered: the effects of the deals on foreign policy and the repercussions of the increase in imports from Russia to Germany which the deals would entail on the German economy.[21]

Speaking for the Prussian Minister President Weismann, the Secretary of State, categorically refused to give any guarantee at all on the grounds that the financial situation was too bad. But the representative of the Prussian Ministry of Trade was of a different opinion and promised to have the standpoints in the Prussian Ministry of State clarified.

Curtius, Reich Foreign Minister, approved the guarantee on the grounds that the earlier guarantee had also been given on the assumption that it would lead to an increase in employment that justified the greater risk. If the Germans did not sign the contract the Americans would.

In answer to a question from Brüning Luther, President of the Reichsbank, said it was not possible to establish beyond doubt that the USSR could pay. The mood was good, but it was significant that the Soviets were not prepared to make any advance payment in gold.

Klöckner pointed out that Italy had granted major loans to the Soviet Union, while the USA was selling it whole plant, such as a tractor factory, costing more than $ 200 million, and giving very long-term loans. General Directors Koettgen, Reuter and Poensgen argued that only Germany could build the smelters the Russians needed. Orders had dropped by 80% over the previous month and prices were falling rapidly, and it was to be feared that the big smelters would have to shut down in two to three months. Without the Russian deals wages and salaries

[20] Loc. cit. p. 937.

[21] Discussion on the Russian business on 16 March 1931, AR, loc. cit., pp. 948f.

in the West would have to be reduced by at least 20% if closures were to be prevented.

Chancellor Brüning indicated that the Reich Government might reach a decision by the end of the week; before that, however, the whole situation in foreign policy would need to be thoroughly reviewed.

The decisive ministerial talks were held on 20 March 1931. Trendelenberg, the Secretary of State, again argued that new loans to Russia would serve Germany's foreign interests, although he felt it was hardly justifiable for the private sector to increase the Russian debt to RM 1 billion. "In general policy terms, however, it does seem right to set more on the Russian card. This is not likely to lead to friction with other countries, and certainly not to the withdrawal of short-term foreign loans. Gradually the other countries should come to realise that things may take a serious turn in Germany if trade with Russia is not stepped up. If the capitalist powers were prepared to grant Germany the appropriate advantages German trade with Russia might be reviewed."[22] So Trendelenburg regarded the expansion of German trade with Russia mainly as a means of exercising pressure on the Western powers, to force them to a more cooperative attitude over the reparation payments, for instance; moreover, it was a form of pressure that could, if necessary, be exchanged for the appropriate concessions. He was in favour of a 70% guarantee.

The Reich Minister of Labour, on the other hand, doubted whether an orientation to the East, which he also felt to be the right course in foreign policy, would have the right results as far as the reparations were concerned. Newspapers in Basle had already pointed out that Germany could hardly ask for foreign loans or any revision of the reparation demands if it was rich enough to grant the Russians loans of such dimensions.

Curtius, the Reich Foreign Minister, on the other hand, argued that it would be easy to answer the Swiss by saying that Germany was being pushed into the East. He saw an advantage for Germany in cooperating with the USSR: France wanted an understanding with Germany to ease it away from Russia, and "in that case",[23] he was in favour of the Russian business, like Trendelenburg seeing this as a way of exerting pressure on France.

Reichsbank President Luther pointed out that before a decision was taken on the loan it must be ensured that the foreign credits would not be jeopardised.

Secretary of State Schäffer of the Finance Ministry also raised the question of how damaging the Russian loans might prove to be in the reparation question, and asked whether RM 300 million could not be put to better use inside Germany than as a guarantee to the Russians. However, the Reich Finance Minister was prepared to give the guarantee.

The Reich Transport Minister expressed serious doubts about the Russian business, pointing out that the Reich Railway claims of $ 150,000 a month were not being met regularly and only partpayments had been received.[24]

---

[22] Ministerial meeting on 20 March 1931, AR, loc. cit., pp. 971f.

[23] Loc. cit., p. 973.

[24] Loc. cit., p. 974.

The Reichsbank President expressed himself in general positively on the envisaged business with the Soviet Union. In his view there were no objections as far as the reparation payments were concerned, on the contrary, he thought this was the positive aspect of the Russian deals: "Action must be taken to show other countries that Germany would have to engage in business of this kind to meet the reparation payments, and would have to borrow from abroad. With a guarantee of this size there was a danger of crossing a psychological threshold. It would always have to be made clear that the guarantee had been given at the request of industry."[25] So Luther, too, thought the Russian business was very welcome in the context of foreign policy. He hoped the danger of undesirable reaction from other countries, such as a withdrawal of credit, could be reduced by stressing the private nature of the business and the risk the private firms were taking.

The Reich Minister for Food and Agriculture was not prepared to give unconditional approval for the guarantee. A guarantee of RM 300 million could be put to better use on the domestic market, e.g. for purchases of agricultural machinery and fertilisers. Schiele was very concerned at Russian dumping of grain and timber.

Dietrich, the Reich Finance Minister, said that for all the doubts that had been expressed it would be difficult to refuse the guarantee, even if foreign reaction – mainly owing to the customs union with Austria that was being forged at the same time – was uncertain.

The Reich Foreign Minister stressed that it would not be possible to find domestic orders to replace the Russian orders for RM 300 million, and it would hardly be possible to sell the goods in any other country. Curtius was hoping that the deals with Russia would improve the economic situation.

The Reich Labour Minister was in favour of the Russian deals for labour market policy considerations, but asked for the decision to be postponed in regard for the Austro-German customs union and the plans to cancel the reparations.

Brüning felt that the wording of the press release on the cabinet decision would be of crucial importance. He regarded it as necessary to point out that a number of other countries had already concluded major deals with the Soviet Government and that the industrialists themselves had approached the Reich Government to ask for a guarantee. His aim was to avoid making a sensation of the deal, which would be highly undesirable in foreign policy, and prevent any impression being given that this was a Government initiative. He felt it was necessary to play down the risk in the business to the public and would have preferred to impose conditions on the industrialists, whose main concern was to obtain contracts for supplies, before they left for the Soviet Union. He also regarded the increase in short-term loans which the business would entail, as dangerous credit policy. Nevertheless, the Reich Government did finally commission the Reichsbank to look into and clarify the question of financing the Russian deals together with the Reich Economics and Finance Ministries and the industrialists concerned

After the Reichsbank had done so the Russian deals went back on to the agenda for a ministerial discussion on 24 March 1931. In the meantime Secretary of State

[25] Loc. cit., p. 975.

Trendelenburg had held negotiations with the representatives of industry who had rejected the proposal to reduce the state guarantee for major firms to 60% altogether. To Trendelenburg the Russian business could only be justified "if it seems useful in terms of policy as a whole. That should be the case, because pressure should be exerted on other countries. It is evident, for example, in a question from the Secretary-General of the International Chamber of Commerce proposing cooperation with France to form a front against Russia."[26] Clearly Trendelenburg was also hoping to be able to win concessions from France and the other Western powers one day in return for moving away from the Soviet Union.

The Reichsbank President again spoke in favour of the deals with Russia; however, the private nature of the business should be stressed in view of the reparation obligations.

The Reich Post Minister did not support the idea of a Reich guarantee because he thought the risk too high and only moderate benefit likely to employment. The Reich Post Office also needed credit to the amount of RM 140 million and similar amounts were needed by the railways and the local authorities.

The Reich Transport Minister expressed his former doubts in this meeting as well, as did the Labour Minister, who thought the deals could easily jeopardise the customs union, the efforts to obtain cancellation of the reparations and the disarmaments question.

But Foreign Minister Curtius again spoke very decisively in favour of the state guarantee. To refuse this would be to move away from existing policy towards Moscow, moreover the domestic economy needed the business.

At the end of the discussion the cabinet by a majority vote authorised the representatives of the Reich departments in the inter-ministerial committee that had been entrusted with issuing the export guarantees "to provide ... the guarantee against default within the framework of the existing authorisation to give guarantees and on the grounds of the existing regulations for supplies to the Soviet Union agreed on principle by German industrialists in Moscow under the conditions known to the Cabinet."[27]

Looking back on the discussions on the Russian deals in the Reich Cabinet one can see that the many doubts expressed by some of the Ministers on economic, finance and credit policy grounds were finally subordinated to a foreign policy strategy in which the "Russian business", as Curtius and Trendelenburg put it, were seen as a means of exerting further pressure on the Western powers to achieve concessions on the reparations and the question of disarmament. This is also the interpretation that seems most compelling from a note written by Hans Schäffer, Secretary of State in the Finance Ministry, on 9 April 1931 on the reparation question, listing all the arguments that might promote a solution to the reparation qustion that would be desirable to the Germans. Schäffer includes the Russian deals among his arguments. It could be pointed out to other countries that the reparation claims meant that Germany "would have to work the Russian market and take the appropriate attitude to Russia in politics and finance which would

[26] Ministerial meeting on 24 March 1931, AR, loc. cit., p. 980.
[27] Loc. cit., pp. 981f.

help the Soviets to carry out their plans for economic expansion and exert pressure on world markets."[28] The point of these considerations was to make other countries aware that Germany could only transfer the reparation sums, now that foreign credits had been withdrawn, through achieving a trade surplus and so must export to the USSR to this extent. It would therefore be in their own best economic interests to waive the reparations. That is precisely the strategy which Brüning has described in his memoirs.[29] But it looks as if the "Russian card" was played mainly by the German Foreign Office, while Brüning was sceptical towards the deals for a variety of reasons although he clearly followed the line taken by his Foreign Minister.

The Russian deals were not without controversy in the German industrial and banking world either. In the spring of 1931 some industrialists and bankers came to believe that Germany should draw back from the Russian market because of the danger of Russian dumping, and the financial and political risks involved. Many industrialists took the view "that a victorious Russian industry would mean the the victory of the Bolshevik idea and be bound to further the bolshevisation of the whole of Western Europe."[30] But the Chairman of the Russian Committee countered fears of Russian dumping by arguing that only in a very few areas could one say there was real dumping, while German industry would find it hard to answer the question "in how many areas are you selling not only below domestic costs but below present production costs as well?"[31] In Krämer's view forming an anti-Soviet or anti-dumping front with the French would inevitably lead to the loss of the existing RM 1.1 billion claims on the Soviet Union. For Germany, therefore, there could be no question of "dropping the Russian card prematurely. We must keep tight hold of it, for political and economic reasons."[32] But it is interesting to see that not even Krämer totally rejected the possibility of "dropping the Russian card" later - for the appropriate concessions. But for the present he saw a great chance for German export goods to push the British and Americans from the Russian market, especially since the British had recently been naming harder conditions and the British banks were increasingly reluctant to take Russian bills.

The German industrialists had not negotiated the details of the various deals in Moscow; this was now done and what was known as the Piatakov Agreement was signed, covering the period 15 April to 31 August 1931. "The Soviets insisted, if only for foreign and domestic propaganda, that as much as possible of the business should be put through, or reach the concerns, within the shortest possible time."[33] Piatakov was the head of the Soviet Supreme Economic Council, and he had told Krämer frankly that "We must get the orders through as fast as possible; we have built the factories, the sheds are standing empty and we need the machines. There

[28] Note by Schäffer dated 9 April 1931 on the reparation question, in: Politik und Wirtschaft in der Krise 1930–1932. Quellen zur Ära Brüning (Quellen zur Geschichte des Parlamentarismus und der politischen Parteien. Third series, vol. 4/1, ed. K. D. Bracher, E. Matthias and R. Morsey), Düsseldorf 1980, p. 592.

[29] See Note 4 to this article.

[30] Director Krämer in an RDI Board meeting on 23 April 1931, minutes, p. 69, BL RDI, microfilm 32.3.

[31] Loc. cit., p. 70.

[32] Loc. cit., p. 71.

[33] Loc. cit., p. 76.

are gaps wherever you look; the people are getting restless and we must start producing now, we must produce more and more."[34] The Soviet organs expressed their interest in buying not only for the present RM 300 million but a further RM 500 million as well. Had all the orders they envisaged materialised the Soviet debt would have been at least RM 1 billion by the end of 1931, but the Russian Committee had always taken the stand that the liability should not go beyond RM 500 million.

To finance the new orders of initially RM 300 million the Russian Committee proposed that the Russians should pay 20% in advance in bills, for which the Reich and the Länder would give 100% guarantees. These bills, which were signed by the Russian Trade Commission, the supplier firm and the Reich Government, were accepted by the banks without demur. It was more difficult to finance the rest of the business that was to be put through in 1931 and which required not only the down payment but the entire amount to be available. The goods were mainly semi-manufactures, wire, sheet metal, supports, and core iron and steel, for which finance to the amount of about RM 75 million was needed. Since the Golddiskontbank could provide about RM 50 million and some of the bills it had accepted were released during the year as the Russians redeemed them, the Russian Committee believed that there would be no problems in financing this part either. Problems would only arise in 1932, for instance, when deliveries of the electrical engineering goods and other products which needed a longer production period started. Should the Soviets make good their word and start negotiations on further deals before the Piatakov Agreement ran out in August the industrialists felt sure "that both the Reich and the Länder will object, for if a new purchase programme is negotiated for the time after 31 December 1931 the Russian debt to Germany could well go up to one and a half billion or even more."[35] A risk of such magnitude was only regarded as acceptable if prices could be achieved for the goods that made the business profitable. But in view of the "shameles undercutting" and the "way the general directors are storming the Russian Trade Mission"[36] this did not seem likely, especially since one company had just offered 22% less for a deal which the Russians had just concluded with a rival German firm. Director Krämer of the Russian Committee took this as occasion to ask the Reich Government to refuse a Reich and Länder guarantee in future for practices of this kind, and this was promised. But this did not prevent the Russians from playing one German firm off against another to get prices down.[37]

How concerned the Reich Government was to see as smooth a course as possible in German-Soviet trade is evident if only in that the Reichsbank intervened at the request of the Soviet trade representative, Liubimov, with the Secretary of State in the Reich Economics Ministry, Trendelenburg, acting as intermediary, to "settle the matter", when the Oberschlesische Hüttenwerke

[34] This was Krämer's version of the gist of it, loc. cit., p. 76.
[35] Loc. cit., p. 81.
[36] Loc. cit.
[37] Knickerbocker, see Note 2, p. 137, described the tactics like this: "The state monopoly in foreign trade was always trying to play at least two firms off against each other". That accords entirely with comments by members of the Russian Committee in RDI Board meetings.

refused to prolong Soviet bills to the amount of RM 450,000, which it was obliged to do under the contract. Some other firms had also "felt they were not in a position" to prolong Soviet bills and the Soviet Ambassador complained of this to the German Foreign Office on 30 July 1931, pointing out that increases in German customs and tariffs and the obligation to were having a negative effect on German trade with the Soviet Union. Foreign Minister Curtius, however, said that negotiations on an increase in Russian exports could not begin until September.[38] On the German side the expected difficulties had materialised in August 1931, and the industrialists regarded further orders for the period after 31 August as essential.[39] However, in a discussion with representatives of the Steel Industry Association on 18 August Brüning said firmly that it would be very difficult to find finance for further orders. For foreign policy reasons he saw no possibility of a further expansion of the Russian business: "The whole world has been antagonistic to the deals. They think the orders are being used for armaments and this has done us a great deal of damage abroad. It will therefore scarcely be possible to finance further Russian orders."[40] The Secretary of State, Trendelenburg, shared his view. Negotiations on an expansion of the Russian business would hardly be possible at present, there were too many risks involved in expanding the business. Dr. Vögler of the Vereinigte Stahlwerke agreed with that view. Brüning laid great stress on the loss of confidence abroad in the German economy and the situation of the banks. The credit crisis was such that a further increase in trade with the USSR did not seem advisable at that point of time.

The German deals with Russia had indeed aroused unease abroad. The British Government in particular was following developments with close attention, since British industry was in direct competition with the Germans on the Russian market. In September the head of the Export Guarantee Department, Nixon, went to the Auswärtiges Amt to negotiate on similar conditions for British and German deals with the Russians (credit terms, interest rates, premiums granted by industry for guarantees against default). The German maximum credit term was about three to four months longer than the British and the industrial premiums were far lower, at about 5% against 14%. The spokesman in the Auswärtiges Amt was dilatory in response to the British desire to see the gap narrowed, pointing out that "We have had to fight hard against pressure from our industrialists to increase the amount guaranteed, and I am convinced that as unemployment grows in Germany this pressure will increase. In my view it would be a great step towards understanding if the British could count on Germany not increasing the present volume of credit or prolonging the terms of the loans."[41] Nixon then indicated that there was a possibility of fiercer British competition in Russia. The British Government was clearly prepared to increase its risk in Russian business from £7 million to £15 million. There were further talks between Nixon and the

[38] Telegram from the ambassador in Moscow von Dirksen, to the Auswärtiges Amt of 6 August 1931, in: Akten zur deutschen auswärtigen Politik (ADAP) 1918–1945, Series B, Vol XVIII, p. 228.
[39] See Klöckner's comments in a discussion with the Chancellor and members of the Steel Industry Association on 18 August 1931, in: Pol. u. Wirtschaft i. d. Krise, as Note 28, Vol. 4/11, p. 909.
[40] Loc. cit.
[41] Note by Schlesinger of 2 September 1931, ADAP, as Note 38, Vol. XVIII, p. 381.

Auswärtiges Amt in October 1931. Since the Piatakov Agreement had by then run out, the Germans were able to point out that the credit terms would now automatically be longer and since the guarantee funds were used up German industry would no longer be a serious competitor to the British. The German authorities, Nixon was informed, would certainly keep to their limit of RM 1 billion for the Russian debt. New guarantee funds would only be available as credits were repaid. Nixon departed with these assurances, but not without expressing the fear that "another German industrial delegation might suddenly go to the Soviet Union and from one day to the next offer the Russians concessions, surprising Britain again as it was surprised by the Piatakov Agreement in the spring of the year."[42]

In September 1931 the Auswärtiges Amt expressed the view that the guarantee of RM 400 million which the Reich had given must on no account be exceeded and new guarantees could only be made available as the Russians redeemed their bills. There was understanding for the Russian pressure for higher exports to Germany, for this was the only way the Soviets could meet their payments obligations in Germany as other countries were also pressing on to the Russian market or putting obstacles in the way of Russian goods entering their own. Secretary of State Bülow put the orders received by German firms from the Soviet Union up to 15 August at RM 684 million. By that date the Soviet payments obligations to German firms for 1932 in the form of bills already totalled RM 565 million, while Soviet exports to Germany only amounted to RM 220 million by August. The Auswärtiges Amt therefore held the view that too great a Russian debt "would constitute a greater risk to the amounts already guaranteed by the authorities in the present economic situation" and German-Soviet trade must first be put on "a sounder basis."[43]

At the end of September 1931 the Reich Government assumed that German exports to Russia would be about RM 1 billion, while Russian exports to Germany would only be about RM 280 million. Von Raumer, a former Reich Minister, therefore expressed the fear, in a talk with Brüning and the Secretaries of State Punder, von Bülow and Trendelenburg, that the Russian business might peter out altogether since the USSR could only pay with what it exported. The business was "of extraordinary importance for the German economy, much more than people generally think. One could say that all German industry that involves technology is only surviving on the Russian deals. Russia is really the only sales area we have left now for these products especially, and other countries are now falling upon it as well. It is certainly in Germany's interests to try and increase Russian exports to Germany."[44] There was largely agreement on this, and it was decided that von Raumer should talk to the departments, especially the Reich Food Ministry, which would be particularly affected by Russian exports of grain, on ways of increasing Soviet exports to Germany (e.g. grain, tobacco and oil).

---

[42] Ditto, 24 October 1931, ADAP, loc. cit., Vol. XIX, p. 114.

[43] Von Bülow, Secretary of State in the German Foreign Office, to the Reich Economics Minister on 16 September 1931, ADAP, Vol. XVIII, p. 415.

[44] Remark by Pünder, Secretary of State, on a discussion on the Russian business on 29 September 1931, AR, as Note 19, p. 1760.

In the view of the Soviet Union the German-Soviet customs and tariff negotiations on 26 August and 3 and 18 September in Berlin were very unsatisfactory. The Soviet Foreign Minister complained to Councillor von Twardowski over the preferences that had been granted to imports of grain from Rumania and Hungary, indicating that the Berlin negotiations could under these conditions have a negative effect on Soviet orders in Germany, especially since Britain, which took nearly one third of total Soviet exports, was exerting heavy pressure on the Soviet Government to achieve a balanced trade account in view of the economic crisis in Britain.[45] This could only be done by increasing British exports to the Soviet Union at the expense of German industry.

Secretary of State von Bülow pointed out in a note to the German embassy in Moscow that there was every understanding for the Soviet complaints on the trade deficit with Germany. But the Soviets should be given to understand that the decline in German imports from the Soviet Union in the first half of 1931 was well within the framework of the general drop in consumption, which was 35%, and that, with such a drop in overall consumption, it was very difficult to create a market for Russian goods in Germany. Von Bülow also stressed that, independent of the German readiness to meet Soviet wishes, the Soviet Union was under an obligation "to find the money to meet its obligations. The Russians seem to be trying to throw a veil over things insofar as they are behaving as if exports to Russia were only in the German interest, while the Soviet Government was the real driving force in the increase in our exports to their country and is still pressing harder for a further increase in the Reich guarantees. The goods Russia imports are urgently needed investment goods, while their exports to Germany would be goods for current consumption."[46]

Von Dirksen, the German Ambassador in Moscow, followed these instructions and gave the People's Commissar, Litvinov, to understand that "the Soviet Government is creating a vicious circle by first complaining that we are not giving enough credits; then, if we do give extensive credits and our exports to the Soviet Union go up, they complain at the resultant trade deficit to them and want us to buy more Soviet goods."[47]

By the end of 1931 the deficit on the Soviet trade balance with Germany was growing rapidly and in view of the obligations towards Germany which the Soviet Union had undertaken for 1931 and 1932 under bills the situation seemed serious, leading the German Foreign Office to the conclusion that Germany must now refrain at all costs from granting any further guarantees to the Soviet Union – even for the amounts released as bills were redeemed.[48] The Reich Economics Ministry held the same view.[49]

---

[45] Telegram from the German Ambassador in Moscow, von Twardowski, to the German Foreign Office of 29 September 1931, ADAP, as Note 38, p. 482.

[46] Secretary of State von Bülow to the German embassy in Moscow, 8 October 1931, ADAP, loc. cit., p. 509.

[47] Note on the discussion with Litvinow, the People's Commissar, on 19 October 1931, ADAP, loc. cit., Vol. XIX, p. 21.

[48] von Bülow to the Reich Finance Ministry on 7 December 1931, ADAP, loc. cit., p. 229.

[49] Loc. cit., p. 230, Note 4.

In the meantime the German-Soviet trade negotiations in Berlin proceeded at a desultory pace. The Soviets thought the Germans should place orders with them to the amount of RM 750 million for 1932, while the Germans argued that the trade negotiations were leading in that direction. The Soviet organs should inform the German authorities of the effects of the Berlin trade negotiations on Soviet exports after three months. The head of the German delegation indicated that in addition to the grain contracts already signed supplies of a further 100,000 tons of Soviet grain might be ordered, assuming price and quality were right, and the Ministry would do its best to see that this order materialised. In return for Soviet agreement to the preferences granted to Rumania and Hungary it was suggested verbally to the Soviet negotiators that Germany should meet the greater part of its need for rye in 1932, should imports be needed, from the Soviet Union. If imports of corn were needed the same percentage should be imported from that country as in 1931.[50]

Further German-Soviet negotiations were held in February 1932 on grain imports, when the Soviet Union insisted that Germany must take 40% of its grain imports from the USSR in 1932. The Germans offered to take between 20 and 25%.[51] In March 1932 the minutes of the German-Soviet trade negotiations that had been signed on 21 December 1931 were ratified, changing the invoicing of German-Soviet trade to the Reichsmark. So the Soviet Union agreed not to insist on payment for the goods imported into Germany in foreign currency, which was a great relief to the German foreign exchange balance. In the summer of 1932 agreement was also reached on new customs and tariffs, giving reduced rates or exemption for important Soviet goods with the aim of increasing Soviet imports to Germany and German exports to the USSR at the same time.

Once the limit of RM 1 billion (= RM 400 million under Reich guarantee) in German exports to the Soviet Union was reached in the autumn of 1931 the Reich Government on principle provided no further guarantees, and only those transactions that were already agreed and which had guarantees were implemented and financed. At the beginning of February the finance needed for the remaining transactions under the Piatakov Agreement, which had now run out, was still around RM 120 million, and the RDI approached the Reichsbank asking for a further discount line. At first the Reichsbank refused, pointing out that it already had a very high involvement in Russian business.[52] A large number of firms, particularly in the machine industry, had concentrated on the Russian business as markets at home and abroad shrank, trusting that finance would be found when the time came, and failure to obtain this finance would have had serious repercussions on the labour market. A number of companies could have been ruined, especially if the Russians had insisted on the contracts being fulfilled. The Reich Economics Ministry therefore regarded it as essential for the Reichsbank to provide a discount line of up to RM 120 million.[53] At the beginning of March

---

[50] Minutes on the plenary session of the German and Soviet delegations at the trade negotiations on 22 December 1931, ADAP, loc. cit., p. 308f. On the proposals made verbally see Note 6 on that page.

[51] Note by Bräutigam, Secretary to the Legation, on 25 February 1932, ADAP, loc. cit., p. 598.

[52] Warmbold, Reich Economics Minister, to the Secretary of State in the Reichskanzlei, 1 February 1932, ADAP, loc. cit., p. 521.

[53] Loc. cit., p. 522.

Warmbold actually put the finance needed at RM 300–600 million (RM 120 million for existing transactions and RM 180 to 300 million for new business). Vereinigte Stahlwerke and Klöckner accounted for up to RM 140 million of the new orders, the railway wagon industry for RM 160 million and the electrical industry RM 40 million. If the iron industry did not take the Russian orders, he said, further redundancies would be inevitable.[54]

A plan was actually circulated among the industrialists to let the workers in the supplier firms share in financing the Russian deals. They were to receive 10% of their wages in the form of credits which would be redeemed as soon as the Russians had paid the bills for 20% of the purchase price given as advance payment on the orders. The companies would give their own guarantee for the part covered by the Reich guarantee.[55] The director of the RDI, Kastl, wanted the amount beyond the 20% advance payment in the form of bills to be financed by the Reich transferring the guarantees that would be released in 1932 to new business totalling RM 350 million. The RDI expected finance to the amount of RM 140 million to be needed for this new business, some of which was to come from the payment of wages in the form of credits, as explained above, and the Reichsbank was to be approached for the rest. Finally the Reichsbank did agree to provide discount lines for further Russian deals to the amount of RM 150 million.[56]

In April it actually agreed to discuss further credits, since the current repayments on credits were keeping the total outstanding liability within acceptable limits.[57].

A great boost to German-Soviet trade came from the conclusion of the framework agreement on exports of 15 June 1932. This by and large repeated the arrangements in the Piatakov Agreement of April 1931, but extended the maximum term for credits on major deals beyond the 28.6 months then usual. Thereupon the Soviets gave further orders for 350,000 tonnes of German machine tools.

The following table shows the development of German-Soviet trade during the years of crisis from 1929 to 1932:

German-Soviet Trade from 1929 to 1932[58]

Year	Imports (RM mill.)	In % of total imports	Exports	In % of total exports
1929	426	3.2	354	2.6
1930	430	4.2	531	3.6
1931	304	4.5	763	7.9
1932	271	5.8	626	10.9

54 Pol. u. Wirtschaft i. d. Krise, see Note 28, Vol. 4/1, p. 1367, Note 2.
55 The plan was put to Luther, President of the Reichsbank, on 8 April 1932, loc. cit., p. 1367.
56 Note by Director Waldhecker on a meeting of the Reich Cabinet, Pol. u. Wirtschaft i. d. Krise, as Note 28, Vol. 4/II, p. 1371.
57 Note on a discussion in the Reichsbank, loc. cit., p. 1391.
58 Kuczynski, see Note 1, p. 67.

So in 1932 German exports to the Soviet Union were 176.8% of the 1929 figure, while German exports to what had been the main trading partners before the slump, the Netherlands, France and Britain had shrunk to 46.8%, 51.6% and 34.3% respectively of the 1929 level. In 1932 more than 10% of total German exports went to the Soviet Union. while Soviet exports to Germany had regained their prewar level by 1932. The slight decline in German exports in 1932 is not least due to the drop in German imports from the USSR. The German surplus in trade with the USSR for 1930, 1931 and 1932 was RM 915 million. In 1931 the Soviet Union became Germany's most important trading partner, taking more than half all the machine tools and metal exported. Nearly one third of total exports of aluminium, pipes, rolled metal, rod and cast iron, and one quarter of German exports of sheet metal, wire, smelters, machine parts, automobiles and similar goods went to the Soviet Union. Whole sectors and works.survived through the crisis very largely or totally thanks to the Russian orders, among them the Ernst Heinckel aircraft works, the Zeiss-Werke in Jena[59], the metal and electrical industries and the machine tool factories in Saxony.[60]

If the economic importance of the Russian orders to German industry was evident, the calculations of the Auswärtiges Amt were also very largely realised. The Wiggin Report of August 1931 commented on the repercussions of the Brüning Government's export promotion policy in these words: "It will accentuate the world depression by reducing the sales by other countries to Germany and by creating intense competition from her exports in other markets", an effect it regarded as "highly undesirable in the general interest"[61], and the authors had mainly the Russian deals in mind. So the intensification of trade with Russia was a very suitable way of promoting the British Government's idea of keeping Germany in the Western camp by inducing gradual concessions to bring about "peaceful change".

In finance policy, admittedly, the Russian business did not match the draconian economy practised by the public authorities in other areas, and the imports of Russian grain and timber also damaged German agriculture. In keeping to this line despite all this, the Reich Government had firstly its reparation policy and secondly labour market policy considerations in mind.[62]

---

59 Wilhelm Treue: Deutschland in der Weltwirtschaftskrise in Augenzeugenberichten, Düsseldorf 1967, pp. 199ff.

60 Hans Münch: Die Bedeutung der sowjetischen Aufträge an die sächsische Werkzeugmaschinenindustrie in der Zeit der Weltwirtschaftskrise 1929 bis 1932, in: Jahrbuch f. Wirtschaftsgesch. 1965, T.4, pp. 54–76.

61 Report of the Committee appointed on the Recommendation of the London Conference ...", Appendix II, in: Documents on British Foreign Policy, 1919–1939, 2nd series, II, London 1947, p. 492.

62 The book by Hans-J. Perrey: Der Russlandausschuss der Deutschen Wirtschaft. Die deutsch-sowjetischen Wirtschaftsbeziehungen der Zwischenkriegszeit. Ein Beitrag zur Geschichte des Ost-West-Handels (stud. z. mod. Gesch. 31), Munich 1985 was not then available to me.

A Review of the New Literature on Business History[1]

Beate Brüninghaus[2]

Foreword

In 1986 the number of publications on business history in the Federal Republic of Germany rose again strongly, with around a quarter more on the subject appearing than in 1985. New was the growing interest in business history in so-called "left" circles, where the main focus used to be on labour and trade union history. Until recently only a small number of professors and company archivists in the Federal Republic of Germany were working on business history, but now a growing number of universities and non-university institutes are showing an interest in this field of research. Since many of the latter come from labour and trade union history, they tend to focus on the social aspects of the subject, and especially in accounts of industry during the Third Reich this often led to controversial discussion on the contents and methods of business history studies, which even went beyond the purely academic field to be fought out in public.

About 400 of the approximately 440 monographs on business history which were published in the Federal Republic of Germany in 1986 were to mark the anniversary of a company or association, or the birthday of an entrepreneur. So these were commemorative publications or commissioned works in the narrowest sense, and not primarily intended for readers with scholarly requirements. In spite of this, many of these commemorative documents contain information which was first published as a paper from a company's archives, and which may well be of interest to economic and particularly business historians. Then there were also publications, some of which were sponsored by companies, concerned not only with one company, entrepreneur or association, and which were mainly written by research workers.

Once again a selection has had to be made of the publications on business history which appeared in 1986. The criterion for the choice was the value of their

---

[1] Publications which appeared in 1986 in the Federal Republic of Germany, except for works on banking history which are mentioned in the article by Monika Pohle. For the rest reference is made to the bibliography which appears periodically in the "Zeitschrift für Unternehmensgeschichte" and which tries to consider all works on business history and biography.

[2] I have received much help in compiling the bibliography and obtaining the books. I am particularly grateful to Mrs. Erika Hermanns of the Institut der deutschen Wirtschaft in Cologne, Mr. Gerhard Alschner in Munich, Mr. Günther Berthmann of the Gesamtverband der Versicherungswirtschaft in Cologne as well as Mrs. Martina Mundorf and Miss Birgit Weitz of my staff. Finally I would like to thank my teacher Prof. Dr. Hans Pohl, University of Bonn, for his critical advice.

German Yearbook on Business History 1987

contribution to research work. If a paper contained new archive material and presented interesting and previously unknown facts, it is mentioned. The selection was not strictly confined to academic publications, and in cases of doubt non-academic publications have also been included.

1. General Studies on Individual Industries

Volume 3 of the *Handbuch der Europäischen Wirtschafts- und Sozialgeschichte* (Handbook of European Economic and Social History), to be six volumes in all, appeared in 1986, edited by the Emeritus Professor of Economic History, Hermann Kellenbenz[3]. It deals with European economic and social history from the end of the Middle Ages to the mid-17th century. First there is a general survey by Kellenbenz himself, which looks beyond individual countries to deal with the economy and society in Europe in the centuries between 1350 and 1650 and also considers individual sectors and their production techniques, as well as the services sector, there are articles on Northern, Western, Southern, Middle and Eastern Europe, written by leading international specialists, who devote large sections to describing economic trends and individual industries in particular. So they provide important background information for publications on company history during the early modern age. The detailed index makes the handbook a valuable reference work.

The volume of papers given at the Graz Conference of the Society for Social and Economic History in 1983 on the subject of trade and industrial landscapes from the late Middle Ages to the twentieth century includes, in addition to the introduction by the chairman Hans Pohl, Professor of Economic and Social History in Bonn, twelve papers, mostly by younger economic historians.[4] After a general survey by Othmar Pickl on Steiermark as a centre of trade and industry from the late Middle Ages to the present come two general papers by Wolfgang von Stromer and Karl Heinrich Kaufhold, covering the late Middle Ages to 1800. These are followed by papers on the production sectors linen, wool, cotton and silk, iron, steel, coal, metal working and mechanical engineering, non-ferrous metals, chemicals, electrical engineering, paper, glass and ceramics, agricultural implements and machines. These papers cover the period from 1800 to 1914.

The thesis by Thomas Meier, written under the direction of Rudolf Braun in Zürich, on non-agrarian activities and sources of income in a traditional crop farming area in the eighteenth century, draws on numerous individual sources to study the crafts, the cottage industry and home labour[5] Every third person earned

---

[3] Wolfram Fischer et al. (Ed.), Europäische Wirtschafts- und Sozialgeschichte vom ausgehenden Mittelalter bis zur Mitte des 17. Jahrhunderts (= Handbuch der europäischen Wirtschafts- und Sozialgeschichte, Vol. 3, ed. by Hermann Kellenbenz), Stuttgart (Klett-Cotta) 1986, 1326 p.

[4] Hans Pohl (Ed.), Gewerbe- und Industrielandschaften vom Spätmittelalter bis ins 20. Jahrhundert (= Vierteljahrschrift für Sozial- und Wirtschaftsgeschichte, Supp. 78), Stuttgart (Steiner) 1986, 497 p.

[5] Thomas Meier, Handwerk, Hauswerk, Heimarbeit. Nichtagrarische Tätigkeiten und Erwerbsformen in einem traditionellen Ackerbaugebiet des 18. Jahrhunderts (Zürcher Unterland), Zürich (Chronos) 1986, 435 p.

their income from non-agrarian activity in the area around Zürich at this time, and we find occupations based on the needs of the farming community, such as smiths, millers and stone-masons, weavers, cartwrights, coopers and small retailers. The thesis corrects the widespread misconception that farming communities were hostile to innovation and so static.

Dietmar Stutzer studies the assets of the 65 monasteries and retreats at the end of their lives during the secularisation in Bavaria, and for what business and employment system they provided an economic basis [6]. He also gives an account of the constitutions of the companies and plants where the assets were managed and run. They include manufacturing and agriculture and forestry. The author also discusses in detail the social constitution, especially the wages and payment in kind. The role of the monasteries as employers around 1800 is described in great detail on the basis of source material from two Benedictine abbeys.

In his Habilitation thesis, written in Braunschweig, Gerhard Schildt discusses the social history of the pre-industrial and industrial workers from 1830 to 1880[7]. In this case study of social change the historian presents an account of day labourers, journeymen and workers, seeing the workers as a newly emergent social class. However, he questions the applicability of the term "class" to craft journeymen, and rural and urban day labourers. A large number of the Braunschweig factory workers were in sugar and tobacco factories. The study is based on sources in the Lower Saxony state archives in Wolfenbüttel, the municipal archive in Braunschweig and church documents.

Until recently the history of workers was seen as the history of the labour movement, but today historical research has turned to the everyday lives of the workers, and so to questions of interest in business history in the narrower sense. The editor Wolfgang Ruppert has assembled thirty authors to tell us about the way of life, everyday conditions and culture of workers from the early industrialization period to the "economic miracle"[8]. These essays are based on new sources: many draw on oral history, household accounts and cookery books; the situation on the job is also described, although the names of the companies are not given. Female labourers are also included, and the book is illustrated with more than 130 photographs, some of which are published here for the first time.

The conference volume edited by the Bielefeld Professor of Economic and Social History, Jürgen Kocka, combines worker and middle class history in a consideration of the relation between workers and the bourgeoisie in the nineteenth century on a European comparison[9]. The book is based on a

---

[6] Dietmar Stutzer, Klöster als Arbeitgeber um 1800. Die bayerischen Klöster als Unternehmenseinheiten und ihre Sozialsysteme zur Zeit der Säkularisation 1803 (= Schriftenreihe der Historischen Komission bei der Bayerischen Akademie der Wissenschaften, Vol. 28), Göttingen (Vandenhoeck & Ruprecht) (1986), 390 p.

[7] Gerhard Schildt, Tagelöhner, Gesellen, Arbeiter: Sozialgeschichte der vorindustriellen und industriellen Arbeiter in Braunschweig 1830–1880 (= Industrielle Welt, Vol. 40), Stuttgart (Klett-Cotta) 1986, 505 p.

[8] Wolfgang Ruppert (Ed.), Die Arbeiter. Lebensformen, Alltag und Kultur von der Frühindustrialisierung bis zum "Wirtschaftswunder", München (C. H. Beck) 1986, 512 p.

[9] Jürgen Kocka (Ed., by assistance of Elisabeth Müller-Luckner), Arbeiter und Bürger im 19. Jahrhundert. Varianten ihres Verhältnisses im europäischen Vergleich (= Schriften des Historischen Kollegs, Kolloquien Vol. 7), München (Oldenbourg) 1986, 342 p.

colloquium held in 1984, the main focus of which was comparative international aspects. The papers relevant for business history include an essay by Heinz Reif on workers and entrepreneurs in cities in the Western Ruhr between 1850 and 1930. The Paris historian Patrick Fridenson has contributed an interesting paper on worker politics in large firms in France and its effects on the workers between 1880 and 1914. Alf Lüdtke entitles his paper "Arbeiterpolitik versus Politik der Arbeiter" (Policy on Workers versus Workers' Policy), considering entrepreneurs' strategies and worker behaviour in large German firms between 1890 and 1914/20. The US historian Gerald Feldman examines entrepreneurs and workers in German heavy industry before 1914. The title of this collected volume is, however, misleading in that most of the papers go on into the twentieth century as well.

The thesis by Rudolf Jaun, written in Zuricha under Rudolf Braun, is concerned with the growth of scientific management, and the americanization and rationalization of working conditions in Switzerland between 1873 and 1959[10]. The author assumes that the analytical approach to management and the attitude of company managements on the one hand and that of the workers on the other are related. The question is why the Swiss workers began to copy the approach of the management and did not group themselves into independent trade unions or even adopt the class war approach. The author sees this as due to the growth in scientific management, which began under American influence after 1870. The thesis is in three parts, the first on the tendency to scientific management from 1873 to 1918 and the second on the adoption of American scientific management after 1918. The third examines the realization and effects of these changes on company working practice, using company studies, with the Bally Shoe factories, Maag Zahnräder AG and the Oerlikon mechanical engineering firm as examples. The work is based on extensive material from many public, company and association archives.

The thesis by Ralph-Rainer Ohlsen, written under FriedrichWilhelm Henning in Cologne, on German exports to Great Britain from 1923 to 1933 deals with political relations between Germany and its First World War opponent[11]. German trade with other countries during the Weimar Republic is still largely unresearched. Britain was at the time the leading industrial nation in Europe beside Germany. Using statistical material, some of which he regroups to enable comparisons and meaningful statements to be made, the author calculates the size of German exports to Great Britain. A particular problem is inflation, and this he attempts to solve using price indices. – Sören Dengg's thesis describes Germany's departure from the League of Nations and Schacht's "New Plan"[12]. Like Ohlsen, Dengg is here dealing with an aspect of foreign economic policy during the transition phase from the Weimar Republic to the Third Reich. Germany's departure from the League of Nations in 1933 and Schacht's "New Plan" in 1934, which switched

[10] Rudolf Jaun, Management und Arbeiterschaft. Verwissenschaftlichung, Amerikanisierung und Rationalisierung der Arbeitsverhältnisse in der Schweiz 1873–1959, Zürich (Chronos) 1986, 505 p.

[11] Ralph-Rainer Ohlsen, Der deutsche Export nach Großbritannien von 1923 bis 1933. Seine Veränderungen und seine Bedeutung, Bergisch Gladbach (Josef Eul) 1986, 256 p.

[12] Sören Dengg, Deutschlands Austritt aus dem Völkerbund und Schachts "Neuer Plan". Zum Verhältnis von Außen- und Außenwirtschaftspolitik in der Übergangsphase von der Weimarer Republik zum Dritten Reich (1929–1934), Frankfurt (Peter Lang) 1986, 480 p.

German foreign trade policy to the principle of "buy from your customer", concluded a long development towards increasing bilateralism. The thesis, which was written under Leo Haupts in Cologne, is based on sources mainly from the Federal archives in Koblenz and the Political Archives of the Foreign Office in Bonn. Dengg concludes that German foreign trade under Hitler and Schacht was subjected to the "primacy of politics", but the German efforts to achieve autarchy, which now only permitted bilateral trade, were preprogrammed in many ways. With due stress on the discontinuity through Hitler's dominant role Dengg shows the continuity in economic policy between Weimar and Hitler as manifest in foreign trade policy.

The Habilitation thesis by Stefan Karner in Graz deal with Steiermark in the Third Reich, from 1938 to 1945, so after the "Anschluß" with the German Reich[13]. This voluminous and detailed work is based on a large number of sources, in company archives and public archives, and it deals with the political, economic, social and cultural development of the Steiermark, touching on business history aspects as well. Also the cruelties of the Third Reich, the genocide of the Jews, the concentration camps in Steiermark, the persecution of Sloveness and gipsies as well as that of the social associations, here for the first time are most far-reachingly worked up.

A Habilitation by Karl-Heinz Schlarp in Hamburg describes the economy and the occupation of Serbia from 1941 to 1944[14]. The National Socialist "Großraum" policy saw Yugoslavia, like the whole of South East Europe, as an area of economic expansion which could be exploited for the German war economy. The area was utilized mainly as a source of raw materials and agricultural produce, but the supplies did not come up to expectations - unlike the transportation of labour.

The "Hermann Göring" Reichswerke was a new armaments factory, and during the Third Reich it was built up until it was the largest in the German Reich. In his study of the works[15] August Meyer attempts to give an account of the controversies between leading members of the regime over economic and business policy aims. The concern succeded, often contravening state instructions, in pursuing its own business policy goals. Basis of the Study are numerous archives at home and abroad as well as the combine archive of the Salzgitter AG. Indexes of persons and places, numerous documents as well as surveys on the complicated structure of combines let the work become a reference book, too.

The "forced labour" used in Germany during the Second World War was a subject not only of political discussion during 1986 but of historical research as well. After the publication of Ulrich Herbert's standard work in 1985, with a second edition in 1986[16], the same author has now followed this up with the history

---

[13] Stefan Karner, Die Steiermark im Dritten Reich 1938–1945. Aspekte ihrer politischen, wirtschaftlich-sozialen und kulturellen Entwicklung, Graz/Wien (Leykam) 1986, 636 p.

[14] Karl-Heinz Schlarp, Wirtschaft und Besatzung in Serbien 1941–1944. Ein Beitrag zur nationalsozialistischen Wirtschaftspolitik in Südosteuropa (= Quellen und Studien zur Geschichte des östlichen Europa, Vol. 25), Stuttgart (Steiner) 1986, 443 p.

[15] August Meyer, Das Syndikat. Reichswerke "Hermann Göring", Wien (Europa-Verlags-GmbH) 1986, 348 p.

[16] Ulrich Herbert, Fremdarbeiter: Politik und Praxis des "Ausländer-Einsatzes" in der Kriegswirtschaft des Dritten Reiches, 2. edition, Berlin et al. (Dietz) 1986, 494 p.

of foreign labour in Germany from 1880 to 1980[17]. He considers seasonal workers, forced labour and foreign workers, giving a summary of the research on this so far in brief and readable form.

The excellent documentation by the Wolfsburg municipal archivist Klaus-Jörg Siegfried on armaments production and forced labour in the Volkswagenwerk from 1939 to 1945[18] is little known. Siegfried presents the main sources and facts on this subject, with an economical but informative commentary. He conducted written interviews with several of the former forced labourers. As a new company, the Volkswagenwerk had fewer core workers than other companies, and so about two thirds of its workforce consisted of forced labour. The share of concentration camp prisoners employed there was also relatively high, some chosen personally by the works manager Ferdinand Porsche.

A school competition on German history for the prize given by the President of the Federal Republic of Germany has produced a local study by Bernd Klewitz on slave labour in Dynamit Nobel[19]. Taking the munitions factory, which was then part of the IG-Farben concern, and its associated concentration out-camps in the district of Marburg-Biedenkopf, Klewitz examines the situation of the forced labourers and concentration camp inmates from 1939 to 1945. He also draws on extensive contemporary reports by eye witnesses, since the written material on this subject is inadequate.

A conference held in 1984 initiated the volume on companies and the state after the Second World War edited by Alois Brusatti and Hans Pohl[20]. The two papers by the Vienna Professor of Economic History, Brusatti, and Horst Albach, Professor of Business Studies in Bonn, clearly show the reasons for the different developments in the two countries, with the high state participation in companies in Austria ultimately proving a handicap to economic development.

The volume edited by Hans Pohl on the emergence and development of the social market economy[21] was also a conference report. Joachim Starbatty, economic historian from Tübingen, spoke on the theoretical bases of the social market economy, which he traced back to the nineteenth century. The spokesman of the Board of Managing Directors of Deutsche Bank AG, Alfred Herrhausen, spoke from the standpoint of the practitioner on the social market economy as the best possible economic system for the Federal Republic of Germany. The panel of leading figures in business, whose contributions are included too, warned of

---

17 Ulrich Herbert, Geschichte der Ausländerbeschäftigung in Deutschland 1880 bis 1980: Saisonarbeiter, Zwangsarbeiter, Gastarbeiter, Berlin et al. (Dietz) 1986, 272 p.

18 Klaus-Jörg Siegfried, Rüstungsproduktion und Zwangsarbeit im Volkswagenwerk 1939–1945. Eine Dokumentation, Frankfurt/New York (Campus) 1986, 239 p.

19 Bernd Klewitz, Die Arbeitssklaven der Dynamit Nobel, Schalksmühle (Engelbrecht) 1986, 319 p.

20 Alois Brusatti/Hans Pohl (Eds.), Unternehmen und Staat nach dem Zweiten Weltkrieg. Ein deutsch-österreichischer Vergleich (= Zeitschrift für Unternehmensgeschichte, Supp. 39), Stuttgart (Steiner) 1986, 68 p.

21 Hans Pohl (Ed.), Entstehung und Entwicklung der sozialen Marktwirtschaft. Referate und Diskussionsbeiträge der 10. öffentlichen Vortragsveranstaltung der Gesellschaft für Unternehmensgeschichte e. V. am 26. 6. 1985 in Frankfurt am Main (= Zeitschrift für Unternehmensgeschichte, Supp. 45), Stuttgart (Steiner) 1986, 76 p.

political errors which were threatening to undermine the meaning of the social market economy.

West German postwar history has increasingly been the focus of research as the appropriate archives have been opened in recent years. A conference held by the Munich Institute for Contemporary History in 1984 gave rise to a volume edited by Ludolf Herbst[22]. Since the institute is now running a research project on this subject further publications may be expected in the next few years. Although the volume concentrates on political history, it also contains several essays on economic developments. The decade between 1945 and 1955 in West Germany was determined by the policy of the Allies, and this can be described in three key terms: subjection, control and finally integration.

Beside Great Britain the Federal Republic of Germany has the most subsidiaries of Japanese firms in Europe. One reason for the growing Japanese presence is the growing fear of protectionism among Japanese exporters. The study by Hans-Peter Merz and Sung-Jo Park on Japanese management in the Federal Republic of Germany[23] gives a statistical account, based on an evaluation of questionnaires, of Japanese subsidiaries in Germany. The inquiry emerged from a research project at the Department of Far Eastern Studies at the Free University Berlin. – In his two-volume economic history of modern Japan[24], the Mainz Professor of Economic History, Volker Hentschel, deals with the conditions, bases and successes of industrialization in Japan from 1600 to 1929 and Japan's road to a world economic power from 1930 to 1983. Japan's present economic strength has three historical roots: firstly, positive economic, social and intellectual traditions existed from the pre-modern age, secondly the political revolution of 1868 ushered in the process of industrialization which went on uninterrupted until the beginning of the Great Depression in 1929. Thirdly, however, the Depression ultimately offered Japan a chance to develop further. After the militari ation of politics and economy Japan's recovery from the collapse of 1945 was only slow, and it was not until the beginning of the fifties that its rise to a world economic power began. In this brief account Hentschel does not present his own research, he summarizes other detailed research studies. Several chapters also deal with industry and money and banking, and so are of direct relevance for business history.

The regional and local studies published in 1986 again include several good accounts of business history. Under the trenchant title "Der Wirtschaftsraum zwischen den Wirtschaftsräumen" (The Economic Area between Economic Areas) Ernst Moritz Spilker deals with the region between the Rhine, the Ruhr, Fulda and

---

[22] Ludolf Herbst (Ed.), Westdeutschland 1945–1955. Unterwerfung, Kontrolle, Integration (= Schriftenreihe der Vierteljahreshefte für Zeitgeschichte, Sondernummer, ed. by Karl Dietrich Bracher and Hans-Peter Schwarz), München (Oldenbourg) 1986, 308 p.

[23] Hans-Peter Merz/Sung-Jo Park, Japanisches Management in der Bundesrepublik Deutschland. Strukturen und Strategien (= Reihe Horizonte Asiens), Berlin (Express Edition) 1986, 227 p.

[24] Volker Hentschel, Wirtschaftsgeschichte des modernen Japans. 1. Die japanische Industrialisierung. Voraussetzungen, Grundlagen, Durchsetzung (1600–1929) (= Wissenschaftliche Paperbacks Sozial- und Wirtschaftsgeschichte, Vol. 22), Stuttgart (Steiner) 1986, 203 p; 2. Japans Weg zur wirtschaftlichen Weltmacht (1930–1983) (= Wissenschaftliche Paperbacks Sozial- und Wirtschaftsgeschichte, Vol. 23), Stuttgart (Steiner) 1986, 174 p.

the lower Main[25]. These medium-range hills on the right of the Rhine and in Upper Hesse were the site of iron production and processing in the pre-industrial age, but the industrialization process went on elsewhere, leaving this area on the side of the main transport routes, as it still is today. This revised thesis for a diploma at the University of Cologne is the first account of the region as a whole, although its economic structure is anything but homogeneous. Above all, Spilker has compiled a great many statistics; in the appendix with its statistical tables, for instance, he also shows the number of firms in individual sectors in the period between 1830 and 1914.

Industrial archaelogy is a field in which research publications have only been appearing since the last decade in the Federal Republic of Germany. The volume edited by Axel Föhl on industrial and technical monuments in Hessen[26] gives equal place to photographs and text, with most of the photos published here for the first time. A list of firms also makes the book interesting to business historians. The authors are on the staff of the Municipal Museum in Rüsselsheim; this is a very appealing series and it is to be continued for all the Federal Länder.

The former municipal archivist of Ludwigshafen, Willi Breunig, has published an account of the economic development of the city of Ludwigshafen on the Rhine from 1820 to 1920[27]. The contributions, based on material from the city's archives, are mainly commentaries to photos. The book is subdivided according to sectors and the main focus is on sectors so far little researched, like banking, postal history, energy supplies, local transport, trade and the crafts, while the development of the chemical industry, which predominates in Ludwigshafen in the form of the large firm BASF and has been frequently described, is deliberately kept brief.

Götz Meidinger has described the development of industry in Heilbronn from the First World War to the beginning of the 80s[28]. Drawing on numerous company and public archives, the author describes the economic history of this town in South West Germany, once a centre of the motor industry. Many details on company history are included. In Heilbronn, where in 1832 its only 17 factories already made in the town to an industrial centre of Württemberg, the number of factories rose to 250 in 1861 and to 271 in 1907. The work deals with the time from 1914 to the present, with a survey of future prospects.

In good time before the celebrations for the 750th anniversary of the City of Berlin the second volume of the series "Industriekultur in Berlin" (Industrial

---

[25] Ernst Moritz Spilker, Der Wirtschaftsraum zwischen den Wirtschaftsräumen: Eine Studie über ausgewählte Kreise der rechtsrheinischen und oberhessischen Mittelgebirgslandschaft im Zeitalter der Industrialisierung von 1830 bis 1914 (= Kölner Vorträge und Abhandlungen zur Sozial- und Wirtschaftsgeschichte, Vol. 38), Köln (publ. by Forschungsinstitut für Sozial- und Wirtschaftsgeschichte at the University of Cologne) 1986, 223 p.

[26] Axel Föhl (Ed.), Hessen. Denkmäler der Industrie und Technik, Berlin (Nicolaische Verlagsbuchhandlung) 1986, 141 p.

[27] Willi Breunig, Vom Handelsplatz zur Industriestadt. Wirtschaftsentwicklung am Rhein 1820–1920 (= Veröffentlichungen des Stadtarchivs Ludwigshafen, Vol. 12), Ludwigshafen am Rhein (publ. by Stadtarchiv Ludwigshafen) 1986, 151 p.

[28] Götz Meidinger, Die Entwicklung der Heilbronner Industrie: Vom Ersten Weltkrieg bis zum Beginn der Achtziger Jahre (= Beiträge zur südwestdeutschen Wirtschafts- und Sozialgeschichte, ed. by Gert Kollmer and Harald Winkel, Vol. 3), St. Katharinen (Scripta Mercaturae) 1986, 263 p.

Culture in Berlin) was published. The first, which appeared in 1984, was devoted to the nineteenth century and this is concerned with the metropolis in the twentieth[29]. Similar publications appeared in 1983 on Nuremberg and in 1984 on Hamburg. The editors are art historians and political scientists, but they have assembled a number of essays that are relevant for business history, on the Treptow Trade Fair in 1896, interest policy and the war aims of the large electrical firms in Berlin from 1914 to 1918, the Rheinmetall-Borsig armaments factory and the normal working day at Siemens. The texts are illustrated with a large number of photographs.

If the entrepreneur was neglected in Federal German historical research for some years while studies concentrated on trade unions, blue or white collar workers or companies, it is evident that interest is now turning back to these figures. The historian Volker Berghahn, now teaching in the United States, has given a brief account of the relation between entrepreneurs and politics in the Federal Republic of Germany[30]. Since the relevant company or association archives are not open to the public Berghahn has relied mainly on the literature on the subject. While the heavy industry in the Ruhr dominated the German economic and sectoral structure until after 1945, and so entrepreneurial policy as well, the late fifties and sixties were dominated by the rise of the manufacturing industry. The anticartel policy transplanted from the United States led to the fragmentation and liberalization of the economy. The American influence brought the recognition of the trade unions as partners in negotiation and a tendency on the part of entrepreneurs to move away from the patriarchal approach to management. The brief, readable account contains numerous references to American and British developments.

The "Rheinisch-Westfälische Wirtschaftsbiographien" (Rhineland-Westphalian Business Biographies) of which the twelfth and thirteenth volumes appeared in 1986[31] have long been highly esteemed in business history. The economic historian Horst A. Wessel here reports on the Cologne entrepreneurs' family of Felten and Guilleaume, whose company of the same name was one of the leading cable manufacturers in Europe, and the rubber and cable manufacturer Franz Clouth. The Cologne economic historian Friedrich Zunkel contributes an informative essay on the Cologne publisher Josef Bachem and the Cologne economic historian Klara van Eyll one on the Cologne master threadmaker, Franz Wilhelm Koenig, who was one of the major guild craftsmen of his day. Wilhelm Treue, Professor of Economic History in Göttingen, writes on three Cologne bankers, Simon, Abraham and Dagobert Oppenheim and their partner Robert Pferdmenges, who also contributed to political history as a friend and advisor to Konrad Adenauer. Two essays come from the Cologne economic historian Guntram Philipp, on the

[29] Jochen Boberg/Tilman Fichter/Eckhart Gillen (Eds.), Die Metropole. Industriekultur in Berlin im 20. Jahrhundert, München (Beck) 1986, 400 p.

[30] Volker Berghahn, Unternehmer und Politik in der Bundesrepublik, Frankfurt (Suhrkamp) 1986, 364 p.

[31] Rheinisch-Westfälische Wirtschaftsbiographien, ed. by Volks- und Betriebswirtschaftliche Vereinigung im Rheinisch-Westfälischen Industriegebiet, the Historischen Kommission für Westfalen, the Rheinisch-Westfälischen Wirtschaftsarchiv and the Westfälischen Wirtschaftsarchiv, Vol. 12: Kölner Unternehmer im 18., 19. und 20. Jahrhundert, Münster (Aschendorff) 1986, 201 p.; Kölner Unternehmer im 19. und 20. Jahrhundert, Münster (Aschendorff) 1986, 245 p.

Mühlheim silk manufacturer Andreae, while the Bonn economic historian Frauke Schönert-Röhlk reports on the Cologne wool and cloth dealers Peter and Gustav Michels. Friedrich Zunkel writes on the Cologne merchant Gustav Mallinkrodt, Klara van Eyll on the sugar manufacturers Johann Jakob Langen and Emil Pfeifer, and Wilhelm Treue on the scent manufacturer Ferdinand Mülhens. A bibliography and indexes of names and subjects provide excellent openings for further research.

The thesis by Hans Hesselmann on the commercial middle class in Bavaria between 1890 and 1914 was written at the University of Bamberg under Karl Möckel[32]. The author describes the ties between the commercial bourgeoisie and the government in four regions: Augsburg, the Palatinate government district, Ludwigshafen and Mannheim. After the formation of the Reich the nobility and the powerful industrialists, merchants and bankers determined social and political power relations. In Augsburg 35 leading personalities in business life controlled industry and banking before the First World War; the group accounted for only 0.027 per cent, of the population at the time and were some of the 65 millionaires in the Swabian metropolis before the outbreak of the war.

2. Studies on Individual Sectors

2.1 Mining

Mining is still one of the most researched areas in German business history. The series "Technische Denkmäler in der Bundesrepublik Deutschland" (Technical Monuments in the Federal Republic of Germany) which is now a standard work, and in which Rainer Slotta has now presented the fifth volume on iron ore mining[33], will cover all the iron, coal and steel monuments when the inventary work is finished. This first part of volume 5, devoted to iron ore mining, lists first the northern areas by regions, divided according to Federal Länder. The pits which were still operating after the Second World War are studied in detail, the others only briefly. The account is divided as follows: first a description of the location, then a description of the historical and business development of the mine and finally a description of existing monuments. – Ore mining is also the subject of the work by Volker Nichelmann[34], who draws on archive material to describe the development of the Amberg ore mine and the Luitpoldhütte from 1800 to 1945, which once helped to make the Upper Palatinate one of the major manufacturing centres in Germany. Herbert Dennert, a former senior mining official, has studied mining and smelting in the Harz from the 16th to the 19th century[35]. Part I

---

[32] Hans Hesselmann, Das Wirtschaftsbürgertum in Bayern 1890–1914 (= Beiträge zur Wirtschafts- und Sozialgeschichte, Vol. 32), Stuttgart (Steiner) 1986, 419 p.

[33] Rainer Slotta, Der Eisenerzbergbau (= Veröffentlichungen aus dem Deutschen Bergbau-Museum, No. 38), Bochum (Deutsches Bergbau-Museum) 1986, 1151 p.

[34] Volker Nichelmann, Der Amberger Erzberg und die Luitpoldhütte von 1800 bis 1945 (= separate print of Verhandlungen des Historischen Vereins für Oberpfalz und Regensburg, Vol. 126), s. l. 1986, p. 99–343.

[35] Herbert Dennert, Bergbau und Hüttenwesen im Harz: Vom 16. bis zum 19. Jahrhundert dargestellt in Lebensbildern führender Persönlichkeiten, Clausthal-Zellerfeld (Pieper) 1986, 195 p.

appeared in 1960, and now we have the complete work. Dennert describes the history of ore and ironstone mining and smelting in the Harz. Two thirds of the book are concerned with the lives of those who worked in this mining area. In addition to original biographical information the volume also includes reprints from periodicals, so that not all the volume has references or a bibliography.

The Antwerp historian Margareta A. Devos has written a thesis in Bonn under Hans Pohl on capital integration in the coal, iron and steel industry between Western Germany and Belgium from about 1830 to 1914[36]. Using a large number of archive sources the author presents an international comparative study, of which there is still a shortage in business history. So far we have also lacked an account of Belgian expansion in Germany in the nineteenth century. Devos restricts herself to the mutual capital integration in the coal, iron and steel industry, dealing with all the firms in Belgium, but only companies in the western part of Germany.

The history of lignite mining in the Rhineland is virtually the history of the whole sector since the division of Germany in 1945, now that the main lignite deposits are in the GDR. While there are a large number of publications on the Ruhr, the work by Arno Kleinebeckel is the first general account of the lignite area in the Rhineland to the west of Cologne[37]. More than 300 photos and illustrations, some published for the first time, supplement the text, which was commissioned by the Rheinische Braunkohlenwerke AG. This is one of the best company publications on business history to appear in 1986. – In his Clausthal thesis the mining official Gunter Gach deals with the historical development of the specialized mining companies in Germany[38]. These companies were mainly concerned with specialized and difficult mining techniques, particularly shaft sinking. The first specialized mining companies were already operating at the end of the 17th century and this account follows their development to the present.

The collection of source material published by Klaus Tenfelde and Helmuth Trischler to mark the centenary of the Mining and Energy Trade Union consists of requests and complaints by miners during the industrialization period[39]. Most of the documents are published here for the first time, and they give information on the living and working conditions of miners from the standpoint of those affected. In time the material covers the years from 1816 to 1933, and it includes business history material on questions of wages, invalidity benefits, failure to observe safety regulations and working time. Each of the sources has a brief commentary, and the book provides a further set of material for scholars beside the frequently quoted workers' memoirs. – The Western Ruhr area serves as example for the economic and social historical thesis of Ullrich Feige[40], written under Friedrich Zunkel in

36 Margareta A. Devos, Kapitalverflechtungen in der Montanindustrie zwischen dem westlichen Deutschland und Belgien von etwa 1830 bis 1914, Bonn 1986, diss., 394 p.

37 Arno Kleinebeckel, Unternehmen Braunkohle. Geschichte eines Rohstoffes, eines Reviers, einer Industrie im Rheinland, ed. by Rheinische Braunkohlewerke AG, Köln (Greven) 1986, 287 p.

38 Gunter Gach, In Schacht & Strecke. Die historische Entwicklung der Bergbau-Spezialgesellschaften in Deutschland, Essen (Glückauf) 1986, 299 p.

39 Klaus Tenfelde/Helmuth Trischler (Eds.), Bis vor die Stufen des Throns. Bittschriften und Beschwerden von Bergleuten im Zeitalter der Industrialisierung, Munich (Beck) 1986, 531 p.

40 Ullrich Feige, Bergarbeiterschaft zwischen Tradition und Emanzipation. Das Verhältnis von Bergleuten und Gewerkschaften zu Unternehmern im westlichen Ruhrgebiet um 1900, Düsseldorf (Schwann) 1986, 184 p.

Cologne, where he examines the developing period of the miners' unions, a phase full of conflicts. This work is based on documents of public archives and its stress lies on the period between 1894 with the establishing of new competing unions and 1905 with the great miners' strike.

After the publication in 1979 of volume one the head of the Bochum mining archive, Evelyn Kroker, presents volume two of "Der Arbeitsplatz des Bergmanns" (The Miner's Workplace)[41]. While the first volume dealt with the development up to the Second World War, the second is concerned with the years from 1939 to the 1960s, entitled 'the road to full mechanization'. The text is illustrated with 385 black and white photos. The main focus is on company level, and this is not intended to be a documentation of the miners' everyday lives. – The thesis completed in 1983 by Rudolf Tschirbs under the Bochum historian Hans Mommsen, deals with collective bargaining policy in the mining industry in the Ruhr from 1918 to 1933[42]. It is also of interest to business historians, for it contains much inner-company research. A large number of pits are mentioned that are becoming accessible through a company register. This work is based on extensive source studies, in Federal, mining, the Westphalian Business and German Trade Union Federation archives and in numerous companies; it also evaluates extensive literature and very greatly widens the state of research on collective bargaining. The author sees the Coal Industry Act of 1919 with its co-determination rights and planned wages' fixing as positive for the economy. The exploitation of crises by the employers to reverse social benefits was bound to destabilize the political system.

2.2 Energy

The Freiburg economic historian Hugo Ott within a main point program of the "Deutsche Forschungsgemeinschaft" (German Research Community) presents the first volume of a new series of historical statistics in Germany, here public electricity supplies from 1890 to 1913[43]. The purpose of the series is to obtain figures of greater historical depth, regional differentiation and thematic breadth through new research in archives and private and semi-official publications from the time before statistics were kept or the early statistical period. This volume is indispensable for anyone who wants to work on the history of public electricity supplies.

---

[41] Evelyn Kroker, Der Arbeitsplatz des Bergmanns, Vol. 2: Der Weg zur Vollmechanisierung (= Veröffentlichungen aus dem Deutschen Bergbau-Museum, Vol 37) (= Schriften des Bergbau-Archivs, No. 4), Bochum (Deutsches Bergbau-Museum) 1986, 448 p.

[42] Rudolf Tschirbs, Tarifpolitik im Ruhrbergbau 1918–1933, (= Veröffentlichungen der Historischen Kommission zu Berlin, Vol. 64) (= Beiträge zu Inflation und Wiederaufbau in Deutschland und Europa 1914–1924, Vol. 5), Berlin/New York (de Gruyter) 1986, 531 p.

[43] Hugo Ott (Ed.), Historische Energiestatistik von Deutschland. Vol. 1: Statistik der öffentlichen Elektrizitätsversorgung Deutschlands 1890–1913 (= Quellen und Forschungen zur historischen Statistik von Deutschland, Vol. 1), St. Katharinen (Scripta Mercaturae) 1986, 654 p.

2.3 Iron and Steel

The business history publications in 1986 on the iron and steel industry are of a very high scholarly level. The Berlin economic historian Rainer Fremdling presents the shortened and revised version of his Habilitation thesis, written under the Münster economic historian Richard Tilly[44]. It deals with technological change and international trade in the iron industries in Great Britain, Belgium, France and Germany during the 18th and 19th centuries. Fremdling includes both qualitative and quantitative aspects in his study, which is one of the products of the New Economic History School. Although the work is economic in orientation, drawing on public archives in Great Britain, Belgium, France and Germany, it provides an account of the economic framework conditions that will prove of value to business historians as well. The extensive tables in the appendix are also impressive. - The revised Darmstadt thesis by Ulrich Wengenroth, which was completed in 1982, deals with company strategies and technical progress in the German and British steel industry from 1865 to 1895[45]. This is a comparative study of an industrial sector in two countries and it is based on a thorough evaluation of archive material on German and British companies, association and cartel records and contemporary specialized literature. The work was awarded the prestigious Rudolf-Kellermann Prize for Technical History in 1982. Wengenroth uses case studies to examine success in rationalization in companies introducing progressive technology to build up mass steel production at the end of the 19th century. He examines the reasons for the success of the German steel producers over their British counterparts, from whom they had learned.

Another thesis completed in 1982 was by Irmgard Steinisch under Gerhard Ritter in Munich. Now an assistant at the Free University in Berlin, she presents an enlarged version of the work, which is concerned with the struggle for the eight-hour shift in the iron and steel industry in Germany and America from 1880 to 1929[46]. The transition from the two twelve-hour shift system to three eight-hour shifts from 1880 to 1929 is described against the background of technical and political developments. The problem of working time was highly politicized in the Weimar Republic in Germany and unlike British industry the resistance to the change was particularly strong in the iron and steel industry in both Germany and America. The study is based mainly on the archives of Gutehoffnungshütte, and it concludes with an exemplary index of subjects, persons, places, countries and firms.

---

[44] Rainer Fremdling, Technologischer Wandel und internationaler Handel im 18. und 19. Jahrhundert. Die Eisenindustrien in Großbritannien, Belgien, Frankreich und Deutschland (= Schriften zur Wirtschafts- und Sozialgeschichte, Vol. 35), Berlin (Duncker & Humblot) 1986, 493 p.

[45] Ulrich Wengenroth, Unternehmensstrategien und technischer Fortschritt. Die deutsche und die britische Stahlindustrie 1865–1895 (= Veröffentlichungen des Deutschen Historischen Instituts London, Vol. 17), Göttingen/Zürich (Vandenhoeck & Ruprecht) 1986, 316 p.

[46] Irmgard Steinisch, Arbeitszeitverkürzung und sozialer Wandel. Der Kampf um die Achtstundenschicht in der deutschen und amerikanischen Eisen- und Stahlindustrie 1880–1929 (= Veröffentlichungen der Historischen Kommission zu Berlin, Vol. 65) (= Beiträge zu Inflation und Wiederaufbau in Deutschland und Europa 1914–1924, Vol. 6), Berlin/New York (de Gruyter) 1986, 640 p.

The work by the Japanese historian Hisashi Yano is the result of a thesis under Dietmar Petzina in Bochum[47]. Using mainly material from company archives Yano examines working and social conditions in Gutehoffnungshütte Aktienverein and Fried. Krupp Aktiengesellschaft up to 1939, so just before the start of the Second World War. The work combines business and regional history in the Ruhr with a study of state economic and social policy, which was dominated by rearmament, and the author relativises the argument that there was a general shortage of labour during this period. – Hermann Schulze, teacher at a senior school, describes in his Braunschweig thesis the influence of Ilseder Hütte on the economic and social structure of the city and southern district of Peine during the years from 1933 to 1952[48]. Using unpublished manuscripts and material from company, municipal and district archives the author traces the development of the firm through three periods of time, up to 1933, during the Third Reich, which is the main section, and the postwar period from 1945 to 1952. But he does not give a full history of the firm, concentrating only on certain aspects, presumably depending on the source material available and his own interests.

Associations are still a neglected area in business history research, and one of the main reasons is probably the lack of source material. Werner Bührer in his Hamburg thesis deals with the Iron and Steel Industry Association and the beginning of European integration from 1945 to 1952[49]. The steel industry on the Rhine and in the Ruhr was in a very bad situation in 1945, with demands for it to be separated and put under international control. Politically greatly disadvantaged, the sector was put under severe restrictions by the Allies, but the reorganization of an effective interest representation and the change in European policy objectives enabled it to recover and rehabilitate itself with astonishing speed. Bührer has engaged in extensive research for his thesis, and in addition to the Federal archives and the main state archive in Düsseldorf he has been able to use the private archives of the director of the association during that period, Salewski and the Günter Henle papers in the Klöckner archives.

The collected volume edited by Rudolf Judith contains 16 essays on the subject of 40 years of codetermination in the iron and steel industry[50]. Most of the authors are scholars close to the trade union movement. The separate solution to the codetermination question in 1947, when the industrial sectors were divided and a separate solution found for the iron and steel industry, is regarded as "half a victory", not a historical compromise. Other essays deal with the codetermination and the controversies over this in the coal, iron and steel industry from 1951 to

---

47 Hisashi Yano, Hüttenarbeiter im Dritten Reich. Betriebsverhältnisse und soziale Lage bei der Gutehoffnungshütte Aktienverein und der Fried. Krupp AG 1936 bis 1939 (= Zeitschrift für Unternehmensgeschichte, Supp. 34), Stuttgart (Steiner) 1986, 193 p.

48 Hermann Schulze, Der Einfluß der Ilseder Hütte auf die ökonomische und soziale Struktur in Stadt und Südkreis Peine 1933–1952, Braunschweig (Uni-Verlag) 1986, 379 p.

49 Werner Bührer, Ruhrstahl und Europa. Die Wirtschaftsvereinigung Eisen- und Stahlindustrie und die Anfänge der europäischen Integration 1945–1952 (= Schriftenreihe der Vierteljahreshefte für Zeitgeschichte, Vol. 53), München (Oldenburg) 1986, 236 p.

50 Rudolf Judith (Ed.), 40 Jahre Mitbestimmung. Erfahrungen, Probleme, Perspektiven, Köln (Bund) 1986, 293 p.

1956. Of interest to business historians are the case studies on Mannesmann, Ilseder Hütte and ARBED Saarstahl.

2.4 Mechanical Engineering

To mark the seventy-fifth anniversary of Maschinenfabrik Alfing Kessler GmbH, Eugen Hafner, company sociologist and university lecturer, has presented an interesting Festschrift[51]. Using interviews and evaluating material from the firm's archive he has written a good account of the history of this Baden-Württemberg company, in which he also mentions the period of the Third Reich, when the factory experienced a rapid upswing on account of its production of crankshafts for aero engines, which was only possible with the use of prisoners of war and foreign workers.

2.5 Production of Rail and Road Vehicles

After the first edition of the book "Axle, Wheel and Carriage", now a standard work, appeared in 1965, the editor Wilhelm Treue has given us the second, completely revised edition[52]. This is a collected volume in which different authors consider 5000 years of cultural and technical history illustrated by the production of axles. Of most interest to business historians is the article by the Cologne economic historian, Bernhard Kuhlmann, on the history of the Bergisch axle factory Fr. Kotz & Söhne in Wiehl, which also commissioned the book. The other articles, by twelve authors in all, are more concerned with technical history, and break new ground for scholarship, particularly as far as the early period is concerned.

A collected volume dedicated to Heinrich Büssing honours the work of the pioneer of commercial vehicle construction[53]. Two of the six authors have written articles of particular interest to business historians: Wilhelm Treue describes the economic development of the Büssing company, most of which now belongs to MAN, and the automobile historian Hans Christoph Graf von Seherr Thoss considers the historical and technical development of the Büssing commercial vehicles.

Ulrich Kubisch, journalist and member of the staff of the Berlin Transport and Technology Museum, deals with vehicle construction in Bremen and Varel up to 1929 in an exhibition catalogue[54]. This is a forgotten chapter of German

[51] Eugen Hafner, 75 Jahre Alfing Kurbelwellen, ed by Maschinenfabrik Alfing Keßler GmbH, (Aalen-Wasseralfingen) (publ. by the firm) 1986, 135 p.

[52] Wilhelm Treue (Ed.), Achse, Rad und Wagen. Fünftausend Jahre Kultur- und Technikgeschichte. Im Auftrag der Bergischen Achsenfabrik Fr. Kotz & Söhne in Wiehl, Göttingen (Vandenhoeck & Ruprecht) 1986, 448 p.

[53] Heinrich Büssing, Mensch - Werk - Erbe. Ed. by MAN Nutzfahrzeuge GmbH, München, Göttingen (Vandenhoeck & Ruprecht) 1986, 303 p.

[54] Ulrich Kubisch, Hansa-Lloyd: Borgward war nicht der Anfang ..., Automobilschau in Bremen und Varel bis 1929, Bremen (Steintor) 1986, 111 p.

automobile history. Norddeutsche Automobil- und Motorenfabrik (NAMAG), founded in 1906 and using the trade name Lloyd, merged in 1914 with Hansa-Automobil-Gesellschaft. During the First World War the company became the biggest producer of lorries for the armed forces, but it did not succeed in changing to peacetime production and in 1929 the trade names Hansa and Hansa-Lloyd and their firms were taken over by Carl Borgward. The two companies once employed more than 10,000 workers. Altogether this is a readable account with interesting illustrations.

The hundredth anniversary sumptuously celebrated by Daimler-Benz AG in 1986 gave rise to a number of interesting publications: the official two-volume history of the firm was written by journalists. Max Kruk and Gerold Lingnau dealt with the history of the firm[55], while Manfred Barthel and Gerold Lingnau wrote the technical history[56]. Both are well written, informative and full of detail. They not only give a comprehensive account of the research on this field to date, but also include original archive research. The authors also succeed in taking a critical look at their subject. - Richard Osswald was head of personnel at Daimler-Benz for seven years, and he has written the social history of Daimler-Benz AG from 1945 to 1985[57]. After 27 years in the company dealing with its social policy, he has provided a comprehensive survey. Interesting is also his statement that he believes both the employers and the trade unions are responsible for the sharper tone now evident in negotiations between the social partners. - The subject of the Third Reich is still often taboo in German company history and the work by Hans Pohl and his two pupils, Stephanie Habeth and Beate Brüninghaus, on Daimler-Benz AG from 1933 to 1945[58] ist the first such study to be commissioned by a firm on this period. The authors provide documentation, half of which consists of material from the Daimler-Benz archive, here published for the first time, and public archives, and half of an account and interpretation of the material, the latter deliberately kept brief. A detailed index of names, places and subjects concludes the book.

The history of the Metalworkers Union since 1945 is given in the book published by the union, regrettably without an author's name[59]. The work not only describes the emergence and development of IG Metall after 1945 but also its policy, which is part of the history of the union movement and the social history of the Federal Republic of Germany. The book is divided into three chronological sections: 1. The period of reconstruction (1945 to 1965/66), 2. Reforms and the economic crisis (1967 to 1980). These are almost identical with the text published by the Board of IG Metall in 1981, "90 Jahre Industriegewerkschaft" (90 Years of

---

55 Max Kruk/Gerold Lingnau, 100 Jahre Daimler-Benz. Das Unternehmen, Mainz (Hase & Koehler) 1986, 339 p.

56 Manfred Barthel/Gerold Lingnau, 100 Jahre Daimler-Benz. Die Technik, Mainz (Hase & Koehler) 1986, 329 p.

57 Richard Osswald, Lebendige Arbeitswelt. Die Sozialgeschichte der Daimler-Benz AG von 1945 bis 1985, Stuttgart (Deutsche Verlags-Anstalt) 1986, 394 p.

58 Hans Pohl/Stephanie Habeth/Beate Brüninghaus, Die Daimler-Benz AG in den Jahren 1933 bis 1945 (= Zeitschrift für Unternehmensgeschichte, Supp. 47), Stuttgart (Steiner) 1986, 394 p.

59 Industriegesellschaft Metall (Ed.), Kampf um soziale Gerechtigkeit, Mitbestimmung, Demokratie und Frieden. Die Geschichte der Industriegewerkschaft Metall seit 1945. Ein Bericht in Wort und Bild, Köln (Bund) 1986, 318 p.

an Industry Union). The third part is new and deals with the period from 1981 to 1985. The book concludes with an index of names and subjects, which contains helpful material, but no information on its sources.

2.6 Electrical Engineering

A centenary was also the occasion for Robert Bosch GmbH to issue several publications. The journalist Hans Konradin Herdt has written a portrait of the firm from 1861 to 1986[60]. The book is to mark the firm's hundredth anniversary and the 125th birthday of its founder, Robert Bosch. This Swabian family firm has succeeded in maintaining an individual company culture to today, as the author shows. The foundation, set up between 1962 and 1964, has preserved the independence of the modern technology firm. Robert Bosch was one of the first to introduce the eighthour day in 1906, for which he was sometimes wrongly accused of being "Red Bosch". In fact, his ideas always combined useful with social considerations. In view of the many excellent historical publications on Bosch the author was not able to add anything new on his subject. – The exhibition catalogue on Robert Bosch 1861 to 1942 and the company Bosch from 1886 to 1986[61] is concerned mainly with Robert Bosch the entrepreneur, the subject of a detailed biography by the future Federal President Theodor Heuss. The catalogue deals with specific themes in headline form, focussing mainly on Robert Bosch himself, who died in 1942, and secondly on the firm's technological developments.

The head of the Siemens Museum, Herbert Goetzeler, and the head of the company's archives, Lothar Schoen, have produced an attractively illustrated book on Wilhelm and Carl Friedrich von Siemens[62]. While the founders' generation has often been described, the authors have been able to draw on some unpublished material on the second generation from the company's archives and they present a very readable account.

Christoph Conrad deals with the subject of wealth sharing and capital formation for employees of Siemens AG between 1887 and 1945 in this revised version of his Bonn master's thesis[63]. At this time Siemens was located in the capital Berlin, and it was already one of the largest companies in the German Reich. Against that background many of the early social achievements are explicable, which were introduced in an attempt to halt the fluctuation, then much higher than today. Provision for old age in particular was designed to create continuity of employment. This work, which is highly theoretical, is supplemented by an

---

60 Hans Konradin Herdt, Bosch 1886–1986. Porträt eines Unternehmens, Stuttgart (Deutsche Verlags-Anstalt) 1986, 174 p.

61 Günter Bolle/Frank-Ulrich Breitsprecher/Hans Cronmüller et al., Robert Bosch 1861–1942. Bosch 1886–1986. Katalog zu der Jubiläums-Ausstellung im Robert-Bosch-Haus, Stuttgart, 24. September bis 16. November 1986, (Stuttgart) (publ. by the firm) 1986, 198 p.

62 Herbert Goetzeler/Lothar Schoen, Wilhelm und Carl Friedrich von Siemens. Die zweite Unternehmergeneration, ed. by Wilhelm Treue and Hans Pohl by order of Gesellschaft für Unternehmensgeschichte, Stuttgart (Steiner) 1986, 131 p.

63 Christoph Conrad, Erfolgsbeteiligung und Vermögensbildung der Arbeitnehmer bei Siemens (1847–1945) (= Zeitschrift für Unternehmensgeschichte, Supp. 36), Stuttgart (Steiner) 1986, 172 p.

introduction by Hans Pohl and Horst A. Wessel into the research project on wealth sharing and capital formation for employees between 1900 and 1945, which the German Society for Business History has been conducting for some years.

Heinz Nixdorf, who died suddenly in 1986 during a trade fair, was one of the German entrepreneurs who played a major part in the "economic miracle". This biography by the business journalist Klaus Kemper[64] describes Heinz Nixdorf as the most successful German entrepreneur of the postwar period, but not as the fiddler of genius he is often thought to be. Nixdorf founded his company in Essen in 1952, when he was still a physics student of 27, and as computer manufacturer he had soon made it one of the largest computer producers in Europe. He was always more successful as entrepreneur than as inventor.

2.7 Iron Goods, Sheet Metal and Other Metal Products

The history of the Rhineland and Westphalia in the nineteenth century is first and foremost a chapter of industrial and social history, and fifteen towns are planning to open museums on this subject. The first branch museum is in Solingen, and it was opened in 1986. A hundred years after the Hendrichs drop forge was founded to produce scissors, typical Solingen articles, in other words, the firm and its staff are to be made into a museum, and the original machines and scissors grinders have been preserved. The text of the museum guidebook[65] is brief and attractive and only a list of the most essential titles has been added.

The Mauser-Werke AG in Oberndorf/Neckar are one of the most important German weapons manufacturers. Although the book by Wolfgang Seel on the Mauser works "Von der Waffenschmiede zum Weltunternehmen" (From a Weapons Forge to a World Company)[66] is mainly for collectors of weapons, it is also of interest to the business historian. It includes material from numerous archives and gives a careful chronological account, with notes, of the history of the firm, which was founded in 1811. The author is also comparatively open in his account of the firm during the Third Reich. This is certainly not something one can take for granted in Federal German business history and it is welcome in view of the role the firm played in weapons production during that time. A large number of black and white photos of weapons and their production will ensure a warm welcome for the book from technical historians as well.

---

64 Klaus Kemper, Heinz Nixdorf – Eine deutsche Karriere, Landsberg/Lech (Verlag Moderne Industrie) 1986, 248 p.

65 Gesenkschmiede Hendrichs: Geschichte einer Solinger Fabrik (= Schriften des Rheinischen Industriemuseums, No. 2), Köln (Rheinland-Verlag) 1986, 92 p.

66 Wolfgang Seel, Mauser. Von der Waffenschmiede zum Weltunternehmen, Dietikon/Zürich (Stocker-Schmidt AG/Motorbuch Verlag) 1986, 147 p.

2.8 Chemicals, Pharmaceuticals, Woodworking and Processing

After the end of the Second World War the United States military government for Germany opened investigations against all the large German companies. The resultant reports are published in German translation and with editorial notes by the Documentation Office on NS Social Policy in Hamburg. Among the politically most significant investigations were those against IG-Farbenindustrie, and these are now generally available, not only in archives[67]. – Since the reports have been edited from a standpoint hostile to industry the interpretations cannot in every case be supported. – That also applies to the account by the journalist Otto Köhler of the history of IG-Farben[68]. The author was aiming to write a readable, popular book taking a critical approach to the history of the IG-Farben concern, once the largest chemical company in Europe. IG-Farben existed from 1925 to 1945, and it was finally split up by the Allies. The book, which relies mainly on the evaluation of the literature, concentrates on the fateful involvement of the management with the National Socialists, which had its terrible culmination in the establishment of the Buna works near Auschwitz.

Several *Festschriften* have appeared in recent years to mark the hundredth anniversary of pension funds, and Hoechst has now presented a brochure on this theme as well[69]. The Hoechst pension fund now has 64,000 members and 12,700 pensioners, making it one of the largest occupational pension funds in the Federal Republic of Germany. Unfortunately the publication deals only very briefly with the fund's history, and the main focus is on present benefits. The fund was set up in 1886, initially only for the firm's white collar workers, since a foundation had been set up in 1879 to make provision for the blue collar workers in old age. – Knoll Aktiengesellschaft in Ludwigshafen on the Rhine, now part of the BASF group, has published a well illustrated and interesting study of its pharmaceutical division by Ulrike Thomas to mark its centenary[70]. The company has a leading position in the manufacture of drugs and substances such as codeine, ephedrine and coffeine, and it now employs 6,000 people. – Renate Riedl-Ehrenberg, archivist at Sandoz AG in Basle, has produced a volume on the founders of Sandoz[71] for the highly praised series "Schweizer Pioniere der Wirtschaft und Technik" (Swiss Pioneers of Business and Technology). Alfred Kern (1850–1893) and Edouard Sandoz (1853–

---

[67] O. M. G. U. S. Militärregierung der Vereinigten Staaten für Deutschland. Ermittlungen gegen die I. G. Farbenindustrie AG – September 1945 – translated and revised by Dokumentationsstelle zur NS-Sozialpolitik Hamburg (= DIE ANDERE BIBLIOTHEK – special volume –), Nördlingen (Franz Greno) 1986, 492 p.

[68] Otto Köhler, ... und heute die ganze Welt. Die Geschichte der IG-Farben und ihrer Väter, Hamburg/Zürich (Rasch und Röhring) 1986, 350 p.

[69] Pensionskasse der Mitarbeiter der Hoechst AG (Ed.), Pensionskasse der Mitarbeiter der Hoechst AG, Versicherungsverein auf Gegenseitigkeit 1886–1986, Frankfurt am Main (publ. by the firm) 1986, 54 p.

[70] Ulrike Thomas, 100 Jahre im Dienst der Gesundheit, 1886–1986, ed. by Knoll Aktiengesellschaft, Ludwigshafen am Rhein (publ. by the firm) 1986, 159 p.

[71] Renate Riedl-Ehrenberg, Alfred Kern (1850–1893), Edouard Sandoz (1853–1928). Gründer der Sandoz AG, Basel (= Schweizer Pioniere der Wirtschaft und Technik, Vol. 44), ed. by Verein für wirtschaftshistorische Studien Zürich, Glarus (Tschudi) 1986, 90 p.

1928) founded the firm on the Rhine, that is now one of the largest pharmaceutical firms in Europe.

The exhibition catalogue to mark the 225th anniversary of Faber-Castell in Stein near Nuremberg, producer of pencils, has contributions by ten different authors[72]. One is an essay on the contract between the generations, in which Jürgen Franzke discusses the family business and the lifestyle of this entrepreneurial dynasty. This is of particular interest to social historians, for the Faber-Castell family is part of the Bavarian nobility and this is the eighth generation to own and direct the firm. It is the authors' express concern to provide an example of how company history can be written, namely with light and shade. A further essay with the same aim is that by Hans-Christian Täubrich on the history of the Faber-Castell firm, showing how it grew from small beginnings as a craft firm. Equally interesting is the contribution by Christian Koch on industrial discipline and social care for the workers since Lothar von Faber, that is, since 1839.

2.9 Textiles, Shoes

Gerhard Adelmann, Professor of Economic and Social History in Bonn, has written a number of articles on the history of trade and industry in the western part of the continent of Europe. The main regions he studies are North West Germany and her western neighbours, and the periods are the second half of the eighteenth century to the First World War. It is very welcome to have these 16 articles by Gerhad Adelmann, which were so far only available in widely scattered publications, in one volume[73]. Most of the essays are on the textile industry, and the author has consulted a large number of company archives in the Rhineland, in Westphalia, Holland and Belgium. He also studies the regional distribution of industry and social aspects of his subject.

As counterpart to the official company *Festschrift,* which came out in 1983 to mark the hundredth anniversary of the firm, Volkmar Leohold has issued a publication on working life in Bremer Wollkämmerei (a wool-combing plant)[74]. The author sees himself as close to the trade union movement, nevertheless the publication has met with criticism from the works council as well as the firm's management. It deals in detail with the widespread use of forced labour in this firm during the Second World War. At the end of the war foreign workers accounted for 45 percent of the workforce. The sources for the book are a large number of interviews with workers, from which many passages are given verbatim.

---

[72] Jürgen Franzke (Ed.), Das Bleistiftschloß. Familie und Unternehmen Faber-Castell in Stein. Eine Ausstellung anläßlich des 225jährigen Bestehens des Unternehmens Faber-Castell, München (H. Hugendubel) 1986, 155 p.

[73] Gerhard Adelmann, Vom Gewerbe zur Industrie im kontinentalen Westeuropa. Gesammelte Aufsätze zur regionalen Wirtschafts- und Sozialgeschichte (= Zeitschrift für Unternehmensgeschichte, Supp. 38), Stuttgart (Steiner) 1986, 419 p.

[74] Volkmar Leohold, Die Kämmeristen. Arbeitsleben auf der Bremer Wollkämmerei (= Schriftenreihe der Arbeiterkammer Bremen), Hamburg (VSA) 1986, 167 p.

Reto Jäger and three co-authors describe the change in working and living conditions through the advance of the cotton industry in a rural industrial area in the Zürich Oberland[75]. The publication draws on records and deals with the major role played by cotton spinning and weaving in this area and the gradual changeover from the cottage industry system to factory work during the period from 1750 to 1920. The case study covers social, cultural and political aspects, as well as the living conditions of workers and entrepreneurs, and with its many illustrations the book gives a very vivid picture of a traditional industrial region.

After a tradition of nearly a hundred years the Berlin fashion industry had achieved a worldwide reputation, and could stand beside Paris, mainly thanks to the Jewish clothing manufacturers. But the National Socialists destroyed the clothes industry in Berlin, by driving the Jews in the firms abroad. Those who failed to flee in time fell victim to the Nazi extermination policy. But although the Jews accounted for a major share in the women's clothing industry in Berlin in the nineteenth century, and they also introduced the serial manufacture of clothing, the role they played is generally overestimated, as Uwe Westphal shows in his history of the fashion industry in Berlin from 1836 to 1939[76]. This account is painstakingly researched and it gives a vivid account of the sector and its fate.

The small town of Hauenstein near Pirmasens is known mainly for its shoe industry. In this account of its hundred-year development in Hauenstein Eugen Klein, a local council official, has traced its growth from a craft sector in a book that is also attractively illustrated with old photographs[77]. The author has included a table listing all the shoe manufacturers from 1886 to 1986, and he also discusses the production methods and workers in detail. One chapter is concerned with foreign forced labour, workers sent from Poland, Russia and France. They were rather better off working in smaller firms than the forced labourers in the larger firms in the armaments industry, as many interviews show. Altogether this is a very readable account written with great love of detail.

2.10 Trade

Gerhard Ahrens, Professor of Social and Economic History in Hamburg, has described the relation between the state and the merchants in Hamburg during the first world economic crisis in 1857[78]. As a leading world trading centre Hamburg was particularly affected by the slump, which threatened to turn into a crisis of state as well. In such a situation the merchants had a very important role to play.

---

75 Reto Jäger et al., Baumwollgarn als Schicksalsfaden. Wirtschaftliche und gesellschaftliche Entwicklungen in einem ländlichen Industriegebiet (Zürcher Oberland) 1750–1920, Zürich (Chronos) 1986, 493 p.

76 Uwe Westphal, Berliner Konfektion und Mode. 1836–1939. Die Zerstörung einer Tradition (= Stätten der Geschichte Berlins, Vol. 14), Berlin (Edition Hentrich Berlin) 1986, 208 p.

77 Eugen Klein, 100 Jahre Schuhindustrie in Hauenstein: 1886–1986, ed. by Gemeinde Hauenstein, Hauenstein (publ. by the ed.) 1986, 252 p.

78 Gerhard Ahrens, Krisenmanagement 1857. Staat und Kaufmannschaft in Hamburg während der ersten Weltwirtschaftskrise (= Veröffentlichungen des Vereins für Hamburgische Geschichte, Vol. 28), Hamburg (Verein für Hamburgische Geschichte) 1986, 136 p.

This is the first detailed account, drawing on records and literature, of what was a major event for Hamburg in the nineteenth century. The book includes an index of names and companies, which will be very useful for those needing to find something quickly.

Harald Pohlmann has also written on the history of trade in Hamburg, giving an account of the life and work of the Hamburg merchant and shipowner Richard C. Krogmann (1859–1932)[79]. Krogmann owned the company Wachsmuth & Krogmann, and he had a major influence on technical and social development in the shipping sector in Hamburg. Pohlmann has used the Krogmann papers deposited in the state archive in Hamburg for his history of the life and family of Richard C. Krogmann, as well as the onesided positive account of the father by his son. He has also used the company archives of the firm, which is one of the oldest shipping companies in Hamburg, and his detailed account of the financial development deserves special mention. The biography divides Krogmann's activities into sailing and rowing, work as a merchant for his own firm, honorary work for the professional associations and finally his political involvement and his carefully cultivated relations to the Kaiser and his family.

Ludwig Berekoven, Professor of Marketing, International Marketing and Trade in Nuremberg, has written a history of the German retail trade[80], which is impressive both for the precision of the narrative and its readibility. Against the background of the overall economic and political situation the author gives a terse account of the major developments in the retail trade from its smallest beginnings to the present. A large number of retail firms are mentioned by name and quoted as examples of new developments in the sector.

2.11 Publishing and Printing

Georg Thieme, publisher of medical books, formerly in Leipzig and now in Stuttgart, has asked a member of its staff, Christian Staehr, to write a *Festschrift* to mark the firm's 100th anniversary[81]. The source material for this history of the firm is the company's main periodical, which is preserved complete since 1875, postwar correspondence, reminiscences by the publisher and the archives of the German Book Trade Association. This has provided the basis for a well written and well illustrated history, the main focus of which is on the firm's many periodicals. The family firm has only been headed by three persons during its 100 years of activity, and altogether they have looked after more than 20,000 authors.

---

79 Harald Pohlmann, Richard C. Krogmann 1859–1932. Leben und Leistung eines hamburgischen Kaufmanns und Reeders (= Beiträge zur Geschichte Hamburgs, Vol. 27), Hamburg (Verein für Hamburgische Geschichte) 1986, 360 p.

80 Ludwig Berekoven, Geschichte des deutschen Einzelhandels, Frankfurt am Main (Deutscher Fachverlag) 1986, 175 p.

81 Christian Staehr, Spurensuche. Ein Wissenschaftsverlag im Spiegel seiner Zeitschriften, 1886–1986, Stuttgart/New York (Thieme) 1986, 144 p.

Another publisher to celebrate a centenary in 1986 was S. Fischer, one of whose most celebrated authors was Thomas Mann. To mark the occasion Fischer have produced a bibliography and a work on the design of the firm's books, and a history of the firm, written by Reiner Stach[82]. The founder of the firm, Samuel Fischer, owned a bookshop and originally came from Hungary. The firm is now one of today's leading literary publishers, and has played a major role in establishing modern literature. Fischer secured a viable foundation for his business with profitable business publications. The location of the firm has changed several times: in 1936 it was in Berlin and Vienna, later in Stockholm as well, then it moved to Amsterdam and London and finally New York; since 1950 it has been domiciled in Frankfurt am Main.

2.12 Trade and Handicrafts

The world famous clocks from the Black Forest have a 300-year tradition, covering both the cottage industry and the clock factories. The Black Forest clockmakers have succeeded in keeping their sector free of foreign capital and maintaining demand in numerous countries throughout Europe for a steadily growing domestic production with the often hard methods of selling on the streets. This knowledgeable account of 300 years of a sector, which is mainly one of craft firms, has been written by Helmut Kahlert[83]. It does go up to the present, but the main emphasis is on the cottage industry and the early factories. The author, Professor of Economics at the Technical College in Furtwangen and advisor to the clock museum there, has written a text that is easy to follow, well documented and illustrated, and which discusses a large number of individual firms in detail.

2.13 Transportation

The biggest shipyards in the Federal Republic of Germany, Hapag-Lloyd AG, has issued two publications to mark the centenary of two of its major routes from German or West European ports to the Far East and Australia[84]. The lines opened in Bremerhaven under the aegis of the Reich Chancellor, Otto von Bismarck, since the government had instigated the shipping routes to the Far East and Australia at the request of German industry and trade. Norddeutscher Lloyd won the tender and operated the line initially with government assistance.

Dieter Schneider, chief editor of now the second largest trade union in the German Trade Union Federation, the Public Service and Transport Workers Union, has described the beginnings of a central organization for local authority

---

[82] Reiner Stach, 100 Jahre S. Fischer Verlag 1886–1986. Kleine Verlagsgeschichte, Frankfurt a. M. (publ. by the firm) 1986, 207 p.

[83] Helmut Kahlert, 300 Jahre Schwarzwälder Uhrenindustrie, Gernsbach (Casimir Katz) 1986, 268 p.

[84] Otto J. Seiler, Einhundert Jahre Australienfahrt 1886–1986. Schiffahrtspolitik und Planung, Einhundert Jahre Ostasienfahrt der Hapag-Lloyd AG 1886–1986. Schiffahrtspolitik und Planung, (Hamburg/Bremen) (publ. by Hapag-Lloyd AG) (1986), 110 p.; 144 p.

and transport workers from 1896/97 to 1906/07[85]. The efforts to set up a central association for transport workers that would cover the whole of Germany, started, like those for many other organizations, in Berlin after a labour dispute. A few months later efforts began in Altenburg to group the many local organizations which had come into being since the 1880s into a central association, which was also to be located in the Reich capital. It was not until 1929/30 that the two merged to form the Federation of Workers in Public Enterprises and Passenger and Goods Transport, which was renamed the Public Service and Transport Workers Union after the Second World War. This well written but sparsely illustrated account is based on minutes of meetings, annual reports, official publications, newspaper reports and secondary literature.

2.14 Insurance Companies

Carl Widmer, former Director-General of Helvetia Schweizerische Feuerversicherungs-Gesellschaft, a company with which he has been associated for altogether 54 years, has produced a publication to mark the 125th anniversary of this fire insurance company in St. Gallen[86]. The work concentrates mainly on the last 25 years. As frequently happens with fire insurance companies the firm was founded after a major fire, in this case in Glarus in 1861. The biggest claim the company ever had to face was for the earthquake in San Francisco in 1906, after which it withdrew from US business until 1957. This knowledgeable publication mentions other failures, like offering holiday weather insurance, and reversals, although the Swiss insurance business as a whole has always had a steady growth.

The journalist Arno Surminski and the legal advisor to the Federation of Public Life and Third Party Insurers, Dieter Vogelsang, have written a Festschrift to mark the 75th anniversary of the Federation[87]. The publication is lavishly and imaginatively illustrated, which was certainly not easy with such a subject, and it is impressive for its attractive style despite the rather dry material.

2.15 Institutions

Four publications have appeared to mark the 125th anniversary of the Federation of German Chambers of Industry and Commerce. One is the bibliography compiled by Sigrid Ernst and Klara van Eyll and others on the history and

---

[85] Dieter Schneider, Anfänge: Zentralorganisation der Gemeinde- und Transportarbeiter 1896/97–1906/07, Stuttgart (Courier) 1986, 152 p.

[86] Carl Widmer, 125 Jahre Helvetia Feuer St. Gallen. Ausschnitte und Betrachtungen, St. Gallen (publ. by Helvetia Schweizerische Feuerversicherungs-Gesellschaft) 1986, 177 p.

[87] Arno Surminski/Dieter Vogelsang, Welche Zeiten! 1911–1986. 75 Jahre Verband öffentlicher Lebens- und Haftpflichtversicherer. Ed. by Verband öffentlicher Lebens- und Haftpflichtversicherer, (Düsseldorf) (publ. by the ed.) (1986), 109 p.

organization of the chambers of industry and commerce and their federation[88], which will provide a welcome aid to research. - Wilfried Reininghaus, Klara van Eyll and others have also issued a collection of sources on the history of the federation, also intended as the basis for further research on this subject and compiled from chamber archives from 1861 to 1918[89]. - For the same occasion a historical exhibition has been designed for which the catalogue has now been published[90]. A large number of documents are added to the text, making this a historical documentation in pictures of the history of the chambers. Theodor Frey, a wine merchant, chairman of the trade guild of the town of Eberbach on the Neckar, made an application in 1860 to the Baden trade federation for a trade federation to be set up in which all the states in the Zollverein (Customs Union) would be represented. The aim of the federation would be to establish the same measures, weights, currencies, a binding code of trade law and foreign representation throughout Germany. - The 125th anniversary of the Federation of German Chambers of Industry and Commerce, which was established as a result of Frey's initiative, was the occasion for publication of a biographical sketch of the initiator, drawing on his own memoirs[91]. These were published in 1896, a few months before his death, and are now reissued in abbreviated form with a commentary by Roland Vetter.

The professions are rarely the subject of business history publications, but in 1972 Wilhelm Treue published the first article on the society of solicitors in Hamburg, founded in 1822 by Dr. Johann Carl Knauth. He has now continued this research down to the present, and taken up legal problems of more general interest[92]. He also discusses the work organization in a legal firm, which at present consists of seven solicitors.

To mark the 60th anniversary of the renowned economic research institute, the Deutsches Institut für Wirtschaftsforschung in Berlin, which played a major part in the compilation of the German national accounts and the input-output accounts, a publication has appeared by Rolf Krengel[93]. The author has spent more than 35 years in the Deutsches Institut für Wirtschaftsforschung, and although this probably meant a rather less objective account of the institute's history, the Institute felt that the benefit of having the records evaluated and interpreted by a

---

88 Sigrid Ernst/Klara van Eyll et al., Bibliographie zur Geschichte und Organisation der Industrie- und Handelskammern und des Deutschen Industrie- und Handelstages, ed. by Deutscher Industrie- und Handelstag (= DIHT-Materialien zur Geschichte), Bonn (publ. by the ed.) 1986, 304 p.

89 Wilfried Reininghaus/Klara van Eyll et al., Quellen zur Geschichte des Deutschen Industrie- und Handelstages in Kammerarchiven 1861–1918, ed. by Deutscher Industrie- und Handelstag (= DIHT-Materialien zur Geschichte), Bonn (publ. by the ed.) 1986, 158 p.

90 DIHT, Bonn (Ed.), Zeugnisse der Zeit. 125 Jahre Deutscher Industrie- und Handelstag, Bonn (publ. by the ed.) 1986, 113 p.

91 Roland Vetter, Theodor Frey. Sein Leben und seine Zeit. Eine biographische Skizze des Initiators des Deutschen Handelstages unter Verwendung seiner Lebenserinnerungen. Special edition for the 125th years' DIHT-Jubilee, Eberbach/Heidelberg (publ. by the firm) 1986, 144 p.

92 Wilhelm Treue, Geschichte einer Hamburgischen Anwaltssozietät. Von der Gründung der Kanzlei im Jahre 1822 bis zur Gegenwart (= Zeitschrift für Unternehmensgeschichte, Supp. 48), Stuttgart (Steiner) 1986, 84 p.

93 Rolf Krengel, Das Deutsche Institut für Wirtschaftsforschung (Institut für Konjunkturforschung) 1925 bis 1979, Berlin/München (Duncker & Humblot) 1986, 230 p.

member of its research staff, who with his greater prior knowledge would approach the task quite differently from an outsider, would be a greater benefit. Krengel also visited a large number of other archives for his account, including that in Potsdam. Founded in 1925 as the Institut für Konjunkturforschung, this was the first non-university research institute in Middle Europe concerned with economic policy and economic theory. A detailed chronological breakdown enables the reader quickly to find his way in this detailed account.

Rolf-Jürgen Gleitsmann, technical historian in Stuttgart, has written an attractive account of the establishment of the nuclear research centre in Karlsruhe, drawing on a wide range of documents[94]. The history of nuclear power has been largely neglected so far by historians, and Gleitsmann shows how the decision was taken in the very last minute by the Federal Chancellor, Konrad Adenauer, to locate the centre in Karlsruhe and not in Munich. Munich was then chosen as the location for the first German nuclear reactor by Professor Werner Heisenberg, Nobel prize winner and nuclear scientist.

---

94 Rolf-Jürgen Gleitsmann, Im Widerstreit der Meinungen: Zur Kontroverse um die Standortfindung für eine deutsche Reaktorstation (1950–1955). Ein Beitrag zur Gründungsgeschichte des Kernforschungszentrums Karlsruhe und zu einem Kapitel deutscher Kernenergiegeschichte (publ. by the Kernforschungszentrum Karlsruhe) 1986, 286 p.

A Review of the New Literature on Banking History

Monika Pohle

To accompany the exhibition organised by the Braunschweig Chamber of Industry and Commerce and the Norddeutsche Landesbank on the Braunschweig Stock Exchange: "From Stormy Beginnings to Far-Reaching Change 1686–1934" (Braunschweiger Börse. Von stürmischer Gründungszeit zum tiefgreifenden Wandel 1686–1934)[1] in December 1986 Rainer Dube wrote a short history of the Braunschweig stock exchange during this period in which he also considers the economic history of the city generally. As well as a large number of illustrations the brochure contains a list of the joint stock corporations founded in Braunschweig between 1800 and 1934, with the date of their establishment and a bibliography. There are no references or footnotes to the text.

In 1909/1910 Paul Wallich, whose father Hermann Wallich was a member of the Board of Managing Directors of the Deutsche Bank and played a major part in the establishment of the Deutsche Überseeische Bank, travelled to visit the South American branches of the Banco Alemán Transatlántico. The journal he kept during the trip has now been published with an introduction by Henry C. Wallich and entitled "Banco Alemán Transatlántico. Eine Reise durch Südamerika" (Banco Alemán Transatlántico. A Journey through South America)[2]. Paul Wallich's observations are of a highly personal nature and of mainly biographical interest.

Jacques Attali, personal advisor to the French President François Mitterand and author of several books on political, economic and historical subjects, wrote a biography of Siegmund G. Warburg in 1985[3], which is now available in German translation: "Siegmund G. Warburg. Das Leben eines grossen Bankiers" (Sieg mund G. Warburg. The Life of a Great Banker)[4]. Written like an novel, the account always combines the description of Warburg as a person with an account of his position in the overall political and economic situation. Individual business transactions are described in great detail. The biography is based i.a. on the as yet unpublished notes of Max M. Warburg and notes by Siegmund G. Warburg

[1] Rainer Dube, Braunschweiger Börse. Von stürmischer Gründungszeit zum tiefgreifenden Wandel 1686–1934. Eine Ausstellung der Industrie- und Handelskammer Braunschweig und der Norddeutschen Landesbank in der Hauptniederlassung Dankwardstraße vom 2.–16. Dezember 1986, (Druckerei Gühne), Braunschweig 1986, 56 S.

[2] Paul Wallich, Banco Alemán Transatlántico. Eine Reise durch Südamerika, mit einer Einführung von Henry C. Wallich, (v. Hase & Koehler), Mainz 1986, 300 S.

[3] Jaques Attali, Un homme d'influence – Sir Siegmund C. Warburg (1902–1982), Paris 1985.

[4] Jaques Attali, Siegmund G. Warburg. Das Leben eines großen Bankiers, (ECON), Düsseldorf, Wien 1986, 504 S.

German Yearbook on Business History 1987

himself. It includes an index of names and subjects and an bibliography, but no references or footnotes.

The history of banking in Hamburg ("Hamburger Bankengeschichte") by Manfred Pohl[5] is the first full account of the history of banking in Hamburg from the Middle Ages to today. It deals mainly with the earlier and present member banks of the Hamburg Banking Association, but considers the other institutions as well as far as this is necessary for the general overview.The extensive source material on which the work is based is from the Hamburg state archives, the archives of Berenberg, Gossler & Co., the Lutteroth family archives, the Warburg archives and the historical archive of Deutsche Bank AG. The work includes a list of the present members of the Hamburg Banking Association and a chronology of the main dates in Hamburg banking history from the founding of the Hamburg stock exchange in 1558 to 1984.

To mark its centenary the Pfälzische Hypothekenbank has published a *Festschrift* in two volumes[6]. Volume 1 is an enlarged version of the jubilee publication on the bank's 75th anniversary: "Epochen einer Bankgeschichte" (Epochs in a Bank's History)[7], while volume 2 contains articles on monetary and financial history in the Palatinate from Roman times to the 1920s; the authors are Heinrich Chantraíne, Bernhard Kirchgässner, Pirmin Spiess, Hans Ammerich, Joachim Kermann and Ernst Otto Bräunche. The first volume is richly illustrated and both have numerous tables and maps.

In his book on vocational training in the German savings bank sector ("Berufsbildung in der deutschen Sparkassenorganisation")[8], Günter Ashauer gives a brief review of this aspect of the history of the savings banks from their emergence and the establishment of their central organisations, through the separation of the training of their bank officials from that of local officials, to the present three-stage basic and advanced training system. The work is a revised version of an article on the history of vocational training in German banking ("Berufsbildung in der deutschen Kreditwirtschaft – ein geschichtlicher Überblick")[9], written in 1983.

The history of the Deutsche Girozentrale – Deutsche Kommunalbank – from its establishment as a branch of the Deutsche Zentral-Giroverband in 1918 to today is the subject of Gerhard Zweig's book "Die Deutsche Girozentrale – Deutsche

[5] Manfred Pohl, Hamburger Bankengeschichte, (v. Hase & Koehler), Mainz 1986, 264 S.

[6] Festschrift zum 100jährigen Bestehen der Pfälfzischen Hypothekenbank 1886–1986, Teil 1: Epochen einer Bankgeschichte, Teil 2: Beiträge zur Pfälzischen Geld- und Finanzgeschichte, hrsg. v. Hans Ammerich und Otto Roller (Veröffentlichungen der Pfälzischen Gesellschaft zur Förderung der Wissenschaften in Speyer, Band 79), hrsg. v. d. Pfälzischen Hypothekenbank AG Ludwigshafen u. a., (Verlag der Pfälzischen Gesellschaft zur Förderung der Wissenschaften), Speyer 1986, 162 S. (1. Teil) und 268 S. (2. Teil).

[7] Epochen einer Bankgeschichte, hrsg. v. d. Pfälzischen Hypothekenbank AG, Speyer 1961.

[8] Günter Ashauer, Berufsbildung in der deutschen Sparkassenorganisation. Ein geschichtlicher Überblick (Sparkassen in der Geschichte, Abteilung 3: Forschung, Bd. 1), (Deutscher Sparkassenverlag), Stuttgart 1986, 139 S.

[9] Günter Ashauer, Host Liefeith, Klaus Weiser, Berufsbildung in der deutschen Kreditwirtschaft – ein geschichtlicher Überblick (Studien zur Entwicklung der deutschen Kreditwirtschaft, Bd. 4), Mainz 1983.

Kommunalbank -"[10]. The review of the periods 1918–1945 and 1945–1964 is followed by a description of the DGZ in Frankfurt am Main and a comparison of the time before and after 1945.

On 4 and 5 September 1985 the Society for the Promotion of Research into Savings and Giro Banks in Bonn held its 1985 historical symposium on the subject: "The Public Obligation of the Savings Banks and their Historical Development" (Der öffentliche Auftrag der Sparkassen in der historischen Entwicklung)[11]. The conference book edited by Jürgen Mura arranges the contributions historically (Friedrich-Wilhelm Henning on the historical roots), in the age of industrialisation (Josef Wysocki), the modern savings banks (Reinfrid Fischer) and systemativally (the savings banks and competition by Albin Gladen).

The conference volume from the 1986 symposium on savings bank history, which dealt with the development of the savings banks to universal banks[12], follows the various phases of this development, from the beginnings to 1908 (Hans Pohl), from 1908 to 1931 (Josef Wysocki) from 1931 to 1958 (Jürgen Mura) and from 1958 to today (Ingo Ellgering). In the final paper Gustav Adolf Schröder deals with the question: Are savings banks the same as universal banks?

The 1986 German Savings Bank Conference was held on 15 and 16 May in Hamburg. The papers and discussions are now published by the Federation of German Savings and Giro Banks[13], and they deal mainly with questions of the form under public law, the use of new technology in customer service and problems of funding.

Josef Wysocki, Professor of History in Salzburg, has specialised on savings bank history, and together with Volker Wehrmann he has written a *Festschrift* to mark the 200th anniversary of the Detmold savings bank, the oldest in Germany: "Lippe: Leben – Arbeit – Geld 1786–1986" (Life, Work and Money on the Lippe, 1786–1986)[14]. In the first part Josef Wysocki shows that the Detmold savings bank really is the oldest of its kind in Germany, and his remarks on the history of this bank in particular and German savings banks in general are followed by articles by Volker Wehrmann on the economic history of the Lippe district.

The *Festschrift* to mark the 150th anniversary of the Vereinigte Sparkassen in the Weilheim district of Upper Bavaria, also by Josef Wysocki[15] documents the

---

[10] Gerhard Zweig, Die Deutsche Girozentrale - Deutsche Kommunalbank - , (Deutscher Sparkassenverlag), Stuttgart 1986, 182 S.

[11] Der öffentliche Auftrag der Sparkassen in der historischen Entwickung. Sparkassenhistorisches Symposium 1985 (Sparkassen in der Geschichte, Abt. 1: Dokumentation, Bd. 1), hrsg. v. d. Gesellschaft zur Förderung der wissenschaftlichen Forschung über das Spar- und Girowesen e.V., (Deutscher Sparkassenverlag), Stuttgart 1986, 113 S.

[12] Die Entwicklung der Sparkassen zu Universalkreditinstituten. Sparkassenhistorisches Symposium 1986 (Sparkassen in der Geschichte, Abt. 1: Dokumentation, Bd. 2), hrsg. v. d. Gesellschaft zur Förderung der wissenschaftlichen Forschung über das Spar- und Girowesen e.V., (Deutscher Sparkassenverlag), Stuttgart 1987, 140 S.

[13] Leistung durch Wettbewerb. Deutscher Sparkassenverlag 1986, hrsg. v. Deutschen Sparkassen- und Giroverband e. V., (Deutscher Sparkassenverlag), Stuttgart 1986, 173 S.

[14] Josef Wysocki, Volker Wehrmann, Lippe. Leben - Arbeit - Geld 1786–1986, hrsg. v. d. Sparkasse Detmold - älteste Sparkasse Deutschlands - aus Anlaß ihres 200jährigen Jubiläums, (Deutscher Sparkassenverlag), Stuttgart 1986, 351 S.

[15] Josef Wysocki, Land und Zeit 1836–1986, hrsg. v. d. Vereinigten Sparkassen im Landkreis Weilheim in Oberbayern zum 150jährigen Jubiläum am 4. Dezember 1986, (ESTA-Druck), Weilheim 1986, 273 S.

main principle on which the savings banks operate: their ties to their local district. The rise of the savings banks is therefore an intrinsic part of the economic and social history of their region.

In 1986 many savings banks celebrated a jubilee. Most of them could look back on an tradition lasting 150 years, and the following institutions documented their history in voluminous publications which go far beyond the picture documentation usual in such anniversary volumes: the Amberg district savings bank[16], the Kaiserslautern savings bank[17], the Landau district and municipal savings bank[18], the Lauf savings bank[19], the Main-Taunus district savings bank (75 years)[20] and the Melle savings bank[21].

The Austrian Postal Savings Bank held its first symposium on 5 December 1985, and the conference book edited by Roland Löffler and Michael Wagner entitled "Stillstand ist Rückschritt. Der erste Postsparkassen-Gouverneur 1910" (To Stand Still is to Regress. The First Postal Savings Bank Governor in 1910)[22] contains the conference papers, each provided with a critical commentary, i.a. on the first governor, Rudolf Schuster-Bennett, the social structure of savers and a comparison of the bank with its model, the British post office savings bank. In addition to many illustrations and tables the book contains extensive notes, a list of sources and an index of names and subjects.

To mark the 100th anniversary of the Raiffeisen banks in Austria the Austrian Raiffeisen association has published an *Festschrift* on Raiffeisen and his work in Austria.[23] The contents include a facsimile print of the book "Die Darlehenskassen-Vereine" by Friedrich Wilhelm Raiffeisen, written in 1887[24], a historical documentation in pictures and the history of the Austrian Raiffeisen organisation from its beginnings to the present. The last part is based on extensive source

---

16 Von der historischen Ratstrinkstube zur Kreissparkasse Amberg. Die Geschichte des umgebauten und renovierten Hauses Marktplatz 3 in Amberg, hrsg. v. d. Kreissparkasse Amberg, (Amberger Zeitung), Amberg 1986, 395 S.

17 Sparkasse zu Kaiserslautern 1836–1986. 150 Jahre Stdtsparkasse. Aus den Anfängen, hrsg. v. ders. aus Anlaß ihres 150jährigen Bestehens, (Georg Gehringer GmbH), Kaiserslautern 1986, 132 S.

18 Kreis- und Stadtsparkasse Landau, seit 150 Jahren. Jubiläumsbericht 1836–1986, hrsg. v. ders., (Pfälzische Verlagsanstalt), Landau 1986, 107 S.

19 150 Jahre Sparkasse in Lauf (Mitteilungsblatt für Lauf a. d. Pegnitz, Sonderausgabe zum Sparkassenjubiläum), Schweig 1986, 107 S.

20 Menschen und Mächte. Geschichte und Geschichten zwischen Main und Taunus. Ein Erinnerungsbuch zum 75. Jahr des Bestehens der Kreissparkasse der Main-Taunus-Kreises, hrsg. v. ders., (Deutscher Sparkassenverlag), Stuttgart 1986, 255 S.

21 Begegnungen im Grönegau. 150 Jahre Sparkasse Melle, mit Beiträgen von Maria Otte, Fritz-Gerd Mittelstädt, Werner Nagel, hrsg. v. d. Kreissparkasse Melle, (Deutscher Sparkassenverlag), Stuttgart 1986, 188 S.

22 Stillstand ist Rückschritt. Der erste Postsparkassen-Gouverneur 1910, hrsg. v. Roland Löffler, Michael Wagner im Auftrag der Österreichischen Postsparkasse, (Agens-Werk Geyer + Reisser), Wien 1986, 95 S.

23 Raiffeisen und sein Werk in Österreich, hrsg. v. Österreichischen Raiffeisenverband, (Rauchdruck), Innsbruck 1986, 439 S.

24 Friedrich-Wilhelm Raiffeisen, Die Darlehnskassen-Vereine als Mittel zur Abhilfe der Noth der ländlichen Bevölkerung, sowie auch der städtischen Handwerker und Arbeiter, 5. Aufl., Neuwied 1887.

material, according to the editor, but unfortunately he gives us neither references nor a list of titles or sources.

Oswald Hahn from Erlangen-Nuremberg, a specialist in the study of banking and finance, gave the address on the occasion of the jubilee celebration to mark the 100th anniversary of the Trommetsheim Raiffeisenkasse, and this is now published in book form[25]. The author discusses the role of the classical Raiffeisen bank today.

Several cooperative banks issued smaller *Festschriften* on their jubilees in 1986 in which historical information plays rather a minor role while most of the publication consists of modern pictures. However, the *Festschrift* by the Süderlügum Raiffeissenbank[26] deserves the interest of banking historians for its extensive source documentation.

The account of the emergence and development of the universal banking system ("Entstehung und Entwicklung des Universalbankensystems") by Manfred Pohl[27] gives a survey of the development of every sector of German banking from its beginnings to the present, with the changes in the sector caused by concentration and crises. The author concludes with a survey of the expected effects of technical change through computerisation. The book includes a chronology of the main dates in the development of German banking from the 16th century to the modern age.

Inge Morawetz, a sociologist, aims to show the connection between economic and political power in her book "Die verborgene Macht. Personelle Verflechtungen zwischen Großbanken, Industrie und Unternehmerverbänden in Österreich" (Hidden Power. Multiple Office-holding in Major Banks, Industry and Employers Associations in Austria)[28], by examining the interlinking at the top of Austria's business life as an indicator of concentration of power. She believes that the basis of this process of concentration of power is the large state share in business in Austria, and she dismisses other theories held by Austrian sociologists with the remark that they are in any case dependent on their sources of funds in what they say.

Heinz-Peter Spahn in his work on the history of theory "Stagnation in der Geldwirtschaft. Dogmengeschichte, Theorie und Politik aus keynesianischer Sicht" (Stagnation in Finance. The History of Dogma, Theory and Politics in the

---

25 Oswald Hahn, Die klassische Raiffeisenbank: Die Dorfbank als Nostalgie oder Notwendigkeit?, Festvortrag anläßlich der Jubiläumsveranstaltung zum 100jährigen Bestehen der Raiffeisenkasse Trommetsheim e.HG. ... am 4. Juli 1986, (Veröffentlichungen des Lehrstuhls für Allgemeine, Bank- und Versicherungs-Betriebswirtschaftslehre an der Friedrich-Alexander-Universität Erlangen-Nürnberg, H. 41), Nürnberg 1986, 32 S.

26 Raiffeisenbank eG Süderlügum 1911–1986, hrsg. v. ders., (Clausen & Bosse), Süderlügum 1986, 143 S.

27 Manfred Pohl, Entstehung und Entwicklung des Universalbankensystems. Konzentration und Krise als wichtige Faktoren (Schriftenreihe des Instituts für bankhistorische Forschung e. V., Bd. 7), (Fritz Knapp Verlag), Frankfurt am Main 1986, 199 S.

28 Inge Morawetz, Die verborgene Macht. Personelle Verflechtungen zwischen Großbanken, Industrie und Unternehmerverbänden in Österreich (Campus Forschung, Band 499), (Campus Verlag), Frankfurt am Main 1986, 200 S.

Keynesian View)[29] deals with the interrelation of stagnation, Keynesian economics and supply policy, taking a critical look at both supporters and opponents of the Keynesian approach to our economic problems.

The authors of volume 1 of the "Weltwirtschaftslehre", which deals with foreign trade and monetary policy[30], offer an analysis of key problems in international economic policy. They explain theoretical causalities, using actual economic policy decisions as examples, with the aim of suggesting possible solutions.

The South West German Central Cooperative Bank has published a collective volume with essays by Hermann Göppe on the general bases of the banking business, Helmut Guthardt on the Third World debt crisis, Arnold Kremer on interest and exchange rates as cyclical determinants and Egon Kremer on banks between regulation and competition[31].

In 1986 the third volume of the handbook of European economic and social history: "Europäische Wirtschafts- und Sozialgeschichte vom ausgehenden Mittelalter bis zur Mitte des 17. Jahrhunderts", covering the period from the late Middle Ages to the midseventeenth century, appeared, edited by Hermann Kellenbenz[32]. Chapter 3 (Services) of Part I, the European Economy and Society from 1350–1650, contains a section on money and banking, which deals with the problems of international payments, the growth in means of payment and the expansion of banking during this period. A large section is also devoted to an account of private and public banks, the development of trade fairs, banking centres and stock exchanges. The second part of the volume, which deals with the development of economy and society in European regions, is by various authors and it deals with the history of banking for the individual countries under a number of headings, such as coins, money and banking (p. 465), investment and capital (p. 600) and the financial system and taxation (p. 702).

"Wandel und Probleme in der internationalen Exportfinanzierung" (Change and Problems in International Export Finance) was the subject of the second international symposium organised by the Institute for Bankhistorical Research on 6 April 1984 in Frankfurt am Main. The papers and discussions are now available in volume form[33]. Jean-François Bergier from the University of Zurich

---

[29] Heinz-Peter Spahn, Stagnation in der Geldwirtschaft. Dogmengeschichte, Theorie und Politik aus keynesianischer Sicht (Arbeitsberichte des Wissenschaftszentrums Berlin, Internationales Institut für Management und Verwaltung/Arbeitsmarktpolitik), (Campus Verlag), Frankfurt am Main 1986, 304 S.

[30] Hans Hinrich Glismann, Ernst-Jürgen Horn, Sighart Nehring, Roland Vaubel, Weltwirtschaftslehre. Eine problemorientierte Einführung. I Außenhandels- und Währungspolitik, 3. u. überarb. Aufl., (Vandenhoeck & Ruprecht), Göttingen 1986, 269 S.

[31] Beiträge zur Bankentheorie und Wirtschaftspolitik, mit Beitr. v. Hermann Göppel, Helmut Guthardt, Arnold Kremer, Egon Kremer, hrsg. v. d. Südwestdeutschen Genossenschafts-Zentralbank AG, (Fritz Knapp Verlag), Frankfurt am Main 1986, 79 S.

[32] Handbuch der Europäischen Wirtschafts- und Sozialgeschichte, Bd. 3: Europäische Wirtschafts- und Sozialgeschichte vom ausgehenden Mittelalter bis zur Mitte des 17. Jahrhunderts, hrsg. v. Wolfram Fischer, Jan A. van Houtte, Hermann Kellenbenz, Ilja Mieck und Friedrich Vittinghoff (Klett-Cotta), Stuttgart 1986, darin: Geld- und Kreditwesen, S. 305–330.

[33] Wandel und Probleme in der internationalen Exportfinanzierung (Bankhistorisches Archiv. Zeitschrift zur Bankengeschichte, Beih. 10), Zweites Internationales Symposium zur Bankengeschichte am 6. April 1984 in Frankfurt am Main, (Fritz Knapp Verlag), Frankfurt am Main 1986, 88 S.

gave a historical survey of export finance from the fourteenth to the nineteenth century, William H. Draper III, President of the Export-Import Bank of the United States, spoke on the establishment of the bank and its development, Jan Ekman, President of Svenska Handelsbanken, spoke on the effects of the debt crisis on export finance and Michel Freyche, President of the Banque Française du Commerce Extérieur, pointed out the dangers of separatism in reaction to the international debt crisis, entitling his paper "Barter Trade".

The development of banking supervision in Switzerland since the nineteenth century is the subject of the thesis by Hugo Bänziger[34]. The author examines the political circumstances which finally led to the Federal Act on Banks and Savings Banks in 1934, with special emphasis on the following aspects of the legislation: protection of banking secrecy, regulations on capital exports in economic policy, trends in interest rates on bonds.

The catalogue for the exhibition of Deutsche Bank AG's Lower Saxony Coin Collection, "Vom Taler zur Mark" (From the Taler to the Mark), published in 1986,[35] provides basic information on the history of money and coin in the modern age.

A survey of 500 years of money and coin history, with the best known coin in the world as an example, comes in the book of the same title to accompany the Munich State Coin Collection's 1986 exhibition "Vom Taler zum Dollar 1486–1986" (From the Taler to the Dollar 1486–1986)[36]. The book is edited by Wolfgang Hess and Dietrich Klose and it includes an extensive bibliography.

"Banco, Species und Courant"[37] is the title chosen by Konrad Schneider for his study of the Hamburg currency in the seventeenth and eighteenth centuries. He is concerned with characteristics that are shared by money generally and shows the Hamburg currency as consisting of three entities dependent on market rates: bank money (banko), money in circulation (courant) and the species dollar. The development of the Hamburger Bank, founded in 1619, is a recurrent additional theme of the study.

Anton Zischka has written a popular account of the American currency, "Der Dollar. Glanz und Elend einer Währung" (The Dollar. Rise and Fall of an Currency)[38], in which he traces the development of US fiscal policy from the creation of the dollar to America's present position as a debtor country. The work has a bibliography but no notes or references.

---

[34] Hugo Bänziger, Die Entwicklung der Bankenaufsicht in der Schweiz seit dem 19. Jahrhundert (Bankwirtschaftliche Forschungen, Bd. 95), (Verlag Paul Haupt), Bern, Stuttgart 1986, 277 S.

[35] Vom Taler zur Mark. Niedersächsisches Münzkabinett der Deutschen Bank, hrsg. v. d. Deutschen Bank AG, Frankfurt am Main 1986, 38 S.

[36] Vom Taler zum Dollar 1486–1986. Staatliche Münzsammlung München 1986. Ausstellung vom 11. Oktober 1986 bis 11. Januar 1987, bearb. v. Wolfgang Heß und Dietrich Klose, (Selbstverlag der Staatlichen Münzsammung München), München 1986, 252 S.

[37] Konrad Schneider, "Banco, Species und Courant". Untersuchungen zur hamburgischen Währung im 17. und 18. Jahrhundert, (Numismatischer Verlag Gerd Martin Forneck), Koblenz 1986, 136 S.

[38] Anton Zischka, Der Dollar. Glanz und Elend einer Währung, (Wirtschaftsverlag Langen-Müller/Herbig), München 1986, 366 S.

The articles in the collected volume "The Adaptation to Inflation"[39] were produced as part of a research project on inflation and reconstruction in Germany and Europe from 1914 to 1924, and are each published in German and English. They deal with the question of in how far the economically active, politicians and social classes, can adjust to the conditions of inflation. The book is divided into four sections. Part 1 has contributions by Claus-Dieter Krohn, Steven B. Webb and Jürgen Jaksch, which examine the theoretical and practical conditions for action by individuals and social groups. The authors of Part 2, Martin Geyer, Norbert Ranft, Gunther Mai, Merith Niehuss, Gerald D. Feldman, Robert Scholz and Andreas Kunz deal with the development of institutional and individual conditions for groups that can only adapt reactively. In Part 3 Gerold Ambrosius, Peter-Christian Witt and Gerald D. Feldmann examine the reaction of local authorities and public enterprises to inflation. Part 4 contains articles by David Barclay, William Matthews and Carl-Ludwig Holtfrerich on economic policy programmes and decisions.

The last publication by the former President of the Deutsche Bundesbank, Otmar Emminger, who died in August 1986, "D-Mark, Dollar, Währungskrisen. Erinnerungen eines ehemaligen Bundesbankpräsidenten" (D-Mark, Dollar and Foreign Exchange Crises. Memoirs by a Former President of the Deutsche Bundesbank)[40] are a kind of "personal commentary on monetary developments from 1950 to 1980".[41] Speaking as an insider, Emminger describes the development of the Federal Republic of Germany to an export country, his struggle against "imported inflation" and for his own proposals for dealing with the situation through a system of flexible exchange rates.

Rainer Klump is the author of the book "Entstehung und Verwendung internationaler Schlüsselwährungen" (The Emergence and Use of International Key Currencies)[42]. He concerns himself with the question why certain national currencies maintain so dominant an international position that they can exert a major influence on the economic development in other countries. From his detailed theoretical and empirical analsys of the emergence and use of key currencies the author deduces the way an international key currency should be managed.

The study by Ernest A. Koch on the Soviet Union and the International Monetary Fund[43] gives an account of the efforts made particularly by the United

---

39 Die Anpassung an die Inflation. The Adaption to Inflation, (Veröffentlichungen der Historischen Kommission zu Berlin, Bd. 67 = Beiträge zu Inflation und Wiederaufbau in Deutschland und Europa 1914–1924, Bd. 8), hrsg. v. Gerald D. Feldman, Carl-Ludwig Holtfrerich, Gerhard A. Ritter, Peter-Christian Witt, (Verlag Walter de Gruyter), Berlin, New York 1986, 512 S.

40 Otmar Emminger, D-Mark, Dollar, Währungskrisen. Erinnerungen eines ehemaligen Bundesbankpräsidenten, (Deutsche Verlags-Anstalt), Stuttgart 1986, 480 S.

41 Volker Hentschel, D-Mark, Dollar, Währungskrisen. Anmerkungen zu den Erinnerungen des ehemaligen Bundesbankpräsidenten Otmar Emminger, in : Bankhistorisches Archiv. Zeitschrift zur Bankengeschichte 1/1987, S. 44–50, hier S. 44.

42 Rainer Klump, Entstehung und Verwendung internationaler Schlüsselwährungen (Veröffentlichungen des Instituts für Wirtschaftsforschung – Hamburg), (Verlag Weltarchiv), Hamburg 1986, 462 S.

43 Ernest A. Koch, Sowjetunion und Internationaler Währungsfonds (IWF). Eine Untersuchung aus wirtschaftshistorischer, wirtschaftstheoretischer und rechtlicher Perspektive, (Europäische Hochschulschriften, Reihe V: Volks- und Betriebswirtschaft, Bd. 752), (Peter Lang), Frankfurt am Main, Bern, New York 1986, 605 S.

States in the 40s, and which were ultimately unsuccessful, to include the USSR in the IMF, and then analyses the main problems of order raised by the membership of Socialist centrally planned economies in a monetary system based on market economy principles.

German monetary history since 1914 is the subject of a work by Herbert Rittmann ("Die deutsche Geldgeschichte seit 1914")[44], a continuance of his "Deutsche Geldgeschichte 1848–1914"[45], written in 1975. The new book is mainly intended for numismaticians and it includes a very detailed discussion of the currency situation during the First and Second World Wars in the scenes of fighting (including prisoner-of-war money and ghetto money) as well as the situation in the former German colonies and the emergence of the currency in the GDR. The book also has an extensive appendix of tables and illustrations of coins and bank notes.

To celebrate the 30th anniversary of the establishment of its first investment fund the German investment company DEKA has issued a study on the subject of money under change[46]. This is more of a sociological study and it traces the change in the attitude to money in two key years, 1956 and 1986, from saving in the fifties to investment in the 80s.

The cultural history of taxation[47] edited by Uwe Schultz, includes contributions from authors such as Karl Häuser, Peter Blickle, Micharl Stürmer, Carl-Ludwig Holtfrerich, Günter Schmölders and others. They document the qualitative variety of the different kinds of taxes and the quantitative increase in taxes from Antiquity to the present. As the title shows, this is not only a list of the legal regulations but an account of the social, military, religious and political reasons for and consequences of imposing taxes.

josef Rosen has examined the annual municipal accounts of the city of Basle[48] for the period from 1360 to 1555. The very detailed account covers the extent, compostion and costs of the municipal administration but offers little interpretation of these facts.

Hans-Peter Ullmann divides his comparative study of the emergence of modern public debt in Bavaria and Baden from 1780 to 1820[49] into two parts. In the first he examines the reasons for the rapid rise of public borrowing, the "debt explosion", and in the second shows the development of public debt management to the legalised, commercialised form which we know today.

---

44 Herbert Rittmann, Deutsche Geldgeschichte seit 1914, (Klinkhardt & Biermann), München 1986, 605 S.

45 Herbert Rittmann, Deutsche Geldgeschichte 1814–1914, München 1975.

46 Arthur und Cornelia Fischer, Geld im Wandel, hrsg. v. d. Deka Deutsche Kapitalanlagegesellschaft mbH, (Hartwig-Braun-Druck), Oberursel 1986, 84 S.

47 Mit dem Zehnten fing es an. Eine Kulturgeschichte der Steuer, hrsg. v. Uwe Schulz, (Verlag C.H. Beck), München 1986, 297 S.

48 Josef Rosen, Verwaltung und Ungeld in Basel 1360–1535. Zwei Studien zu Stadtfinanzen im Mittelalter (Vierteljahrschrift für Sozial- und Wirtschaftsgeschichte, Beih. 77), (Franz Steiner Verlag), Stuttgart 1986, 231 S.

49 Hans Peter Ullmann, Staatsschulden und Reformpolitik. Die Entstehung moderner öffentlicher Schulden in Bayern und Baden 1780–1820 (Veröffentlichungen des Max-Planck-Instituts für Geschichte, Band 82, Teil 1 und 2), (Vandenhoeck & Ruprecht), Göttingen 1986, 842 S.

Starting from the premise that public finance is one of the determinants of economic and social development, Rudolf Kroboth analyses fiscal and tax policy and the development of money and capital markets from 1909 to 1913–14 for their effects on the political, economic and social constitution of the German Reich on the eve of the First World War.[50]

[50] Rudolf Kroboth, Die Finanzierungspolitik des Deutschen Reiches während der Reichskanzlerschaft Bethmann-Hollwegs und die Geld- und Kapitalmarktverhältnisse (1909–1913/14), (Europäische Hochschulschriften, Reihe 3: Geschichte und ihre Hilfswissenschaften, Bd. 305), (Peter Lang), Frankfurt am Main 1986, 511 S.

Technical Reconstruction After 1945

The VDI's Techno-historical Annual Conference 13 and 14 February 1986
in Dusseldorf

Manfred Mai

The recovery after the end of the Second World War occured under conceivably unfacourable conditions. Demolition of production plants, annihilation and requisition of important construction plants, an inconsistent occupation policy from the Allies and above all the dismantling of available manufacturing sites mark the memories of many contemporaries of the early post-war years. The aim of the VDI's annual techno-historical conference was to examine the details of the technical reconstruction with special reference to case studies.

In his introductory talk Werner Abelshauser (University of Bochum) opposed the idea that there was an new beginning to the economy and society after the end of the war. The paradigm of restoration was equally unconvincing. Much more to the point was that the Federal Republic had, after 1945, continued on from the existing situation and traditions but had, however, managed to find its own new structure.

Even today the economical-political discussion is still extensively marred by experiences and myths from the early post-war years. The stereotypes "collapse", "chaos", and "stagnation" are often used to characterise the post-war period. The three stages: Marshall plan, currency reform and market economy, as the initiators of the recovery of the German economy, have been critically examined by research. Hence the recovery had already started in summer 1945 and was finally completely underway after the autumn of 1947. The currency reform did indeed regulate the distribution of manufactured goods, but did not noticeably hasten the growth in production. The policy of occupation favoured the recovery of the West German economy insofar that the restrictive principles of the Allies policy for Germany never limited the growth of the zonal economy during occupation. As there was no external aid before 1945 it is all the more important to assess the material balance of resources in the western zones with respect to its significance for the recovery. There was a positive balance of industrial invested capital in 1945. In spite of the effects of the industrial dismantlings the industrial capital stock of the western zones remains clearly higher than that of pre-war years. If any funds from the Marshall plan were used in the western zones these resources had no necessary connection with the American programme of aid, but were linked with the Marshall plan for reasons of political opportunism. An important prerequisite for the recovery was the decision against nationalisation taken in 1947. However, as soon as the economic plan had satisfactorily fulfilled its main task of legally and politically regulating the production process and distribution, its significance was reduced below that of the strengths of reconstruction.

Manfred Rasch (University of Bochum) showed how the reconstruction of the "Ruhr-Chemie AG" (Ruhr chemical works) in Oberhausen was possible under the conditions of the British policy of occupation. The main topic was the events connected with the dismantling in late summer 1949. After the end of the War the major products of the Ruhr-Chemie AG (synthetic fuels and nitrogens) were amongst those products affected by the Allies production bans. Although the share-holders of the Ruhr-Chemie were under Allied control the British Military government did not employ a trustee, but the precious board of directors of Ruhr-Chemie could Minitially continue to fulfill its task. As there was a need for fertilizer Ruhr-Chemie had already received a production licence for nitrogen by 30 November 1945 and three months later for motor methane. After the Petersberg agreement the management could no longer make the decision to take up the Fischer-Tropsch systhesis.

Dietmar Voß (Klöckner-Humbolt-Deutz AG, Cologne) reported on the reconstruction of an industrial firm after the Second World War using the KHD-AG in Cologne as an example. The 262 air raids up to 1945 on the urban area of Cologne caused enormous manufacturing losses at KHD. At the turn of the year 1944/45 there was hardly any chance of production. The production of small parts, gear wheels and large motors was removed elsewhere. In total 105 relocations were carried out. The works in Oberursel and Ulm were on the whole spared this measure. Production could, with some limitations, be maintained until the end of the war. Intensive talks with the occupying authorities lead, in mid-June 1945, to new production permission which was however repealed in October. Only production for mining was allowed. It was not until July 1948 that the works in Cologne were permitted to produce without restrictions.

Ulrich Tolkiehn (University of Hamburg) illustrated the post-war phase using the reconstruction of the public electricity supply in Hamburg. He concludes that the electricity works in Hamburg were able to secure a satisfactory electricity supply from the end of the war onwards despite massive damages. In addition to the general problems of supply of material and spare parts and the provision of man-power for repairs, measures of the British occupying power were also made responsible for the power plants increasing susceptibility to break-downs. They meant for example, that firms, authorized to deal with repair-work, could only take on work classified an top priority. According to the intentions of the military government repair work was to be concentrated on only certain parts of the works. Using examples of costs it is possible to show that the electricity supply in Hamburg would have completely broken down if the Hamburger Elektrizitätswerde had only used the machine performance officially permitted by the military government. The supply of fuels became a particular problem. Approx. 60% of all interruptions were connected more or less with the poor quality of the coal. It was not until 1947 that some continuity could be achieved in the supply and repair programme and the electricity supply in Hamburg became steadier.

The technical reconstruction of the West Germany pipe industry was illustrated by Horst A. Wessel (Mannesmann-AG Dusseldorf) in his speech. The demolition caused by the war as well as lack of energy and man-power meant that none of the industrial plants were working. In December 1945 there were still no pipes being produced in the previous province of Westphalia; in Rhineland 7900 tons were being produced in the Mannesmann factories. At the beginning of 1946 the German Pipeworks joined them, initially the Mülheim factory and, as soon as the energy supply could be guarantied, Lierenfeld too. In 1949 there were eleven works with altogether 37 plants and a total capacity of 59,990 tons per month. 25,000, tons of this monthly capacity were destined for reparation. All of the rolling mill plants were from before the War. New constructions could at the best only be partially completed.

Klaus Luther (M.A.N., Augsburg) reported on the technical reconstruction at M.A.N. in Augsburg. The Augsburg plant had been extensively damaged in air raids. At the end of April 1945 the production was completely stopped by the occupation of the American troops. A large number of skilled workers and management had to leave the firm which was itself placed under trustees. The recovery was planned and carried out in three phases. Due to the type of equipment used the works was able to provide is contribution to the general recovery by adjusting relatively quickly to a production process suited to the period. In spite of recognition for this achievement from the occupying forces there were several demands for restitution and reparation. Following exensive bargaining it was possible to reduce both demands to an minimum. However it was not possible to avoid a considerable loss in technical knowledge.

Dierk Hobein (University of Bochum) reported on the recovery of the Widia-Fabrik in Essen in his speech entitled "From the Lack of a Concept to the Lack of Alternatives". The initial position for a rapid recovery of the Widia-Fabrik was favourable; damage to building, supply equipment and services were almost completely repaired by August 1945, the raw materials and energy supply could be secured, the labour potential was sufficient, technical equipment was on the whole undamaged. Howeyer, a problem arose in the apparent lack of concept of the British occupying forces: they alternated between an orientation towards the requirements of security politics on one side and the economic-political aspirations on the other. As a result of these incompatible political extremes the British plans moved between stopping production and continuing with the authorisation of production first granted in August 1946. The determining factor was, in the end, the recognition by the British military government that hard metal was irreplacable, a fact which also affected the British economy.

Max Gerrit von Pein's (Daimler-Benz-AG) report on the reconstruction of the Daimler Benz AG started with a citation from the directors report for 1945 to 1948: "The company had at this point almost ceased to exist". In spite of the occupation by troops of various triumphant forces the company upkept most of the firms structure after the collapse. In particular the Americans recognized that the recovery of the German economy was in their own interest. However it was impossible to think of an orderly production. The Allies initially only allowed clearing up work and vehicle repair. In autumn 1945 the factories Mannheim and Gaggenau were able to restart the heavy vehicle production of the pre-war models. Many of the vehicles were remade from remains or parts taken out of other vehicles, in the first few months 150 units of a 3 ton vehicles were being produced. In 1946 the first Mercedes-Benz 170 V were produced as a box-type or platform truck. However production suffered in particular from lack of materials and dismantling measures. In Sindelfingen almost half of the intact machinery was taken away, vehicles from the Manheim production had to be delivered without wheels in May 1946 since it was impossible to get either rims or tyres. Four years after the end of the War the reconstruction measures had on the whole been completed. At the 1949 export exhibition in Hannover Daimler-Benz AG presented in its new delivery programme the first new models after the war.

Armin E. Möller, an economic journalist from Westdeutschen Rundfunk, Cologne, interviewed personalities who had originally been involved in the reconstruction for his contribution "Searching for the Recovery Generation". Most remarkable is his conversation with Sir Alex Cairncross who, as a British officer in Germany directly after the end of the war, dealt with the reparations and industrial dismantling by the victorious forces. Cairncross concludes that whenever the representatives of the occupying forces added together what had been left of German industry, it always appeared to be of a greater volume than that of German industry in 1932. The objectives of the occupying forces were, however, that Germany should be able to recover but not quicker than its neighbours. Möller's interviews with several entrepreneurs of the post-war period (Oetker, Kurt Hansen, Max Grundig, Konrad Henkel) show in particular the variety of problems which hardly allow any general statements about the technical reconstruction.

Most of the speeches held at this conference have been published in Reports Nr. 4/1986 and 1/1987 of the journal Technikgeschichte.

The Medium Scale Enterprises and the Labour Market. Do the Medium Scale Enterprises Solve the Employment Problems of the German Economy?

11th Conference for the Public held by the German Society for Business History on 10th June 1986 in Munich[1]

Beate Brüninghaus

At least every one in two workers today is employed in a medium scale enterprise; the great significance of the medium scale enterprises for the development of the labour market today and in the future is an topic for constant debate. Research in the USA has shown that employment rates in big firms are on the decline whereas an increase in employment is expected above all in smaller and medium-sized firms.

This year's conference took place in Munich on the occasion of the 10th anniversary of the German Society for Business History founded in Cologne, and it focused on the question of whether and to what extent the labour market has been influenced by the positive effects of the medium scale enterprises on employment from as far back as the 19th century. How has this development taken course since the foundation of the Federal Republic of Germany? What do the medium scale enterprises offer workers as far as prospects for the future are concerned? A subject was therefore found which is – in accordance with the conception of the German Society for Business History – equally topically and historically interesting.

Prof. Dr. Karl Heinrich Kaufhold, an economic and social historian and recognized researcher in the field of the history of small trade from Göttingen, examined the importance of the medium scale enterprises for the labour market from the 19th century up to the middle of the 20th century. Due to the lack of research work relative to the subject he was forced to limit himself to a few theses based on the outline of the development. Kaufhold emphasized the stabilizing function of the medium scale enterprises for the labour market during various economic trends since the 19th century. On the eve of industrialization (in around 1850), the independent medium scale enterprises employed at least 80% of all workers in the fields of industry and small trade. This share lay between 50 and 60% in the fully industrialized economy between 1880 and 1940, and even between 80 and 90% in trade and the transport system. In the phase before 1914 in particular, the medium scale enterprises supplied big businesses with to a large extent skilled labour force and made it easier for them to solve their employment problems.

Its development during the great unemployment of the 1920s and especially during the World Economic Crisis however, was different. According to Kaufhold the view that the medium scale enterprises were a stabilizing factor also in this

[1] The papers and discussions are published as a supplement to the periodical Zeitschrift für Unternehmensgeschichte, Beiheft 45, Franz Steiner Verlag Wiesbaden GmbH, Stuttgart 1988.

period should be reconsidered. In 1933 the unemployment figures of economic branches determined by the medium scale enterprises were considerably higher than those of branches marked by big business.

Prof. Dr. Dres. h.c. Horst Albach, economist and director of the Institute for Medium Scale Enterprises Research in Bonn, based his study on purchase tax and cost, structure figures from official statistics. He showed that even in the Federal Republic of Germany smaller firms employed labour whereas larger firms discharged labour. Up to 1984 the net effect - so Albach - was a reduction in personnel.

It was also shown in this regional study that big firms had a larger share of dismissal than employment schemes in agglomerations as well as in less concentrated areas. In the case of smaller firms, however, the situation was the opposite. According to the analysis of the economic situation undertaken by the Institute for Medium Scale Enterprises Research the "turn to the labour market" first became noticeable in smaller and medium-sized firms, while in bigger firms dismissals were predominant. Albach points out that in the meantime the employment aims of medium-sized firms had increased and those of larger firms had been stabilized so that employment as a whole increased in 1985 for the first time. Albach predicted a stengthening of this trend for the year 1986.

The final discussion was led by Dr. Hans-J. Barth, member of the management of Prognos AG, Basel. Besides the speakers Kaufhold and Albach Dr. Anne-Rose Iber-Schade, president of the Society of Femal Entrepreneurs, Cologne, Günther Spiegl, president of the State Labour Office (Landesarbeitsamt South Bavaria), Munich, and Prof. Dr. Gerhard Zeitel, University of Mannheim participated in the discussion. The subjects discussed arose little controversy. The participants were largely in agreement on the great importance of the medium scale enterprises for the labour market and for economic development. It was complained that the public and politics do not yet appreciate this fact and that the medium scale enterprises are being promoted correspondingly.

Innovations and Changes in the Employment Structure in Banking

Report on the First Scientific Colloquium of the Institute for Bankhistorical Research, held on 20th June 1986 on the premises of the Bayerische Hypotheken- und Wechsel-Bank Aktiengesellschaft, Munich[1]

Monika Pohle

"Computer money", "home banking", "POS Systems". Such are the catchword titles of articles in magazines and publications in recent times. New techniques in banking in the areas of information and communication aim at ensuring that payments and remittences can be carried out quicker and in a manner which is more customer-oriented. However, in doing this, on the one hand the security requirements of banks and on the other hand the behaviour of a competition-conscious market must be carefully weighed one against the other. The effects of financial innovations and technical innovations on the employment structure in credit institutions is judged in varying ways in the press. Although the topic innovations has been systematically researched for only sixty years, if we interpret the term innovation broadly we can trace it back to the exchange offices of the later Middle Ages.

Speakers and participants at the First Scientific Colloquium of the Institute for Bankhistorical Research therefore looked at an aspect which had never been dealt with before and attempted to establish a relationship between innovations and the employment structure from the 13th/14th centuries to this day.

Professor Hans Pohl of the University of Bonn based his introduction on Schumpeter's definition of the term "innovation", which describes innovation as "the process by which new products and techniques are introduced into the economic system". He said that it was difficult, however, to examine and determine the continuous development of employment structures in banking. There was very little recent research into this. He said there was also a lack of research dealing with the connection between the key terms "innovations" and "employment structure".

Professor Jürgen Schneider of the University of Bamberg, who examined the development of innovations from the later Middle Ages to the middle of the 19th century, traced the development from commodity markets to exchange markets, in other words the way banking evolved from trading. At the beginning of the 17th century all legal bodies which are characteristic of modern banking were already in existence. A new stage was marked by the emergence of national banks at the beginning of the 19th century, which served both the state and the industrial sectors and enforced the bank note as means of payment and of lending.

[1] The papers and discussions are published as a supplement to Bankhistorisches Archiv (12. Beiheft), ed.: Research Advisory Council of the Institute for Bankhistorical Research, Fritz Knapp Verlag, Frankfurt am Main 1988.

Professor Friedrich-Wilhelm Henning of the University of Cologne came to the conclusion that from the middle of the 19th century to 1948 innovations resulted in a decisive increase in the number employed, that the employment of women, in particular in the lower wage scales, increased considerably and that professional training improved. Despite greater distinction being made between functions in the employment structure, the "allround banking associate" continued to predominate over the specialist as time went by. Henning believed that the inclusion of new areas of performance in the course of financial innovations was decisive in creating higher employment figures and that the technical innovations utilised to cope with increases in transactions did not lead to the abolition of jobs.

Professor Hans-Jacob Krümmel, Bonn, who examined the connection between financial innovations and changes in the employment structure from 1948 to the present day, confirmed that the need for innovations had grown since the end of the 60's, resulting from competitive pressures, greater familiarity of the general public with banking and greater expectations being placed on the banks by customers. Due to the strong influence of other factors on statistics it was not possible, he said, to extract a connection between financial innovations and an increase in employment levels. Nor could the effects of innovation procedures on qualification structures be statistically proven. The statistics on salary scales, at least of the private banks and savings banks, indicated that there was a strong movement towards higher wage scales. However, a connection could not be established between developments in salary scales and the evolution of financial innovations.

Research into the effects of technical innovations on the employment structure in the present day by Professor Erich Priewasser of the University of Marburg confirmed that structures had improved noticeably in favour of better qualified jobs. This tendency disproved Rossier's theory (J. A. Rossier, Umbruch in der Bankorganisation. Der Bankier vor den Realitäten des industriellen Managements, in: Die Unternehmung 2/1973, page 64) that the process of automation results in the lowering of employee's qualifications.

At the discussion groups the participants were concerned mainly with the definition of the term "innovation". Should differentiation between functions be regarded as an innovation? Is the mere expansion of business activities an innovation? There was also disagreement over the definition of the term "banking", at least in former times. It was agreed that there was a causal relationship between innovations and changes in the employment structure, considering the remarkable specialisation of bank employees on account of financial innovations. In addition to current developments e.g. information services as a form of banking, the other topic of great interest pertaining to the present day was the connection between the employment structure and financial innovations and innovations in products. Those participating in the discussion considered the effects to be less significant than generally maintained in the press.

The Development of Savings Banks to Full-Service Credit Institutes

Report on the Symposium on the History of Savings Banks in Lüneburg, September 24/25, 1986

Jürgen Mura

The general theme of the 1986 Symposium on the History of Savings Banks co-chaired by Gustav Adolf Schröder, Executive Director of the German Savings Banks and Giro Association, Bonn, and by Professor Dr. Bernd Rudolph, University of Frankfurt/Main, was the develoment of savings banks into full-service credit institutes. The symposium was held by the Gesellschaft zur Förderung der wissenschaftlichen Forschung über das Spar- und Girowesen e.V., Bonn, in Lüneburg on September 24/25, 1986.

In his opening remarks, Mr. Schröder underlined the rediscovered interest in history rangings from curiosity and nostalgia to the scientific desire to go back to one's own roots and representing, at least sub-consciously, an attempt to define one's own position. The credit industry's perspectives over the long term could not be definded either without knowledge, reflection and the evaluation of past developments, i.e. without thinking in historical dimensions. The process of defining one's own position invarably involved an evaluation of historical data and, in this context, a critical analysis helped to identify historical relations and made the proper assessment and subsequent treatment of present and future problems easier.

Professor Rudolph, who chaired the discussions among experts posed the question in his introductory to the general theme whether the universality of savings-bank services having increased over time had changed the character of savings banks and whether – in this process of change – the savings banks had developed into Commercial banks or might be doing so in future. It was also possible that the savings banks had come first in the development of part of the universal range of banking services and, thus, of the universality concept and had so redefinded certain functions of the financial sector at the same time.

In his introductory, Professor Dr. Hans Pohl, professor of economic history at the University of Bonn, reviewed "the development of savings banks into credit institutes" and covered the period from the early days of the savings bank movement up to 1908, when savings banks began to extend their activities into banking for the first time. In his paper, Professor Pohl outlined the general development of the savings banks founded upon private initiative in the last quarter of the 18th century – increasingsly – on an municipal basis from the beginning of the 19th century and briefly described the discussions conducted on the future tasks of the savings banks since the 1880s.

Special points of emphasis in that paper were the motives of the foundation of savings banks, business and business policy trends observed, the rising governmental influence on the savings bank movement, legal regulations, the formation of savings bank association as well as the aforementioned lengthy reform discussions especially aimed at the launching of non-cash pay systems by the savings banks and the expansion of their range of business. The gradual opening of the giro service after 1908 finally became the focal point in the development of the German "savings bank unit" and allowed the savings banks to overcome their "atomization" (Eberle).

Professor Wysocki of the University of Salzburg subsequently reported on "the development of the savings banks' banking activities" between 1908 and 1931 which commenced by the successive introduction of the giro service on the basis of the check Act of 1908 enabling them to obtain the legal capacity of drawee banks. This set in motion a complex and persistant innovation process. Reference to this "epochal" move as the "key to innovation" is justified by the fact that it made the integrated savings bank system not only feasible, but even necessary.

However, in spite of the enthusiastic efforts by Dr. Johann Christian Eberle, the promotor of the idea to give the savings banks access to the giro service, the diffusion process was fairly slow, initially. Later the exigencies of World War II economy allowed the institutional brakes to be released, after the German government and central bank had advocated non-cash payment systems.

The giro service was an new attractive product which enabled the savings banks to render services and to enforce innovations according to different patterns in the individual German states. Deposit banking and the giro business meant the development as banks.

The great inflation after World War I was another driving force in the bank-like development of savings banks as well as for the giro centres primarily set up to handle the giro transactions of the saving banks and resulted in a substantial expansion of their product ranges.

After monetary stabilization in 1923, competition with the private banks actually commenced. They had already begun to make front against the bank-like development of saving banks before World War I. In each of their campaigns against the development of savings banks into banks, the private banks tried to represent this trend as "contrary to the character of savings banks". They based their arguments on historical grounds and conjured up the motives that had led to the foundation of savings banks. In 1927, this dispute escalated upon the big banks' decision to take up savings banking as a regular line of business. However, this did not induce savings banks to confine theis activities to their traditional lines of business again. The savings banks' bank-like development meant that they were omnipresent with their range of modern banking service. After the 1927 escalation of the dispute the realization that the savings banks would not step back again was unavoidable, which led to an armistice one year later. The groups of the credit industry entered into their first competition agreement.

The subject "crises and continuity of the savings bank movement" between 1931 and 1958 was discussed by Dr. Jürgen Mura of the Savings Bank Historical Documentation Centre of the German Savings Bank and Giro Association in Bonn. The paper also spanning a long period underlined landmarks in the history of the German savings banks: the bank crisis of 1931 which brought the savings banks their legal independence, the Bank Enquiry of 1933 which recognized the savings banks' business strategy after fierce fighting, the 1934 credit industry Act which recognized the savings banks as credit institutes with equal rights, the integration also of the savings banks into the national socialist economic system focusing on job creation and later on financing war activities, which gave a new political dimension also to the savings banks and their transactions. The secound part of the paper described the development of the savings banks after World War II up to 1958 (key notes: reconstruction, savings bank law reform, technological progress, new business strategy action parameters, growing competition). In this period, the savings banks together with the Landesbanken/Girozentralen succeeded in becoming the most important group of the German credit industry. On the basis of the social market economy, retaining their organizational principles, i.e. non-profit making/task orientation, limitation of their activities to the area of jurisdiction of the municipal/regional government backing their liabilities they and their associa-from manager to build up a strong position in banking, economic and monetary policy.

Dr. Ingo Ellgering, board member of the Cologne Kreissparkasse, reported on the "expansion and Structural change of savings banks in the recent past (from 1958)". This roughly 25-year period has been characterized by the further development of savings banks into full-service credit institutes with increasing market orientation, forced application of technology and growing competition. This development took place withing the framework of a major expansion of the German credit industry in which the savings banks had an decisive part. Such stronger market orientation has resulted in a considerable expansion of the product ranges in the lending deposits and services sectors. Major institutional events having led to a substantial intensification of competition in the German credit industry were the abolition of the public need test preceding the approval to set up bank branches by the Federal Constitutional Court in 1958, the lifting of the interest rate regulations in 1967 still retained from the 1930s as well as the cancellation of the competition agreement also in 1967.

The last paper was that of Mr. Gustav Adolf Schröder who asked: "Are savings banks full-service commercial banks?" He reviewed most recent aspects of the development of the savings banks and reached the conclusion that savings banks undoubtedly are full-service *credit institutes,* but that they are not full-service commercial *banks.*

The symposium ended on a roughly 90-minute podium discussion among renowned managers of the German savings bank organization which was moderated by Professor Rudolph. This review of historical and present trends resulted in a multitude of new ideas and in kicks for thinking about this subject of fundamental importance for the definition of the savings banks' own position and identity and to their opinion-formation process.

In order to spread the results of this symposium and make them available also to the non-participating interested public, the papers read at the symposium and the discussion were again published in brochure form.[1]

---

[1] Gesellschaft zur Förderung der wissenschaftlichen Forschung über das Spar- und Girowesen e.V., Bonn (Hrsg.), Sparkassenhistorisches Symposium 1986. Die Entwicklung der Sparkassen zu Universalkreditinstituten. Deutscher Sparkassenverlag, Stuttgart 1987.

Credit Institutions and Securities Markets[1]

10th National Symposium of the Institute for Bankhistorical Research held at the Bank für Gemeinwirtschaft AG, Frankfurt am Main, on October 24, 1986

Monika Pohle

"Big Bang" took place in London on October 27, 1986, that is to say, the transition from the local to the new electronic stock exchange system as the final step within the shift from the system of separate fields of activity for the different types of banks towards unibanking by all-purpose banks. This event, together with the law passed by the German parliament on October 23, 1986 on stock exchange listings, which facilitates medium-sized companies' access to the stock exchange through the creation of a "regulated market", lent a highly topical note to the symposium organised by the Institue für Bankhistorical Research.

Professor Dr. Karl Häuser from the Institute for Capital Market Research traced in his speech the development of the stock exchanges into capital market centres from the beginning of the industrialization process in the nineteenth century, with its enormous demand for finance, through to the 1970s. Credit institutions have been able to maintain their role as the connecting link between the public and the stock exchange, and lenders and borrowers. The close ties between banks and industry, which are characteristic of the German economy, have been additionally favoured by the unibanking system. In the early years, fixed-interest securities and shares were, to a considerable extent, placed long-term with the public, as there were hardly any institutional investors. The volatility of the market remained relatively small. Following World War II, the securities market was above all a market for banks, as private investors were slow in overcoming their aversion to the market that had been split as a result of the Capital Market Encouragement Law. However, the securities market was turned into a bank market primarily by the central bank-controlled money market interest rate, which was transferred via a transmission mechanism from the banking system to the capital market.

Dr. Wolfgang Röller, Chairman of the Board of Management of the Dresdner Bank AG, spoke on how, after the Second World War, economic growth and the concurrent formation of savings, the rapid growth in the demand for capital by public authorities, the internationalisation of the markets and the worldwide acceleration of inflation brought about a profound change in bank's securities business until the seventies. In the eighties, the growth in securities operations acquired completely new proportions. The substantial rise in the volume of

[1] The papers and contributions to the discussion are published as a supplement to Bankhistorisches Archiv (14. Beiheft), ed.: Research Advisory Council of the Institute for Bankhistorical Research, Fritz Knapp Verlag, Frankfurt am Main 1988.

trading, which is due to above-average turnover velocity and the increase in the share of foreign currency bonds in investors' portfolios, reflects the changed structure. Increased utilisation of bonds as financing instruments by institutional investors could be observed in the last few years in the same way as the growing number of newcomers to the stock exchange. The change in securities business as a result of the trend making itself felt among borrowers towards securitisation presents a challenge to the banks which they can only meet by providing in due time the necessary human, financial and technological resources.

The discussion following the two speeches was chaired by Dr. Hans D. Barbier of the Frankfurter Allgemeine Zeitung and dealt above all with the question of competition among the various groups of institutions in the German banking industry as well as from non-banks and foreign brokers with regard to companies going public. Theo Meinz, Member of the Board of Management of the Hessische Landesbank - Girozentrale -, called for a deeper involvement of central institutions of the savings bank and credit cooperative sectors and said he considered as small the threat of competition from non-banks to the lasting relationships between banks and their customers as a result of the custody and administration of securities. This view was also shared by Herbert Jacobi, spokesman of the managing partners of the Bankhaus Trinkaus & Burkhardt KGaA. Dr. Friedrich Wilhelm Christians, Chairman of the Board of Management of the Deutsche Bank AG, who said that assisting companies, and especially medium-sized companies, to go public was the very task of the all-purpose banks and that he deplored that this task had been neglected, felt that globalisation was more likely to stiffen competition among credit institutions themselves. As a response to "Big Bang", he recommended an interpenetration of areas of activity and the broadening of the range of services.

The question of the pertinent risk management, which has acquired greater urgency as a result of the financial innovations of recent years, was answered by the members of the podium with a demand for greater disclosure of positions and satisfaction of the need for information through more publicity.

The Influences of Motorisation on the Transport Industry from 1886 to 1986

11th Research Symposium of the German Society For Business History e.V., Cologne on 27/28 November 1986 in Fellbach

Stephanie Habeth-Allhorn

In 1986 the Daimler-Benz AG celebrated the centenary of the motorcar. The German Society for Business History took the opportunity on the occasion of the jubilee to make a specialists' contribution to the festivities. The subject of the 11th research symposium was how motorisation has influenced the transport industry in the past 100 years. What possibilities did and does it offer, how was and is it being used and where does it show its limits?

The conference received a wide response despite a great number of other events. Approximately 140 participants from home and abroad from the spheres of research, economics and the press followed 8 lectures and the platform discussion in which the situation of competition between traffic systems of the past, the present and the future was debated.

Professor Dr. Hans Pohl from the University of Bonn and chairman of the research committee of the German Society of Business History gave a historical introduction on the development of the transport industry. The invention of the steam engine, the high-speed petrol engine and the heavy-oil engine triggered the development of our present transport situation. Until roughly the middle of our century the railway held the largest share of passenger and goods transportation, whilst water transport had to increasingly specialize in the transportation of bulk articles. The lorry had already asserted itself as a supplement to the railway in goods transportation after the end of the First World War. The motor-car and the aeroplane on the other hand only gained significance after 1945, but caught up very quickly with the other modes of transport and are today the main means of private and long-distance transport.

Professor Dr. Rainer Willeke from the University of Cologne considered the importance of motorisation for the national economy with emphasis placed on transport economics, the motorisation of the individual, the motor industry and road construction. At present the motor industry is occupying a key position in highly developed economies. The number of goods which are of high-quality and have to be transported quickly is increasing, leading to an expansion in the volume of transportation by lorry. Personal mobility is growing through the increasing supply of cars, and is bringing with it a decentralisation of location and an enlargement of the labour market. Increasing motorisation always places new demands on infrastructure. Following the phase of expansion approximately 50% of road construction expenses today are being used for repairs and maintenance. Encumbrances on and damages to the environment as well as accidents must be considered in addition to gain in productivity and mobility. According to Willeke individual and political willingness to pay show however, that the standard of living is rated higher than the costs and risks.

Professor Dr. Friedrich Fürstenberg from the University of Bonn described the changing relationship between motorisation and labour market as one passing through a series of phases. Motorisation begins gradually, then shows a decidedly accelerating growth and finally drops near saturation point. The same development, namely that of market expansion, market differentiation and market integration, is also evident in those labour markets dependent on the motor-car. Political and economic catastrophees cause clear breaks in this flow of development. Market fluctuations repeatedly exercise effects in the same way. Quantitative employment fluctuations caused by the employment policy of enterprises, and qualitative changes in structure e.g. when all-purpose skilled workers are exchanged with specialists or assistant technicians, directly influence the labour market.

At the beginning of his lecture Professor Dr. Volker Hentschel from the University of Mainz stated that transport should be regulated by the state as a competitive and political area of exception, and then went on to discuss the aims, means and effects of state powers on the transportation of commercial goods and the conveyance of passengers. For example, from around 1880 the USA, Great Britain, France and Germany strove to satisfy the existing demand for transport, to separate traffic into different modes of transport, to balance competition conditions and to determine prices rationally. In order to realise these aims the public took over control. Taxes were and are being raised and subsidies paid. The state is able to determine prices and capacities. Although it is difficult to judge the effect of these measures, according to Hentschel it may be established on a global scale that state intervention does not bring an optimal result. It becomes clear from the example of personal transport that economic optimisation causes the social environment to suffer. Therefore in this case state regulation is urgently necessary.

Being the main means of transport the car influences society, infrastructure and regional planning. Mass mobility has been evident in the Federal Republic of Germany since the sixties. The bus and motor-cycle were the first mass means of mobility, so it was from the end of the fifties that the car rose to become the most important mode of transport. It was then possible, according to Professor Dr. Peter Borscheid from the University of Münster, to locate industry and housing in the outskirts. Private car traffic replaced other modes of transport and even made the surmounting of greater distances possible which can be seen particularly in the increase in leisure-time and holiday traffic. The distance covered daily per person by car is growing steadily, whereas the distance covered on foot is decreasing. Communication has changed as has the cultural discrepancy between town and country.

Robert Braunschweig, former chief editor of the Automobile Revue in Bern, came to the conclusion that public opinion in the past 25 years towards motorised vehicles has changed greatly parallel to its expansion. What was at first celebrated as a positive and civilizing enrichment is being increasingly met with criticism. Motorised vehicles pollute the air with toxic agents from exhaust, they cause noise pollution and injure or kill people in traffic accidents.

Motor-car producers respond by further developments of and improvements to their products, whilst public transport is trying to exploit points of criticism to its favour. However the arguments to date have only brought little change to the volume of private, motorised transport.

Not the past but the present and the future were the focal point of the talk by Professor Dr. Hans-Jürgen Warnecke from the University of Stuttgart on production technologies. Today the economic efficiency of an enterprise shows more how quickly and flexibly it reacts to market demands. Flexible production systems e.g. computers and robots and the flexible employment of labour are thereforce necessary in order to be able to economically balance out the decreasing durability of products and far-reaching innovations. It is not a question of whether new technologies have to be introduced, but of how. Only a conscious union between man and machine in the organisation of work can guarantee that production demands are satisfied and that the economic efficiency of the enterprise is secured.

According to Professor Dr. Hermann Sabel from the University of Bonn the highs and lows in the history of the motor industry result from competition circumstances. In world-wide competition German inventors and managers have initiated innovations which have then been further developed by the North Americans and the Japanese, for example the Americans have introduced mass production of the motor-car, and the Japanese are pioneers of cost cutting in car production. According to Sabel, whether motor-car firms are successful in competition depends on four components. Do firms have a strategy which is capable of survival e. g. does what they offer correspond to the demands of the customer? Are they in the position to adapt to changing conditions? Is the framework within which they produce and sell capable of survival? Do firms go on the decline because different makes disappear or because product regularisation is implemented?

Professor Dr. Werner Breitschwerdt, chairman of the board of directors of the Daimler-Benz AG, Stuttgart, Dr. Reiner Gohlke, chairman of the board of directors of the Deutsche Bundesbahn, Frankfurt/Main, Heinz Ruhnau, chairman of the board of directors of the Deutsche Lufthansa AG, Cologne, and Professor Dr. Rainer Willeke, director of the Institute for Transport Studies at the University of Cologne took part in the closing platform discussion which was led by Professor Dr. Gerhard Fels, director and member of the presidency of the Institut der Deutschen Wirtschaft, Cologne. All advocated free competition in the German market between the car, the railway and the aeroplane. The railway in particular must strengthen its stand in the competition between the 3 modes of transport and discover possibilities of winning new market shares. In the past state protection measures have damaged rather than made use of this mode of transport. Rail has suffered great losses in favour of roads. Future transport planning should place less emphasis on intensifying the competition between car and railway and much more importance on the question of sensible supplementation. The rivalry between the railway and the aeroplane is at present not as distinct as that between the car and the aeroplane. Reductions in the cost of petrol once again make the car attractive for long-distance journeys as well. In the future the railway should be more strongly connected as a conveyer with the aeroplane. The participants of the discussion were also united in the opinion that the role the state plays regarding transport systems is too strong and that it restricts the economic control of transport companies.

Symposium on the Economic Development and Economic History of the Euregio Maas-Rhein

Immo Zapp

In November 1986 the Institute for Economic and Social History (Prof. Dr. Francesca Schinzinger) at the Rheinisch-Westfälische Technische Hochschule Aachen organised a symposium on the historical and contemporary problems caused by economic development in the Euregio Maas-Rhein. Trans-border aspects were considered in particular, as they formed the basis of a longterm research project on the economic and manufacturing history of the Aachen area.

The subject has become particularly relevant as the triple-border economic area surrounding Aachen is moving from a peripheral to a central position, under the conditions of a united European economic region.

The opportunities accompanying these changes - but also the disadvantages which exist in relation to the future development regarded as necessary by political circles - were discussed in several lectures.

Dr. O. Eschweiler (Managing Director of the Industrie- und Handelskammer zu Aachen) clearly presented the many advantages of the economic development in contrast to the "mini-war" of bureaucracy. Consul P. G. Meyer-Viol (former President of the Kamer van Koophandel en Fabrieken voor Maastricht en Omstreken) particularly emphasised the demands every manufacturer in the border area must make of himself if he wants to exploit the possibilities offered by a wider economic field. Not only tariff barriers and trade restrictions are dominant in a border area, under certain historical conditions cross-border forces can actually be encouraging, as revealed in the contribution from Dr. Klara van Eyll (Director of the Rheinisch-Westfälisches Wirtschaftsarchiv zu Köln). Personal initiative and daring, and capital and technology transfer across state borders at the turn of the 18th to the 19th century were an example of this, and mark several entrepreneurs' biographies and business histories of the Belgian-Dutch-German economic area.

The specific demands of an international economy on transport infrastructure and the conflicting national peculiarities and egoisms were examined in lectures by Professor Dr. H. Breuer (Rheinisch-West. Tech. Hochschule Aachen) and Dr. H. Leipold (Director of the IHK in Aachen).

The lectures and discussions clearly revealed the advantages which can result from economic historical research on an interdisciplinary level with the cooperation of economic associations.

The contributions have been printed as Volume 3 of the "Aachener Gespräche zur Wirtschafts- und Sozialgeschichte" under the title:

"Prägende Wirtschaftsfaktoren in der Euregio Maas-Rhein. Historische und aktuelle Bezüge", edited by Francesca Schinzinger and Immo Zapp, in association with the Industrie- und Handelskammer zu Aachen, 1987.

The Contributions to the Yearbook Were First Published in the Following Journals

Yearbook 1987

Beate Brüninghaus
A Review of the New Literature on Business History (first printing)

Beate Brüninghaus
Mittelstand und Arbeitsmarkt. Löst der Mittelstand die Beschäftigungsprobleme der Wirtschaft? 11. Öffentliche Vortragsveranstaltung der Gesellschaft für Unternehmensgeschichte e.V. am 10. Juni 1986 in München. In: Arbeitsgemeinschaft außeruniversitärer historischer Forschungseinrichtungen in der Bundesrepublik Deutschland e.V. Nr. 41 vom 19. 9. 1986

Otmar Emminger †
Die Entwicklung des Wechselkurses von der "sakrosankten" Parität zum flexiblen Instrument der Währungspolitik. In: Bankhistorisches Archiv. Zeitschrift zur Bankengeschichte 1/1986, pp. 3–19

Stephanie Habeth-Allhorn
Die Einflüsse der Motorisierung auf das Verkehrswesen von 1886 bis 1986. 11. Wissenschaftliches Symposium der Gesellschaft für Unternehmensgeschichte e.V. am 27./28. November 1986 in Fellbach. In: Arbeitsgemeinschaft außeruniversitärer Forschungseinrichtungen in der Bundesrepublik Deutschland e. V. Nr. 7 vom 25. 2. 1987

Manfred Mai
Der technische Aufbau nach 1945. Technikgeschichtliche Jahrestagung des Vereins Deutscher Ingenieure am 13. und 14. Februar 1986 in Düsseldorf. In: Berichte zur Wissenschaftsgeschichte 10 (1987), pp. 48–51

Jürgen Mura
The Development of Savings Banks to Full-Service Credit Institutes. Report on the Symposium on the History of Savings Banks in Lüneburg, September 24/25, 1986 (first printing)

Hans-Werner Niemann
Die Russengeschäfte in der Ära Brüning. In: Vierteljahrschrift für Sozial- und Wirtschaftsgeschichte 72 (1985) H. 2, pp. 153–174

Hans Pohl
Ein Jahrzehnt Gesellschaft für Unternehmensgeschichte. In: Zeitschrift für Unternehmensgeschichte 31 (1986) H. 1, pp. 5–30

Monika Pohle
A Review of the New Literature on Banking History. Revised Version of the "Literaturbericht 1986". In: Bankhistorisches Archiv. Zeitschrift zur Bankengeschichte 2/1987, pp. 48–63

Monika Pohle
Innovations and Changes in the Employment Structure in Banking. Report on the First Scientific Colloquium of the Institute for Bankhistorical Research, held on 20th June 1986 on the premises of the Bayerische Hypotheken- und Wechsel-Bank AG, Munich (first printing)

Monika Pohle
Credit Institutions and Securities Markets. Report on the 10th National Symposium of the Institute for Bankhistorical Research held at the Bank für Gemeinwirtschaft AG, Frankfurt am Main, on October 24, 1986 (first printing)

Wilhelm Treue
Die Bankiers Simon und Abraham Oppenheim 1828–1880. Der private Hintergrund ihrer beruflichen Tätigkeit, ihre Rolle in der Politik und ihre Nobilitierung. In: Zeitschrift für Unternehmensgeschichte 31 (1986) H.3, pp. 31–72

Immo Zapp
The Economic Development and Economic History of the Euregio Maas-Rhein (first printing)

MIX
Papier aus verantwortungsvollen Quellen
Paper from responsible sources
FSC® C105338

If you have any concerns about our products,
you can contact us on
ProductSafety@springernature.com

In case Publisher is established outside the EU,
the EU authorized representative is:
Springer Nature Customer Service Center GmbH
Europaplatz 3, 69115 Heidelberg, Germany

Printed by Libri Plureos GmbH
in Hamburg, Germany